Table of Contents

4

Early Childhood and Science

A Collection of Articles Reprinted from *Science and Children.*

MARGARET McINTYRE

NATIONAL SCIENCE TEACHERS ASSOCIATION

Margaret McIntyre was professor of early childhood at the George Washington University in Washington, DC. She served on the GWU faculty for 19 years and retired as professor emeritus in 1982. For nine years (1974–83), Mrs. McIntyre prepared and supervised the popular "Early Childhood" column in Science and Children.

NSTA stock number 501250
Price: $7.50
ISBN 0-87355-029-3

Printed in the United States of America

PREFACE

When asked to put together a collection of articles published in my "Early Childhood" section of *Science and Children**, I thought back to October 1974, when I started writing the column. At that time, little attention was being given to science in the preschool classroom beyond the ubiquitous science corner. Magnets, potted plants, an aquarium, and sometimes a visiting pet usually made up these displays. My objective then, as now, was to alert teachers to the breadth of science opportunities available everywhere. We need to remember that young children are active scientists; seeking, curious, and intent on finding out all they possibly can about their wonderful world.

To young children, science is not an isolated subject. *We* teach them to separate the events in their educational experience into compartments—reading, numbers, music, art, block building, science. However, teachers who are aware of what children are saying and thinking as they manipulate and interact with their environment soon realize that basic science activity is going on.

A young child quickly perceives an adult's attitude toward science. If we are excited about exploration, if we ask questions, and demonstrate the "let's find out" attitude basic to science learning, children know it and they absorb the enthusiasm. Learning becomes an enjoyable experience.

As I began choosing which articles to include, I found that many other authors had contributed pieces to *Science and Children* that belonged in this collection. Some of these articles focus on philosophy, some on novel teaching ideas, and some on topics of special interest. All the articles reprinted here are the result of practical experiences with children, knowledge of child development, and years of observing how children learn. I hope that the material will help you, the teachers, administrators, aides, and parents, to think about the science in your everyday activities with young children, whether in day care centers, nursery schools, kindergartens, early primary grades, or at home. Every article offers dozens of starting points and ideas that you and a child can use to explore your world.

Margaret McIntyre, 1984

**Science and Children* is the preschool through middle school journal of the National Science Teachers Association. The magazine is published monthly during the school year except in December and is available through membership in NSTA.

CHAPTER I

What Is Science for Young Children?

Science is the process of becoming aware of and understanding ourselves, other living things, and the environment through the senses and personal exploration. For young children, this awareness and understanding comes as they become active learners in their own way and in their own time. The articles in this chapter discuss the science inherent in most early childhood experiences.

David Williams' article, "On Science for Young Children" makes the point that labeling certain activities as "science activities" is not important for young children. He lists activities in which children may learn about the world through science and asks teachers to rethink teaching strategies to nurture this learning. It is important for teachers, however, to make a distinction between facts and concepts, since concept understanding is a gradual process in children.

Science readiness is the theme of Mary Iatridis' "Teaching Science to Preschoolers." Her research-based article indicates one way to handle a science readiness curriculum. The readiness is linked to experiences in four broad topics selected by educators in science and early childhood. This interesting article combines a research project with planned practical activities. Her work is based on Jean Piaget's philosophy and reiterates the idea that experience is the core of science for young children.

Science touches the broad area of aesthetics as well. The senses are important in aesthetics, and sensory use is basic to science investigation. You can easily use aesthetic experiences in developing science concepts. "Art Experiences: Opening the Doors to Science" has teachers work with colors, use various types of paper, and introduce a wide variety of art media. Art experiences can introduce or strengthen concepts in physics, chemistry, and botany.

In "Color Awareness," young children explore primary colors, shades, and tints. Even nursery school children can match colors as long as the number of colors is not overwhelming. Visual perception skills develop as children work through the many suggested experiences.

"The Sounds of Music" relates the science of sound to music. Suggestions are given for music making by two-to-five-year olds. The piano and human voice are two instruments to include. Methods for developing listening ability and musical sounds discrimination are described. "The Sound Connection" looks at sounds from learning center activities and the sounds of the weather.

Use "Science and Poetry" ideas to reinforce science concepts. Through its succinctness and precise language, poetry can put into words what children experience. Young children, like scientists, frequently speak in poetic prose. Although poetry can be found on library shelves, this article will give you ideas for starting your own collection of science poetry.

Another basic concept to be explored with young children is their understanding of space. The ideas are often presented through movement activities. However, space is a science issue. Jean Piaget's dictum that knowledge is constructed by the child's own interaction with the environment is nowhere more apparent than in children's use of their bodies. Tie children's observations of the movements of vehicles, animals, and people to their own body movements. Developing directional awareness, understanding what is meant by starting/stopping, keeping on track, discovering space constraints, and experiencing pushing/pulling experiences are starters for children's investigation. These concepts are basic to understanding the force of gravity.

What Piaget calls the "spatial concept" develops slowly. Children primarily use sight, hearing and smelling to perceive space. The article "Spatial Concepts" will help teachers initiate activities to spur children's thinking about physical space. The language associated with these concepts is so important that its proper use could be the teacher's most important contribution to the child's development.

"Are You in Front or Behind?" is a natural sequel to the previous article. Children's use of a phrase such as "in front of" introduces activities in spatial relationships among objects. But do children really *know* what "in front of" means with respect to relative position? We must continually repeat and clarify the terms children use. The many ideas for investigation of opposites and relative position enable youngsters to work through these aspects of spatial concept development.

Reprinted from *Science and Children*, October 1975, Copyright NSTA.

> *Make your pupil attentive to natural phenomena and you will soon make him curious: but in order to nourish his curiosity never be in haste to satisfy it. Ask questions that are within his comprehension, and leave him to resolve them. Let him know nothing because you have told it to him, but because he has comprehended it himself; he is not to learn science, but to discover it. If you ever substitute in his mind authority for reason, he will no longer reason.*
>
> *. . . in your search for the laws of nature, always begin with the most common and most obvious phenomena . . .**

DAVID L. WILLIAMS

Department of Early
Childhood-Elementary Education
and
Science Teaching Center
University of Maryland
College Park, Maryland

AS TEACHERS, parents, and friends we often miss good opportunities to foster children's intellectual development and to assist them in expanding their awareness, understanding, and appreciation of their environment.

Possibly we forget that we do what we have learned to do . . . we are what we have learned to be. Science is whatever we have learned it to be;

* Rousseau, J.J. *Emile.* Quoted in Parker, Samuel Chester. *History of Modern Elementary Education.* Ginn and Company, Boston, Massachusetts. 1912. Pp. 198-99.

On Science for Young Children

and, whatever our children have learned or are learning about science will be science to them.

Science may be described as our way of studying, interpreting, learning about the natural environment. Science is not only the knowledge that we acquire and have acquired from our study, but it is also the process or the way we study our physical world and the attitude we develop toward our world.

Labeling the activities and processes of learning about the environment as "science" is not really necessary. Far more important to the child as a learner is his involvement and his expanded skill and knowledge resulting from his activities. The involvement and incorporation of the skills of investigation may be more important to the child than the factual knowledge acquired from investigations; the child's active participation is essential to learning.

A good guide, a good model, young or old, whether friend, teacher, parent or other relative, is also considered important to the furtherance of a child's success in learning and consequently in living.

There should be a multiplicity of opportunities for children to interact with their environments. You can share with children the excitement, the joy, the sadness of investigating the natural environment by listening to *them*, by talking with them about what *they* observe and what *they* think about what they observe.

Patience and Understanding

Children do not have to learn everything about their world in a day, or a week, or a school year. They will spend their entire lifetime learning. We can help each child that we are fortunate enough to work with by

not forcing a premature closure on curiosity and acquisition of knowledge. If a child asks for immediate closure to a problem that does not have an immediate solution, and shows distress because there cannot be immediate closure, it is probably because someone has taught him or her that problems are immediately solvable. The child can learn patience if we are patient and understanding.

Science for young children *may* take place; *may* be taking place; *may* have an opportunity to take place when

. . . a child takes a walk . . . in the yard, the park, the street, the woods, the zoo, the beach . . . with someone or alone

. . . a child squats down and watches an earthworm try to move from a drying sidewalk to damp grass and moist soil underneath

. . . a child puts a fallen tree branch on top of the already full garden cart and the branch falls off the cart

. . . a child notices pencils or crayons roll off a table or desk

. . . a child looks at a white cat through a piece of red cellophane

. . . a child hears a jet airplane and searches the sky for it

. . . a child's pet dies or gives birth to the young of its kind

. . . a child tries to move a heavy box of blocks in the nursery-kindergarten classroom or at home

. . . a child plants seeds and they grow or they do not grow . . . plants rocks and they do not grow . . . places a coleus leaf in water and it grows . . . places a fallen branch in water and it does not grow

. . . a child sees the sun shining brightly yet feels cold . . . plays hard and becomes very tired . . . calls a beagle a beagle and a collie a collie . . . sees fish swimming in an aquarium . . . sees a snowman disappear . . . and . . . and . . .

John Dewey, Jean Piaget, and Jean-Jacques Rousseau have each advocated active involvement of children in the process of learning about their environment. Today, you read and hear about "hands-on activities." Children manipulate materials and objects to learn more about them. Telling is not a sufficient basis for their learning. Activity is the key. Thinking and talking about the activity makes it more significant to the growth of thought, cognitive development.

We Are Responsible

What are we doing to foster, to encourage the intellectual development of children who are in our zone of influence? And another question, what are we actively doing to rethink our teaching strategies to make our teaching more effective?

There is much that we can do to create additional interest in helping children learn about their world, our world, by simply using the environment as a place to study, to live, to respect and to enjoy. We *can* do it . . .

——— **Mary Iatridis** ———

Preschool educators make a determined effort to develop curricula which build "readiness" in children to learn reading and arithmetic. But where is the *science* readiness curriculum that will help preschoolers survive in this age of technology? In teaching preschool science, we must consider the cognitive level of the learner as well as the appropriateness of the educational materials we select. The challenge is to identify the learning capabilities of four-to-five-year-olds, and design a science curriculum that will contribute to their cognitive growth while nurturing their interest in technology and the physical environment.

Mary Iatridis is an Assistant Professor of Early Childhood Education at Wheelock College, Boston, Massachusetts. Photo by the author. Art by Katy Kelly.

According to Piaget, the preschooler's capacity to think and reason is limited by extreme dependence on experience. Piaget also observed that the thought of the pre-operational child is much closer to overt action than is that of older children and adults. Therefore, it

---

Experiences rather than experiments should form the core of preschool science.

---

is in the activities and interactions of young children that we observe their learning. Experiences rather than experiments should form the core of preschool science. (5)*

————
*See References.

Science-Based Curriculum

In a recent study, a year-long science-based curriculum was developed for a class of 19 four-to-five-year-olds in a nursery-kindergarten class. A comparable class in the same school served as a control group; it did not use science-based materials. Both classrooms maintained their original equipment: dress-up corner, art and music supplies, blocks, and water play. The science-based curriculum embraced five broad topics: water; air; environmental terraria and small animals; magnets, batteries, and bulbs; and gadgetry, including simple machines.

We selected materials based on three criteria: potential to reveal natural phenomena, ability to be used in different ways and to encourage experimentation, and capacity to motivate preschoolers. Educators in science and early childhood ranked each item on a five-point scale (5-high, 1-low). The

Reprinted from *Science and Children*, October 1981, Copyright NSTA.

Teaching Science to Preschoolers

preselected acceptance level for each item was four. All of the materials were accepted, except the ones designed for the air unit; those items we eliminated from the curriculum.

At the beginning of the academic year, we watched children in both classrooms use the Stanford Research Institute observation instrument, and recorded the frequency of certain behavioral patterns—mastery, questioning, and self-directed discovery.

Three times during the shcool year—at the beginning, middle, and end—two experimenters observed each child in both classrooms for a limited time. They found that by the end of the year, mastery behaviors had increased in both the control and the experimental groups. But the experimental group enjoyed one significant advantage: Children exposed to the science-based curriculum increased their self-directed discovery (active, child-initiated exploration rather than aimless handling of materials) and verbalized curiosity more often than the control children did. Educators and researchers have stressed the importance of these experiences and behaviors in preschool science education. (1-7)

Science Experiences for Preschoolers

Water Play: The water-play table, already a fixture in most preschool classrooms, seemed a natural starting point for the science-based curriculum. Focusing on familiar properties of water, we developed a series of activities that changed the quality of the children's water play.

We explored the tendencies of classroom materials (paint brushes, scissors, pencils, and crayons) to sink or float. Children documented their findings on

a large chart with columns labelled "float" and "sink." The children's notations reflected their cognitive skills. Some students pasted the items in the appropriate columns; others drew pictures; a few attempted a symbol system. We challenged the youngsters to find ways to make things that float sink and things that sink float. This raised questions about boats and bridges. Intense experimentation produced boats made of clay, aluminum foil, and styrofoam, designed to carry materials that would otherwise sink.

In science-based environments, teachers encourage children to observe, question, compare, and classify what

they see, and to make their own discoveries: "Look, my crayons on my boat do not sink anymore." In addition, the teacher monitors the level of the students' interest. Interest in the sink-and-float activities lasted about a month. Several months later, activities related to the snow and ice of winter ("Who can melt snow fastest?", "Who can keep it the longest?") were met with renewed interest. Meanwhile, varied sizes and shapes of plastic containers, funnels, and strainers appeared. "Which will fill faster?" we asked the students. "Which will hold the most?" Siphons, clear plastic tubing, and hose clamps encourage children to experiment with the flow of water and its flexibility.

Food coloring offered opportunities to experience the combination of water and color. Students enjoyed blowing large bubbles using mild detergent and a few drops of glycerin. Such activities kept interest high and promoted questioning as well as intricate self-directed discovery.

Small Creatures: Another part of our science curriculum dealt with small animals and their habitats. Throughout the school year, an assortment of small animals came to live in the classroom. The hamster population increased from one to ten; pet shop recruits included a goldfish, lizard, gerbil, newts, crayfish, land turtle, hermit crab, garter snake, and land snails. Following advice from the pet shop and Stein's book, *Great Pets*, we established classroom habitats for these creatures—a desert terrarium for the lizard and plastic pools for the crayfish. (9, 10) The children helped construct the habitats and feed the animals.

We tried to introduce new animal guests as interest in preceding visitors lagged. An interval of two weeks was

established, based on the children's level of interest and involvement. The arrival of a new creature became an important event, with children guessing, "Is it ugly?"; "Can I hold it?"; "What does it eat?"

When a snake arrived in the classroom, the children became excited. Some admitted, "I'm scared," or warned, "Watch out, it's poisonous." Others asked, "Does it bite?" The teacher responded with more questions: "Would I be holding it if it were poisonous?"; "Do you see teeth?"; "How would it bite?" In this way, the teacher allayed fears, piqued curiosity, and encouraged handling by handling the snake gently herself.

This procedure encouraged further questions. The children wondered aloud about the snake's tiny, darting tongue. The teacher asked how their previous experiences with snakes compared to this one. She asked, "What do you think the skin feels like when you touch it?" and "Who wants to be first?", encouraging her students to feel comfortable with this visitor from the natural world. Later, the snake turned up in the children's artwork, represented in plasticene and bits of foam rubber.

The children drew charts comparing human skin to snake scales, then expanded the comparison to include other animals in the room. They also became involved in the snake's eating habits. With hands and legs tied, the children slithered across the floor like snakes, and tried to eat cookies as snakes would.

Books such as *Crictor*, a story about a snake, and a trip to a natural science museum to see a boa constrictor expanded our preschoolers' understanding of snakes.

Classroom Garden: A third set of science activities centered on a classroom garden planted in an old wading pool. The children became involved in establishing the garden, layering pebbles, sand, potting soil, and staking out plots with stones or popsicle sticks. Small plants found outdoors, at home, or at the supermarket were transplanted to this new environment.

During the year, the garden became a yard for the animals and a burial ground for one of our newts. In spring, the garden became a pond. The teacher, in agreement with the children, emptied the garden, and brought in several buckets of pond water complete with polliwogs. The children added the goldfish and newts, but decided against adding crayfish, fearing they would consume everything else in the pool. Individual polliwogs were removed and observed in plastic cups with a large magnifying glass. Comparisons were drawn between polliwogs and the rest of the animal life in the classroom.

Gadgetry: A fourth area to be explored was gadgetry. Our students showed great interest in taking apart and putting together pieces of simple machines.

We introduced intricate pieces of machinery that featured wires, screws, and movable parts—the insides of control boxes or discarded circuits obtained from the telephone company. Boys and girls worked in small groups using screwdrivers and pliers. For some, it was the first time they had used these tools.

The children's comments revealed varied perceptions of technology: "Watch out how you take this wire out; you can get electrocuted," and, "I think this is a spaceship, and I can make it work." The teacher encouraged each child to invent his or her own devices out of the pieces of dismantled machin-ery: cleaning machines, cheese cutters, and spaceships.

Findings

Our work with these children convinced us that the time to begin science studies is in preschool. The program need not be ambitious, even an inexpensive curriculum based on common materials can boost preschoolers' cognitive development. Disadvantaged students and girls, both underrepresented in science professions, may especially benefit from such programs. Although further research is needed, our study suggests that early science education not only strengthens skills of observation, data collection, and classification, but may also encourage students to aim for careers in science.

References

1. Brearly, M., *et al. The Teaching of Young Children*. Schoken Books. New York, NY. 1969.
2. Flavell, John H. *Developmental Psychology of Jean Piaget*. Van Nostrand. New York, NY. 1963.
3. Hawkins, D. "Messing About in Science." *Science and Children* 2:5-9; February 1965.
4. Hein, G. "Children's Science in Another Culture." *Technology Review*. 1968.
5. Hochman, V., and M. Greenwald. *Science Experiences in Early Childhood*. Bank Street College of Education Publications. New York, NY. 1963.
6. Lansdown, B., P. E. Blackwood, and P. F. Brandwein. *Teaching Elementary Science Through Investigation and Colloquium*. Harcourt, Brace and Jovanovich. New York, NY. 1971.
7. Piaget, J. *The Child and Reality*. Grossman Publishers. New York, NY. 1972.
8. Yardley, A. *Discovering the Physical World*. Citation Press. New York, NY. 1970.
9. E.S.S. Guides: *Sink and Float, Colored Solutions, Pond Water, Clay Boats, Ice Cubes*. Webster Division, McGraw Hill Co. New York, NY.
10. Stein, Sara. *Great Pets*. Workman Publishing Company, Inc. New York, NY. 1976.
11. Skelsey, A., and G. Juskaby. *Growing Up Green*. Workman Publishing Company, Inc. New York, NY. 1973.

Reprinted from *Science and Children*,
April 1978, Copyright NSTA.

Art Experiences: Opening the Door to Science

HAVE YOU ever used creative art experiences as science concepts? Classroom work with color, the use of different kinds of paper, and a variety of art media can introduce science.

Colors with Paint or Chalk

Put the primary colors, using tempera paint, into three plastic glasses. Ask the children to make the secondary colors by mixing equal parts of two primary colors in another glass. Have them name the colors. Encourage them to paint pictures using any or all of the colors.

Have a glass of white paint available. What happens when the children add white to each color? Add small spoonfuls of white gradually, observing the changes. Let the children paint with the colors they have mixed.

Try the same procedure but add black paint. What happens? Have the children paint with the resulting colors. Looking at changes in colors is not enough. Paint dots or lines, letting the children see the results of gradually blending two colors. Note the difference in each color as the paintings dry. Discuss "tints." Have the children add large amounts of white paint to both primary and secondary colors.

Science walks could focus on color. What about a spring "green" walk? How many different kinds of green can be observed? Are they light or dark? What about a walk to observe primary colors? The children could later personalize their observations with crayons or paint.

Rubbings

Making rubbings with crayons is an excellent way for young children to gain tactile experiences. Language

— Margaret McIntyre —

can be developed by talking about the textures associated with materials used for rubbings.

To make rubbings, peel the paper from crayons. Rub the side of the crayon over a sheet of paper that has been placed over an object. If the object is bulky, a cushion of newspaper will facilitate rubbing without tearing too easily.

Natural materials make interesting rubbings. Children can learn about the items they gather, investigating by sight and touch. Leaves, grasses, weeds, flowers, tree bark, flat twigs—all are possible rubbings sources.

Some materials are too bulky for rubbings and pressing down will tear the paper. Let the children face this problem. Problem solving is a tool of both the scientist and the artist.

Painting on Different Kinds of Paper

Paper used in art activities presents further opportunities for observing how paint reacts on smooth, rough, thin, heavy, absorbent, and nonabsorbent paper. A learning center would be ideal for this

What happens when you paint with soap?

activity. Have children test the feel of painting on different surfaces. How does the paint look when it is dry? Do the drying times vary? Why do you think so? Start with tempera paints. Later, let the children use water colors.

Try different textured surfaces. Use tempera paint on rough paper or even sandpaper. Have the children try painting on the burlap textures of wallpaper samples, shiny white paper, or on foil. The foils in wallpaper sample books are a source. What about painting on waxed paper? How do you handle the brush when you use tempera on tissue paper? On paper toweling?

Explorations with colored chalk can be used, too. For example, soak 22 × 30 cm sheets of manila paper in water. Have the children draw a picture with colored chalk on the wet paper. They must work quickly, or the paper will dry out.

In contrast, wet the chalk instead. Encourage the children to draw with the wet chalk on dry paper. Let them discover the need to keep the chalk wet. Try using colored chalk soaked for 15 minutes in a one part sugar, three parts very warm water solution. Let the children use the chalk to draw on white paper. How do the resulting colors differ from using chalk soaked only in water? Discuss the differences in the two techniques.

When the pictures are dry, have the children make further comparisons. On which surface does the color come off when handled? Which technique seems to hold the chalk color on the paper best?

Painting with Soap

Half fill a bowl with warm water and gradually add soap flakes. Beat with a rotary beater until the mixture is frothy, but not thick. Stir in a spoonful of tempera paint. Why is the color a tint? Use a flat brush to paint. How does the paint feel? What happens to the paint when it dries if you put it on thickly? Let the children discover what happens if too many soap flakes are added, making the mixture too thick. Add more water if necessary.

Modeling Materials

Water-based pottery clay is one of the easiest and most responsive manipulative materials for young children. Children enjoy the feel and experience of working their fingers through pliable substances. The amount of moisture in clay is important and provides an opportunity for children to discover this delicate relationship between water content and pliability. What happens when clay is left uncovered for a day or so?

MARJORIE SPINGARN

What does the dry clay look like? How does it feel? If the clay is very wet and covered tightly, what happens?

What can you do to make dried-out clay useable? Clay that is too wet? If you work for a long time with clay, what happens when you try to make something? Let children make objects of varying thicknesses, observing how long it takes bulky objects to dry compared with thin ones. Will they dry faster in a warm or cold place? When children make animals, mass comes into consideration. Some child is sure to make a fat and heavy clay animal and then affix four tiny legs, with the inevitable result.

Oil-based Plasticene is a pliable material that does not stick to hands or working surfaces in the same way clay does. How does Plasticene feel? Is the feel different from clay? How does it smell, compared with clay?* How do you clean up after using these materials?

Put Plasticene in a cold place. Try to use it. How does it feel? Put it in a warm place. Talk about how it feels. Does Plasticene dry out like clay? What are some differences between Plasticene and clay? Does Plasticene "dry" differently from clay? Why? If the material does become dry, give the children petroleum jelly to knead into the Plasticene until it is pliable.

Creative art experiences can be more than simply aesthetic or motor development experiences for young children. There are opportunities for introduction of concepts in physics, chemistry, and botany. How many more can you think you think of?

---

* Make sure the children do not ingest Plasticene or clay.

Color Awareness

——— Margaret McIntyre ———

The color of objects has a powerful effect on the young child, and the endless variety of concepts inherent in the attribute of color is a topic worth exploring in early childhood classrooms.

Very young children often don't know the name of a color, but can compare the object with something of the same color, as in, "My pants are a sun color."

Color matching and sorting are perfect activities for developing a child's growing awareness of color. Visual perception skills associated with these activities provide the basis for a commonality of knowledge that is prerequisite to naming colors.

Many early childhood educators prefer the term *labeling* to *naming*, believing the first to be more accurate. I feel that the youngest children respond more easily to the concept of *name* rather than *label*, but the terminology can be extended to include either *name* or *label* depending on the individual child's development level.

Once color matching skills are mastered through card games, paint chip matching, and the like, children enjoy sorting objects of similar colors such as vegetables, fruit, nuts, cloth, paper, and clothing. Naming the colors is not necessary at this time, but can be encouraged if appropriate. Visual comparisons remain the principal concept for young children to master.

Primary Colors

The primary colors—red, yellow, and blue—can be used in an initial approach to exploring color when naming and labeling become important. Children need time to explore and interpret *each* of the primary colors.

Understanding *redness*, for example, requires a variety of experiences with objects labeled red—not merely asking a child to name the color on a simple color wheel. As they grow older, children will be delighting in the red color of objects they see, slowly learning that the color never remains the same. Now is a good time for them to realize that many factors influence their visual impressions of red. How can children become aware of these influences?

The amount of light shining on an object influences its color. Have children compare red objects outdoors in the sun and indoors in the shade. Have them look at the same red object in a classroom with fluorescent light, then again near a lamp with an incandescent bulb. How do these conditions affect the color red they see? Does the red paint on a toy car, for example, look the same under a 40-watt bulb as under a 100-watt? Under which bulb does the color red seem brighter? Which bulb makes the car's color seem more red and shiny? Children should repeat similar activities with all of the primary colors.

Secondary Colors

Once very young children know the primary colors, they need to experiment producing the secondary colors in as many ways as possible. Too often this process is hurried through as a one-time experience. The concept of secondary colors is basic to further work with such aspects of color as shades, tints, and "warm" and "cool" colors, and clearly, children need many experiences over time.

Mixing colors in liquids is an easy way for children to experiment with combining colors. By having small glasses of water, food colors, and medicine droppers available in a color center, children can add drops of one color to another and name the results. Children should not be told what colors to mix but should be permitted to mix colors that result in secondary colors as well as black or brown.

Mixing a more opaque medium such as tempera paints will produce secondary colors that differ from the food colors. Allow children to experiment with tempera and talk over their findings with peers and interested adults.

Finger paints are an excellent medium for color mixing. Choose a primary color as a base and provide children with a small amount of another primary color to mix with the base. Trays designed to hold a sheet of finger paint paper make hanging the paintings and cleaning up very easy. Initially, encourage children to work in one color. Another time, add a second color and watch what happens. The relationship of the quantity of each color mixed to the final resulting color is another subject for investigation. Gradually, children learn that equal parts of any two primary colors produce a secondary color. Five- and six-year-olds make this discovery quite readily.

Non-liquid materials can also be used to experiment with colors. Staple pieces of heavy, bright plastic or cellophane of the three primary colors in a cardboard frame. Make one for every three or four children assembled in a center.

Art by Ford Button

Reprinted from *Science and Children*, April 1981, Copyright NSTA.

The children can position one primary color over another, and label the resulting color. Have them hold the frames up to sunlight by a window, observe the resulting colors, and talk about the differences of sunlight versus classroom light.

Shades and Tints

Spring is ideal for experimenting with tints. Spring flowers, Easter eggs, and new green leaves suggest colors softer than the pure primary colors.

Obtain plastic foam egg cartons and place a little tempera of the six basic colors and white in the slots. Children can add small amounts of white to each of the colors, and create a spring picture. Allow them to add varying amounts of the white tempera. Use the word *tint* with five- and six-year-olds, but do not expect all of them to remember the term. Talk about the tints that result—pink, lavender, and rose. Children can also add white tempera over the surface of a previously painted picture and observe the results.

Coloring with Crayons

Paint is not the only medium which children can use to explore color. Crayons permit a different way of looking at color and add another dimension to the concept of color.

Crayons are a natural for observing color intensity. The amount of pressure a child applies using the crayon provides immediate color feedback. For example, a red crayon can be used to produce an intense or very light color. It can completely cover the object drawn on paper or permit the color of the paper to show through. Children need to experiment with crayons to achieve different color intensities.

If one crayon is good, sometimes two are better. When children use two crayons at once and really bear down, they can see the shiny color that a wax crayon makes. By feeling the picture's surface, they are aware of the smooth, slippery texture of the wax. Multicolored crayon sticks can be made or bought and can produce many color effects children will enjoy seeing and feeling.

Old crayons can be shaved or broken into pieces that kindergarten children can arrange on a sheet of wax paper. Under strict teacher supervision, have the children place another sheet of wax paper on top of the crayons, then press the top sheet with a warm iron. What an opportunity for the children to see the effects of heat on the different colors and to note how the colors blend together. Frame the art in cardboard and hang it in the window where sunlight will produce an effect of stained glass.

Chalk Painting

Chalk is yet another color medium. Large, hard pieces are the best to use. If the paper is painted with buttermilk or liquid starch and used with the chalk while still wet, the chalk does not easily rub off when the paper is dry. The different colors of chalk are in sharp contrast to the same colors of wax crayons. The feel of the chalk and the amount of strength required to fill in an area of a picture are different from what is experienced with crayons. Children should discover this on their own and talk about it with their peers.

Visual Differences

Using paint, chalk, and crayons on colored paper, newsprint, cardboard, and tissue paper will produce a variety of results. Children need experiences with all of these products in order to become aware of visual differences.

To compare visual differences, have children choose a basic color tempera paint—blue, for example—and use this same paint for different activities over several days. The following suggestions are appropriate for five-year-olds:

Monday: Dip the tip of a plastic straw into the blue tempera. Then gently blow the paint out onto a sheet of white paper to create a design.

Tuesday: Use a potato masher, fork, pastry blender, or the like as a printing object. Dip the object into a saucer of blue tempera and print with it on white paper.

Wednesday: Place a small amount of the blue tempera into an empty plastic dish detergent container. Drip the paint slowly out the cap onto a sheet of white construction paper.

Thursday: Create a spatter box by covering the top of a cigar or heavy shoe box with thin wire screening. Tape the edges so there are no sharp corners. Place smaller paper designs on top of white paper in the bottom of the box and spatter the blue paint using a toothbrush to create silhouette designs.

Friday: Use an empty dish detergent container to drop blue tempera on paper towels or old sheets to create designs.

At week's end the children will have created five products using the same blue tempera. Do all the creations seem to be the same color? Question the children about what they see.

These activities are merely an invitation to adults to provide children with a wide variety of experiences using the concept of color. Since an awareness of color is developed and enjoyed throughout life, start early.

The Sounds Of Music

——— **Margaret McIntyre** ———

From birth, children become increasingly aware of sound. Listening to, making, and sharing sounds with others are enjoyable activities for young children and provide a base for simple generalizations and understandings related to the science of sound. Music has a strong relationship to sound. Instead of teaching the customary science of sound, why not teach the sounds of music?

Music Making

Young children eagerly explore the wide range of sounds made by objects and instruments. Music centers are ideal for such exploration.

Two and Three-Year-Olds

Hang several wind chimes within reach of the children. Use chimes made of metal, bamboo, shells, or wood. You may purchase these or make your own. What special sounds (timbre) does each make? How are the qualities of sound different if the chimes hang outdoors, or indoors near an open window or air vent? Why are they called wind chimes?

If the children listen to specific chime sounds and even identify one or two, can they discover what it is that makes the musical sounds? Observing what happens to the chimes as the sounds are heard may be difficult for very young children. How can children get the chimes to make musical sounds?

Four and Five-Year-Olds

Place bells, maracas, and tambourines in the music center. The children can make sounds with each instrument, one at a time. What do they have to do to each instrument to make the sounds of music? Encourage children to label such actions as shaking, hitting, and tapping.

Once children have worked with ways of producing musical sounds, station an adult in the center to acquaint children with the dynamics of music. Make the music of bells sound lightly/heavily, quietly/noisily. Ask children to label what sounds they are making and explain how they do this with the instrument. How does tempo affect sound? Can they make the music seem slow/fast? How do they do this?

More Musical Instruments

Put out small drums, triangles, and tone bars. What sounds do these instruments make? How many ways can the children get music from each one? What force do they use to hit a drum? What about the force used to strike a triangle?

Encourage the children to experience the vibrations caused by these actions. Can any child actually see the vibrations of a particular instrument? Which instrument?

After the triangle is struck, how long can the children still hear the sound? Try counting softly to see how far they can count. Is there a way to stop the sound as soon as it begins? Ask the children to describe what they have to do. Adults should consistently use the term *vibrations* to label this phenomenon accurately. Children will need to play around with producing and stopping musical sounds to integrate the notion that vibrations cause sounds.

Chording instruments such as ukuleles and guitars appeal to youngsters. Children like to explore the different kinds of sounds made with these string instruments. Stimulate further exploration by describing the quality of music they are making—loud/soft, pleasant/unpleasant, funny/sad.

Reprinted from *Science and Children*, February 1981, Copyright NSTA.

A xylophone is an ideal instrument to use in illustrating musical sounds. Hold the instrument up, in a vertical position, so children can see the striker going up and coming down the instrument and associate the sound heard with a particular position. Up and down are locational terms as are high and low. Children should practice using descriptive vocabulary in music.

Tone bars are useful in follow-up explorations with pitch. Use three or four bars, reflecting low, medium, and high. Children can experiment with producing their own music by rearranging the bars. Have the children examine the tone bars closely to note their construction. How can they stop the music as soon as you have played it?

The Voice as an Instrument

Voices as instruments may be a new concept to children, but voices do make musical sounds. Very young children can sing their names, or other significant single words. How do the children make their voices louder or softer? Play games and make up songs to reinforce the change in quality of voice.

Children may now be ready to explore the whole concept of *pitch*, as related to voice, using *high* and *low* to describe the different pitches. Not only must children recognize pitch differences, but they must have opportunities to use the vocabulary to describe these differences.

Try using your voice to climb three steps up a ladder, singing one-two-three. How does your voice feel as you sing? Can you climb even higher to four, perhaps five? Try reversing, climb-ing down, three, two, one. Do this in a very small group. Use a pitch pipe or piano to give the base or one sound. Five and six-year-olds will rise to the challenge of the concept of pitch in terms of up/down, high/low, and perhaps even medium/in-between.

The concept of pitch can be further developed through the familiar stories of *The Three Billy Goats Gruff, Little Red Riding Hood, The Three Little Pigs,* and *Goldilocks and the Three Bears.* Each of these stories has built-in pitch changes related to the main characters. Children can move easily from acting out with speaking to singing their own words, demonstrating pitch appropriate to the story character they are singing.

The Piano

Many classrooms have pianos. This large instrument is valuable in further-ing understanding related to basic concepts in pitch. Children can experiment singly or in pairs, using left to right progression on the keyboard. They begin to grasp the concept of pitch through seeing, hearing, and moving their fingers along the keys. If possible, the children should be able to see the internal workings of the piano. A complete picture of the instrument will stimulate moving the fingers key by key along the keyboard as well as associating the resultant sound with the direction of movement.

Up and *down* on the keyboard is very different from vertical movement in space. Much activity, as well as talking about movement from left to right or *up* and *down* on the keyboard, needs to be shared. Young children can be easily confused by the terminology.

Through activities involving musical instruments or their own voices, young children can learn to listen to and discriminate between musical sounds made by striking and vibrating.

The Sound Connection

———— Margaret McIntyre ————

Young children learn through their senses. Hearing is especially important in the learning process. Some children do not really hear sounds, though their physical hearing is not impaired. Children tune out many of the sounds of their environment, just as adults do. Children cannot see sounds. They have to associate sounds they hear with the object producing sound. Children need to make connections between sounds and sources. Through experimentation and exploration, they will remember the different sounds and be able to understand and talk about what they hear. This article suggests learning centers and outdoor activities that can develop children's ability to identify sounds and discriminate between sounds.

Understanding Sounds

Develop a learning center where children listen to specific sounds. Let children see and handle the objects that make sounds. This will clarify the connection between sound and its distinctive source. An adult should be in the learning center to ask questions, encourage exploration, and help children find the appropriate words to express what they hear.

In the learning center show how the nature of materials helps determine sound. Set up the center using wooden beads and a variety of containers—plastic, tin, aluminum, wood, and cardboard. The various containers will help show how different materials produce different sounds. Have children explore the sound of a bead dropped into each container. Talk about the resulting sounds. Which is most pleasant? loudest? Put several beads in each container, fasten lids, and shake the containers. What do children notice? Is the sound the same as when children dropped beads into the container? Is there a different sound when the beads hit the sides, the lid, or the bottom of the container?

Next, place different objects in several of the same type of containers. For example, place rice, paper clips, thumb tacks, sand, or gravel in film cans. Have children distinguish the sounds made by the different materials in the same type of containers.

Follow this activity with one in which children study the relationship of sound to the qualities of sound-making objects. Hand out drawing paper. What sounds can children make with the paper? Try the same experiment with other types of material: aluminum foil, newspaper, tissue paper, and paper towels. What kind of noises do children hear? If children apply the same action (crumpling, for example) to each material, are the sounds the same?

Place a nested set of aluminum or stainless steel mixing bowls, wooden and metal mixing spoons, rubber spatulas, and plastic cutlery in the learning center. What kinds of sounds can be made? Have children try making different kinds of sounds with the same utensils. Try rubbing versus hitting the mixing bowls.

Hearing Weather

Nature provides distinctive sounds that are available to everyone. Blowing wind, crackling ice, tinkling sleet, and pattering rain are a conglomerate of weather noises that children can observe and discuss.

During a spring thunderstorm, what do children hear? Have them listen to the thunder. Is the storm near or far? Is it coming or going? When the wind blows, what noises can children hear? What makes the noise—leaves fluttering, debris flying against walls, trees thrashing, doors slamming, windows rattling? How can children tell when rain begins if they cannot see the rain? Does light rain sound different than heavy rain? When the rain stops, what sounds of water continue?

A Listening Walk

Outdoor walks in the spring are fun and an excellent culminating activity on sound and listening. Prepare children to listen to sounds during the walk. Once back in the classroom, discuss what they heard and what made the sounds. Categorizing sounds on the walk will help children remember sounds.

After the walk, discuss what was the loudest sound. What made it? Why was it so loud? Was it near or far? Was it something big or small? What was the quietest sound? What made it? Why was it so quiet? What kind of people noises did you hear? What about animal noises? Weather noises? What made lots of continuous noise (not necessarily the loudest)? Which sounds did you enjoy? Dislike?

The sounds available will vary greatly, depending on where you walk—in a city, suburbs, or country. Take a variety of listening walks so children associate certain sounds with certain settings. Busy streets, parks, playgrounds, and even school corridors give opportunities for different sounds.

Reprinted from *Science and Children*, April 1980, Copyright NSTA.

Spatial Concepts

—————— Margaret McIntyre ——————

Active young children cover a lot of space in a few hours. They are not aware of doing so. What Piaget calls "spatial concept" develops slowly over the years. Children primarily use the sense of sight to perceive space, although the senses of smell and hearing also play a part. Teachers can support development of spatial concepts through planning.

Exploring Outdoor Space

A playground, usually connected to a school or center, is a convenient place to start. "Playground" denotes both pleasure and active child participation. Inevitably children run to the playground. Why? You can use the playground to get children to think about space by using the distance involved in playground activities. Use a stopwatch as children run from the school door to the fence at the farthest point. How long does it take? Now have the children walk the same route, again timing them. What differences did they feel between walking and running? Talk about moving faster or slower over the same space.

Ask for volunteers to be blindfolded. Always use a fresh blindfold on each child to prevent eye infections. Have the blindfolded children walk the same distance. Does it take a longer or shorter time when blindfolded? Why?

Draw two straight lines a good distance apart but leading to a goal. Blindfold two children. Have them start walking down the lines until you call "stop." Ask the children to tell you if they have reached the goal, have barely started, or are halfway there. Take off the blindfolds so each can check the accuracy of their answers. Let them talk about the activity.

From a designated starting line, draw 4, 8, 12, and 16 m finish lines on a flat area of the playground. Ask the children to walk, run, and skip the various distances. Encourage them to talk about the shortest and longest distances.

Peanuts in their hulls make fine materials to use in exploring space. Have children throw peanuts up in the air. How high can they throw a peanut? Discuss the need for some sort of reference point, such as the top of a door, fence, or a tree limb. Compare the up and down speeds of the peanut. Children will engage in friendly rivalry as to whose peanut goes up the highest. Do children relate height to the upward force of their throws?

Move to throwing the peanut like a ball. One child can throw while others watch. Talk about the slowness or fastness of the throw, how the peanut seems to reach a certain point and then falls. Have the children work in pairs, one throwing from a marked line while the other marks the spot where the peanut lands. By taking turns, children can see how far each can throw the peanut.

Afterwards, have the entire class walk around to see the different distances. Children could measure how many strides the length of a throw is, adding another dimension to their exploration of space.

You might have the children make metric measurements. However, don't rush use of standard measurement. Children need the background of many, many experiences in space using nonstandard measurement first.

Using a jump rope with five- and six-year-olds can reinforce spatial concept development. Children gain an understanding of the effects of pushing up through space with varying degrees of energy. The harder a child pushes, the higher the jump. Pushing up is hard work, but jumping down is easy. Can the children tell you why? Children must judge space in jumping rope to make the jump clean and accurate so that the rope will clear the body during jumping. Only active practice will accomplish this.

Exploring Indoor Space

On the floor use chalk to draw a circle about half a meter in diameter. How many children can stand, sit, or lie down inside the circle? Let them experiment. Does the children's height make a difference? Measure off a half meter square. Have the children try to fit themselves inside this. Is there a difference in the number who can occupy the space?

Unit blocks are an excellent medium for children to use to demonstrate spatial understanding. Building bridges, archways, elevated roadways, and wall structures means children must experiment, thus gaining knowledge about space, equilibrium, balance, and stability. When children build enclosures within enclosures or put objects within enclosures, they make space allowances. The floor space available for block building limits the structure pattern, forcing children to build vertically or horizontally.

The child's own body in space is also a factor in block building. The more children work with blocks, the less often they will knock the blocks over. Children will realize they have to make allowances for feet, legs, and arms as they sit or kneel to build.

Large hollow blocks lend themselves to a different type of spatial orientation. Children enjoy building large enclosed spaces in which they can fit inside, perhaps using a board roof. Crawling inside and being hidden gives a special feeling of space—far different from peering out an opening that serves as a window. I once watched a child lying on her back, her head barely outside such a window, fascinated by orienting herself to the ceiling and her own self in relation to her surroundings.

Even the sense of smell can play a part in a space orientation. Can students find the cafeteria by following their noses? Could you tell where the gerbils are in a classroom if you were blindfolded? How could you?

Teachers need to be alert to what amount of information can be absorbed and what form it should take to be understood. The language associated with the activities designed for spatial concept building may be the greatest contribution adults can make.

Reprinted from Science and Children, Nov/Dec 1979, Copyright NSTA.

Science And Poetry

—— Margaret McIntyre ——

Good poetry for children reinforces early science experiences. Preschoolers find the sights, sounds, smells, and textures of their world reflected in every verse. Poetry can also encourage exploration of new territory: the ways of insects or the healing of broken skin.

Reading or hearing poetry inspires children to write their own. You may be surprised by even the youngest child's ability to capture in language the violence of thunderstorms or the frailty of butterflies. First, though, introduce your students to the sound and cadence of poetry by reading them some written by adults. Try to choose poems that are relevant to the children's recent experiences.

Summer is nearly over as children return to school. Children who vaca-

tioned near the shore may have seen sea gulls. After talking about the gulls they saw, or after an excursion to the shore, read this brief poem by Leroy F. Jackson about *The Sea Gull*.

> I watched the pretty white sea gull
> Come riding into town;
> The waves came up when he came up,
> Went down when he went down.

"The Sea Gull" from Under the Tent of the Sky. *Originally published in* Child Life Magazine: *Copyright, 1925, by Leroy F. Jackson. By permission of Robert C. Jackson.*

The children might enjoy moving like sea gulls, soaring and swooping over imaginary waves.

If the children saw gulls catch fish, they will enjoy Elizabeth Coatsworth's *The Sea Gull Curves His Wings*.

> The sea gull curves his wings,
> The sea gull turns his eyes.
> Get down into the water, fish!
> (If you are wise.)
>
> The sea gull slants his wings,
> The sea gull turns his head.
> Get down into the water, fish!
> (Or else you'll be dead.)

"The Sea Gull Curves His Wings" from Summer Green: *Copyright, 1947, 1975, by Elizabeth Coatsworth Beston. By permission of Macmillan Publishing Co., Inc.*

This poem suggests pictures children could draw, and prompts questions about marine ecology.

On warmer fall days, when school doors are open, flies often appear in classrooms. Watching the movement of a fly suggested this poem, entitled *Flies*, by Dorothy Aldis.

> Flies walk on ceilings
> And straight up the walls
> Not even the littlest
> Fly ever falls.
>
> And I am quite certain
> If I were a fly
> I'd leave my home to go
> Walk on the sky.

"Flies" from Everything and Anything: *Copyright, 1925-27, 1953-55, by Dorothy Aldis. By permission of G.P. Putnam's Sons, Publishers.*

Your students might want to catch a fly, put it in an insect cage, feed, observe, and later release it outdoors.

Bugs fascinate two- and three-year-

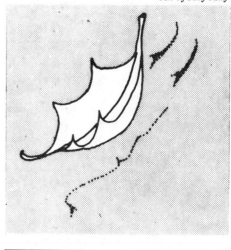

olds. After observing insects with the children, read them the first two verses of *Little Black Bug* by Margaret Wise Brown.

> Little black bug,
> Little black bug,
> Where have you been?
> I've been under the rug.
> Said the black bug.
> Bug - ug - ug - ug.
>
> Little green fly,
> Little green fly,
> Where have you been?
> I've been way up high,
> Said the little green fly.
> Bzzzzzzzzzzzzz.

"Little Black Bug" from Let's Enjoy Poetry: *Copyright, 1958, by Margaret Wise Brown. By permission of J.M. Dent & Sons, Publishers.*

A walk to find spiders spinning webs is a fun way to start the day. What does the web look like? Watch how the spider works. John Travers Moore wrote *Spider*.

> I am a spider—roundabout I go,
> Tie here, tie there, spin a strand so;
> Tie on, move on, busy at a pace
> Only a spider knows, when making lace.

"Spider" from Cinnamon Seed: *Copyright, 1967, by John Travers Moore. Published by Houghton Mifflin Co., Publishers. Used by permission.*

Soon leaves will turn color and fall. When this happens, find a leafy park. The children may want to collect leaves, press them, classify them, or just jump

Reprinted from *Science and Children*,
September 1981, Copyright NSTA.

Mrs. Peck-Pigeon
Is pecking for bread
Bob-bob-bob
Goes her little round head.
Tame as a pussy cat
In the street,
Step - step - step
Go her little red feet.
With her little red feet
And her little round head,
Mrs. Peck-Pigeon
Goes pecking for bread.

"Mrs. Peck Pigeon" from Eleanor Farjeon's Poems for Children. *Originally published in* Over the Garden Wall: *Copyright, 1933, 1961, by Eleanor Farjeon. By permission of J.B. Lippincott, Publishers.*

All children cry from time to time. The next time they cry, ask them to tell you what they feel when they cry. Are

Judith Thurman wrote *Skinned Knees* for children who are forever falling in their energetic exploration of the environment.

My knee
knits itself
with in-and-out
stitches.

A rough patch
that itches—
but don't scratch.
There's skin
below,
still soft,
still

whole.

"Skinned Knees" from Flashlight and Other Poems: *Copyright, 1976, by Judith Thurman. By permission of Atheneum, Publishers.*

Poetry for children reinforces early science experiences.

in them. Eleanor Farjeon's *Down! Down!* says it all, succinctly:

Down, down!
Yellow and brown
The leaves are falling over the town.

"Down! Down!" from Eleanor Farjeon's Poems for Children. *Originally published in* Joan's Door: *Copyright, 1926, 1954, by Eleanor Farjeon. By permission of J.B. Lippincott, Publishers.*

A.R. Ammons looked at leaves and wrote *Poem*.

In a high wind the
leaves don't
fall but fly
straight out of the
tree like birds.

"Poem" from Diversifications: *Copyright, 1975, by A.R. Ammons. By permission of W.W. Norton & Co., Publishers.*

At this point, perhaps the children could compose their own brief poems. Younger children could dictate a poetic sentence about falling leaves. Illustrate the poems using leaves collected outdoors.

Urban children can visit a city park and feed the pigeons crumbs. Watch the birds closely; imitate their walk and the way they eat. On returning to school, introduce Eleanor Farjeon's *Mrs. Peck-Pigeon*.

tears warm or cold? How do tears fall? How do they feel on your cheek? Where do tears go? In what part of the eye do tears seem to start? They will need to look in a mirror or observe a younger child who is crying.

Fourth-grader Wendy Kraus wrote *Tears*.

When I'm sad
Tears fall from my eyes.
Sometimes they fall into my mouth,
And they taste salty.
But they tickle when they roll down my cheeks.

Reprinted from C.E. Schaefer and K.C. Mellor, Young Voices: *Copyright, 1971, by permission of The Bruce Publishing Co.*

Wouldn't it be fun to watch your skinned knee heal? Why shouldn't you scratch the wound? Describe the rough patch that forms over the wound. What happens to the rough patch? Feel it gently with clean hands. What do we call this kind of skin?

With colder weather coming, children catch colds. Discuss good nutrition, adequate rest, and hygiene with the class. When a child sneezes, have this poem, and a tissue, handy. *Sneezing* is by Marie Louise Allen.

Air comes in tickly
Through my nose,
Then very quickly—
Out it goes:
Ahhh—CHOO!

With every sneeze
I have to do,
I make a breeze—
Ahhh—CHOO!—Ahhh—CHOO!

"Sneezing" from Let's Enjoy Poetry: *Copyright, 1958, by Marie Louise Allen. By permission of J.M. Dent & Sons, Publishers.*

Poetry can send children on new adventures, or give them new insight into adventures past. Either way, the child who meets science and poetry at the same time develops keen senses and a joy in discovery.

Are You In Front Or Behind?

———— Margaret McIntyre ————

Young children need considerable firsthand experience if they are to understand the spatial relationships among objects. Begin with a simple concept and present it to children in a variety of situations.

You may be able to begin this exploration informally by picking up on a child's use of a word or phrase. For example, *in front of* is a phrase used by young children, who frequently associate being in front of with being first. You can bring a more precise meaning to the phrase by using it in a physical context. As you are lining up the children to walk to another room or outside to the bus, say, "Danny, you stand by the wall here. Mary, stand in front of Danny. Lisa, stand in front of Mary. John, stand in front of Lisa." This gives all the children in the group an opportunity to understand the literal meaning of the concept and to use it in an everyday routine.

Another way to build on the concept of spatial relationships is to use your key phrases during the children's exercise period. For the very young, keep it simple: ask them to put their hands in

Herman, the zookeeper, was **in front of** the elephant giving her a bath. Her baby, who was standing right **beside** her, was supposed to get a bath too. But Lazy Earl was snoozing on the job as usual **behind** the mother Elephant.

Reprinted from *Science and Children*, March 1983, Copyright NSTA.

front of them. Then, see if they can figure out how to put their feet (and their heads) in front of them. For older children use the more complex *right* and *left*. As children get comfortable enough with these exercises to begin thinking of directions themselves, allow some to lead the activity. But keep an eye out for any who seem confused or who

always look at other children before carrying out instructions. Since there is no specific timetable for grasping this concept, children should not feel pressured.

Attracting with Opposites

Children as young as four years old begin to demonstrate an awareness of

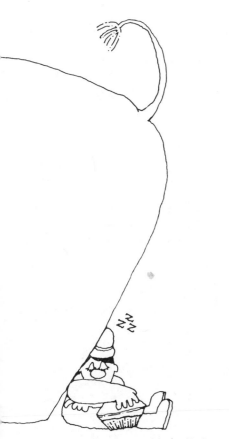

Marilyn Kaufman

indicated for *in front of*. Young children take a keen interest in discovering what they can make their bodies do, and directional commands such as these fit this need.

Classroom puppets can be excellent vehicles for direction giving. They add spice to the activities, and shy children frequently respond to puppets more easily than to people. Furthermore, teachers as well as children may feel freer to use puppets to illustrate position commands.

Other opposites that can be explored during the course of the year include *in/out, inside/outside, on the top of/on the bottom of, above/below, high/low, left/right*. Some single words are also important: *between, beside, (in the) middle (of)*. Include those and other terms in such classroom routines as putting equipment away. Where appropriate, use children's bodies as reference points. With very young children, you may stay at that level for a long time.

Relative Positions

With older children, begin to vary the position directions by using materials and equipment both in the classroom and outdoors. Varying the verbs as well as the objects in your instructions will help maintain the children's interest and build their vocabularies: "Put the Cuisenaire rods inside the box." "Put the trash can outside the door." "Put the blocks on their shelves." "Put the doll carriage outside the play center." "Swing your rhythm sticks high in the air." "Drop the rhythm sticks down low." "Find something under the snow." You may also find a game approach useful with individuals and small groups.

The concept that a child's position determines relative location is not an

easy one to understand. As older four- and five-year-olds begin to incorporate this into their play, you can help by clarifying and repeating the terms they should be using. The following activity may also be helpful.

Seat a small group of children around a table in the center of which you have put a block. Have the children take turns putting a colored cube in front of the block. How many will put the cube in front of the block by repeating what their neighbors did? Which children notice that in front of is not the same position for every child?

Now, put the table against the wall so that no one can sit on the wall side, and ask the children to put the cube in front of the block. What has happened? Move the table away from the wall and repeat the first activity, but have children sit in different seats. Is it the location of the child or of the seat that decides whether the cube is in front of or behind? How many children can figure out and explain that the cube may be behind one child at the same time as it is in front of another?

This same concept can be used in setting the table with knife, fork, and spoon. Use play utensils. Have children set the table for two persons, one on each side. Are the knives exactly across from each other? The forks? Spoons? Why not? If children have difficulty, use only knives and forks. Allow plenty of time for children to experiment.

Children will work through the concept of relative location during the next few years. Use as many different ways as you can devise to let the children practice this concept so that it really makes sense and is not something learned by rote, which will work only under specific conditions. Why not begin such explorations this month?

opposites. The opposite of *in front of* is one that they start to use without instruction. However, you will find that many children are just becoming aware that the meaning of *in back of* is the same as *behind*. Accept either usage.

Extending the concept of *in back of* and *behind* can be done with children's bodies as reference points in the way

CHAPTER II

Your Choice—Approaches to Science Teaching

There are numerous approaches to teaching science to young children. You will use several during the year, depending on the philosophy of their school, children's ages and needs, and presence or absence of a formal curriculum in science.

Nursery schools have long used play to bring about children's understanding and mastery of their environment. Much of what children use in play leads them to develop concepts and lay a foundation for higher level critical thinking.

"Exploratory Play: Beginning the Development of Scientific Concepts" capitalizes on young children's active exploration of the physical properties of materials. Playing implies doing something to a material, and it is this that the article discusses.

"Fascinating Fasteners" focuses on planned play opportunities for investigating a variety of fasteners that children use daily. Perhaps you have never considered the basic science concepts illustrated by the lowly fastener.

You can also enrich children's experiences by the use of program routines that are often neglected because they are so commonplace. "Snack Time Science" by Jacqueline Rosenstein offers examples of this approach. The simple act of questioning offers limitless possibilities for almost every snack or meal. Snack preparation by children provides even more science-related opportunities. Best of all, children get to eat the lesson materials.

Consider integrating science into traditional interest centers and play corners. Most nursery schools have a woodworking or carpentry play center.

"Working With Wood" lists 12 instructional objectives to structure the woodworking center with a science orientation. The objectives use a forestry approach and help children develop concepts of the properties of wood as a raw material. The approach encourages youngsters to discuss what they are doing, and this is precisely how children process and integrate their experiences into learning. This assimilation and accommodation are mentioned frequently by Piaget as being basic to children's internalization of their learning.

Another familiar center is the sand/water table, indoors or outside. In "Discovering Through Sand Play," teachers provide materials that encourage active exploration and discovery of the properties of dry and wet sand. Using beach sand and builder's sand permits simple comparisons about qualities and use. With the addition of accessories such as sieves and funnels, this center continues to focus interest in science.

"The Science Learning Center for the Preschool" is a detailed blueprint for organizing a center. Criteria for material selection and learning center management procedures are highlighted. This article stresses once again the need for teachers to be knowledgeable about materials appropriate to individual learning and developmental needs.

"Kinesthetic-Tactile Learning" suggests science experiences to heighten children's tactile-sensory awareness.

Children learn through their skin in a progression of activities involving barefoot walks, clay play, and "tactile detective" games.

Select a concept and direct all activities toward an understanding of that concept. Cynthia and Dennis W. Sunal show you how in "Creatively Exploring Change." They use four questions as a framework for the study of change. Three questions pertain to observing, comparing objects and properties, and comparing timing; the fourth question uses answers to the previous three to ask what caused the change. The authors use kitchen activities as an introduction.

Exploration and discovery are often referred to as problem solving. Problem solving skills are those learned through activities where teachers ask questions rather than give solutions. The outdoor environment of a playground provides daily opportunities. "Problem Solving on the Playground" by Rita Swedlow provides both a philosophical basis for this approach and practical ways to make use of the playground environment as a learning science laboratory.

Walking trips fit beautifully into Piaget's theory of how young children learn—children must be actively involved. Barry A. Van Deman's "Take A Hike" suggests many themes for hikes.

"It's Not Fair" by Nancy Kaplan demonstrates a useful technique for helping children think about what they are observing.

Reprinted from *Science and Children*, October 1977, Copyright NSTA.

Exploratory Play

--------------- **Margaret McIntyre** ---------------

CHILDREN BEGIN EARLY to investigate their world. Exploratory play is the means by which children gain understanding as they move in the world of living things. The child is a natural investigator — testing, fumbling, and endlessly repeating. All objects have to be examined, explored, and experimented with to discover their inherent qualities. The means by which this searching is done varies according to the individual child's developmental age.

Initially the emphasis is on the physical properties of an object. Thus, the child consciously and unconsciously asks himself/herself such questions as:

What is it?   What is it like?   What does it do?

By "playing" with the material the children make discoveries that provide a base for scientific conceptual development on which they will build for the rest of their lives.

If these explorations and subsequent discoveries sound like play, they are. Garvey (1)* says that children tend to follow a progression of exploration, manipulation, practice, and repetition as they increasingly adapt to an object in play. This progression moves from the grasping, banging, and mouthing by the infant to the more precise investigations of toddlers. Actions done to or with an object by the child become increasingly important as a way to explore materials. Children are active learners on their own behalf, not passive. Watching someone else *do* something is not effective learning for the preschooler.

Adults need to provide the materials and set up the environment for exploratory play. This preparation is one of the most important tasks of adults working with young children. Collect a group of materials and make them freely accessible. The number can vary from as few as five items for toddlers to as many as ten for kindergarten children. Add new materials if the children show interest. A facilitating adult can be stationed at the table or learning center where the materials are placed to encourage, comment, or elaborate on children's comments. Several children (2-4) can be encouraged to explore at the same time as a small group creates a social learning atmosphere for four-and five-year olds. With twos and young threes, you may want to keep the play more individualized.

Provide diverse materials, thus encouraging comparison and extended language development.

Check all materials for safety. No sharp edges, or items too large or heavy for a young child to handle, should be included.

Children are free to explore these materials while playing with them. Answers to the questions listed earlier will be discovered through free exploration. Although there may be little or no verbal indication of what questions the children are asking themselves, the sensitive adult will listen for their comments and make inferences about their actions. Sometimes a question may help to stimulate additional actions.

"What happens if I do this to it?" is a divergent question that stimulates action. Most young children are very creative in answering it. The adult may have to make a suggestion for a "do" action, thus encouraging the child to think of others. Somerset (2) suggests a list of such "do" actions:

pull	bend	crush	hit	tear
push	squeeze	drop	poke	rub

Children can add their own action verbs nonverbally by acting out an event or doing something to the material being explored.

Actions, of course, result in reactions, but you do not need to use this expression with the toddlers. With kindergarten children, the word "reactions" could be used by adults, thus extending the child's understanding of a new term. Materials do react in many different ways to the same action. How does the result of hitting clay compare with hitting wood or water?

Other science concepts are built by using these same materials. Light and heavy as a concept can begin being internalized by the child who is dropping a feather, metal, wood, or paper. There are many sizes and shapes of materials to be examined and named, and objects made from these materials.

A child can note the force used in crushing the materials. Children like to show how strong they are. It is easy to crush tissue paper and fabrics, but what about wood? Classification of easy- and hard-to-crush materials could be made. What happens in trying to bend these materials? Is the classification the same? The more materials used, the greater the opportunity to explore the ideas of what can happen to materials.

Children will not necessarily "do" all the suggested actions to the materials. There is no need to. A child is the best judge of how long to work with the materials and what to *do* to them. Some materials are simply more attractive to children than others. The more manipulations done with materials, the greater the learning potential for children. This exploration can continue during the early childhood years, provided adults allow time, freedom, and the opportunity for exploratory play.

1. Garvey, Catherine. *Play.* Harvard University Press, Cambridge, Massachusetts. 1977. P. 46.
2. Somerset, Gwenn. *Vital Play in Early Childhood.* New Zealand Playcentre Federation, Auckland, New Zealand. 1976. P. 49.

Fascinating Fasteners

———— Margaret McIntyre ————

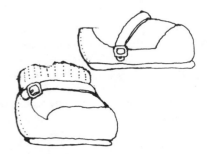

Nursery and kindergarten children never get tired of investigating their world and discovering the way things work. This month, why not try them on fasteners? You'll be amazed at the wide scope of investigation possible and at the excitement these inanimate, but important, items arouse.

Children will probably ask themselves questions as they go about their explorations: What is this? What do you use this for? What can we do with it? Their discoveries in answering these questions are the beginnings of scientific thinking, and your role is that of a careful listener and an astute questioner.

Fasteners Children Wear

Begin with the familiar—fasteners that children wear. Ask your students what the word "fastener" means, and expect answers like "hitch stuff together," "tie," "close," "stick things together." Get the children to look at the clothes they are wearing. Do they find any fasteners? Write their answers on the chalkboard so you can read back what they have told you. Allow plenty of time for children to show each fastener they discover and talk about it.

You might expect them to find and identify buttons, zippers, belt buckles, shoe laces, Velcro closures,® and shoe buckles. Less obvious fasteners could include bobby pins, barrettes, hair ribbons, safety pins, and clasps on jewelry. Perhaps you'll have to lead children toward talking about things they might not have thought of as fasteners with questions like, "What keeps the hair from Debbie's eyes?" or "How does Mary keep the bracelet on her arm?" And you may want to save the less obvious fasteners for another day's exploration. You could begin it then by making the items available in the play area for children to use before talking about them. Be sure safety pins are diaper size and are used only with older preschoolers, unless the children are very closely supervised.

A further look at fasteners in clothing might involve dolls. The three-year-olds will do little more than try to dress the dolls, but, by asking questions and expanding on their answers, you will help children attach names to the items they are handling and the actions they are performing.

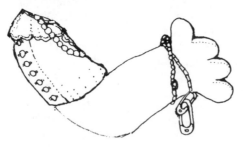

Fasteners in Art

Children are probably unaware of the wide variety of fasteners they use in art activities, and they are certainly unaware that they make choices about which fastener to use in a particular project based on its fitness for the purpose. Children often like to use paste and glue to fasten what they have cut out of paper or cloth, but they may prefer staples, various types of tape, and even paper clips, depending on the project. As they work, children need to be able to talk to you about the materials, what they are trying to do, and why they have selected a particular fastener.

Paper and wood projects also involve fasteners. Rubber bands hold pieces of wood or cardboard together. Special cements can also be used with careful adult supervision. Even straight pins or thumbtacks may be used by older fours and fives, again under supervision. With wood, of course, the fasteners will be screws, nails, and tacks.

If children choose to make their drawings into a book, they have to fasten the pages together. Help them punch holes in the pages and join them with colorful yarn, string, or paper fasteners. They may never have made a book, and, if this is the case, you should provide the opportunity: children derive a great deal of satisfaction from doing so.

Fasteners All Around

The discussions of fasteners used in artwork will be a good preparation for getting children to see the fasteners that abound in their physical environment. How do you make a door close or fasten? Are all doorknobs alike? How do they work? Investigate as many

Reprinted from *Science and Children*,
February 1983, Copyright NSTA.

doors as possible. What about cupboards in the classroom? In the office? Do they have doorknobs or latches? How are these fasteners different from the ones on doors? Get the children to look at the furniture in the play center. Does the child-size refrigerator close with a latch, a hook, or a magnet?

How do pictures stay up on the walls? What about the wall clock, the window shades, and the light fixtures? Borrow a ladder if necessary, so children can look at those fasteners. Be very careful to supervise this climbing closely, even in a room with a low ceiling.

Next, ask the children to find out how materials stay on the bulletin board. On the flannel board. The flannel board exploration could be done as a learning center, with a range of materials to test as fasteners and non-fasteners. Grouping these and trying to figure out why some materials adhere to the flannel board and others do not will help children to become more aware of the texture and weight of materials. This month you could tie the February holidays to appropriate flannel board materials—cut-outs relating to the lives of the Presidents or the history of Valentines—thus integrating science and social studies.

To close your classroom exploration, have the children dictate a list of all the fasteners they have found. Some kindergarten children will want to count them. They could add to the list as they become more aware of fasteners as a class of objects. Encourage them to bring new materials into the classroom and discuss their use.

Marilyn Kaufman

A Fastener Walk

Even in February, an around-the-school walk with a *small* group of children is refreshing and instructive. A fastener walk is unique and will heighten the children's curiosity. Before leaving, ask them what kinds of fasteners they might see outdoors?

As you go out the door, ask the children what holds the door to the door frame? Why doesn't the door fall out? How big are the hinges? How many screws are in each hinge? How do hinges seem to work?

Are there any gates around the school? If so, what fasteners keep them closed? How many kinds of fasteners do you see on gates during the walk? Do any gates have padlocks? Why?

When you walk past houses in the neighborhood, get the children to look for clotheslines with clothes hung out to dry. How are clothes fastened to the lines? A friendly neighbor may let a small group investigate.

Other fastener walk explorations might include looking into how your school's flag is fastened to its pole. The custodian may be able to help with this if you think to ask in advance. Get the children to take a look at the walls of the school or of a nearby house. How are pieces of wood put together to make the house? What about the bricks? What other kinds of fasteners are used in the construction of buildings?

The list of fastener topics could go on and on, and your children will enjoy bringing in additional suggestions for areas to be investigated. They will also enjoy the feeling that they understand something more about how the world is put together, thanks to their exploration of fasteners.

MARJORIE SPINGARN

Margaret McIntyre

Using Hand Tools and Machines To Do Work

ENERGY IS THE capacity to do work.* The challenge to early childhood teachers is to make that definition a concept understandable to young children at their experience level. Since children are interested in what makes things operate, have them explore hand tools and simple machines and how they are used. The basic concepts can be reinforced through the operation of familar machines in and around the schoolroom.

Without Energy, Tools and Machines Cannot Work

Tools and machines in themselves do not supply energy. They only control the energy that is delivered to them. Even the youngest child can activate some tools and machines.

Equip a learning center with a wide variety of hand tools and materials that children can use. Small cross-cut saws in medium size, a coping saw, light-weight broad-headed claw hammers, a drill, screwdrivers, and pliers are good choices for tools. Also, roofing nails, thumb tacks, four-, six-, eight-, and ten-penny nails, plywood pieces, and short lengths of soft yellow or white pine or poplar, as well as chunks of rigid plastic foam should be available.

At first, allow the children to familiarize themselves with the tools. Can they select the appropriate tool for a particular task and can they perform the action required? As a by-product of these efforts, children will

begin to conceptualize the amount of their energy they must use to do work. Questions such as the following could be used periodically:

1. What tool can you use to drive a nail into the board?
2. What tool can remove the nail if it is driven in crooked?
3. What tool will make a hole in the board?
4. What tool can you use to cut a piece of plywood in half?
5. What tools do you use to insert a screw into a switch-plate to mount on a board?

Tools Require Varying Amounts of Energy

After the children have had ample opportunity to work with the tools and materials, focus on discussions about the varying amounts of energy the children feel they must exert to perform certain tasks. They might compare the amount of effort it takes to saw a board in half with sawing the plastic foam.

Use a coping saw to cut thin plywood and then a cross-cut saw to cut white pine; compare the hardness or easiness of the work involved. Do thick boards take longer to cut than thin ones? Use a timer to see how long it takes to cut varying sizes of boards. If it takes longer, is it necessarily more work? Can they give an explanation? Why do some children saw right along while others have to stop to rest? Does this difference affect the amount of work performed? Are some children exerting more force? The answers will make interesting listening.

---

*Work is force (a push or pull) moving an object over a distance.

Be sure the children try driving different lengths of nails into the same piece of board. Which nail can be driven all the way with the least effort? Which hammer is easier to use? Why? If available, try using a toy hammer. Why doesn't that work very well?

Compare driving in a roofing nail with driving an eight-penny nail. Which seems to require more energy to drive it into the board? Can they figure out why?

Have the children stick a thumbtack into a chunk of plastic foam. Try it in soft pine. Can you still do it only with your fingers or thumb? What hand tool could you use? Does that make it easier or harder for you?

Hand Tools in the Kitchen

Tools for woodworking are not the only tools children can compare. The kitchen in a house or school or a cooking center in the classroom has all kinds of tools that can be explored.

An eggbeater is a fascinating hand tool. There is much to watch and listen to. How much work does it take to whip two egg yolks until they are thick and very yellow? Now whip two egg whites until stiff and standing in peaks. Is more energy needed to whip the whites than the yolks? When you are whipping, is it easier to whip slowly but steadily or as fast as you can without stopping?

Children are usually familiar with a rolling pin. Have them roll one around to get the feel of it. Then the children can use it to crush graham crackers into fine crumbs—the beginning of a fine dessert for their parents who are coming to visit. Have some children crush the crackers by hand (be sure they wash their hands prior to the activity). Which method makes the most crumbs? The finest-ground crumbs? Which requires the least amount of energy?

Machines Save Human Energy in School and Home

Custodians in schools or centers would be delighted to demonstrate the machines they use to keep rooms clean and shiny. After an art lesson, many small scraps of paper may be left on the floor or rug. Test various clean-up methods. Clean one side of the room by picking up the scraps by hand and with dustpan and broom.

On the other side, the custodian can show how a vacuum cleaner picks up the litter. Why does the

Reprinted from *Science and Children*, March 1978, Copyright NSTA.

custodian use this machine instead of a dustpan and broom? Discussion can be centered about where the source of energy comes from to run the machine. The children can note where the machine is plugged into an electrical outlet. Will the machine clean if there is no electric energy source? How can you try this?

Machines for floor waxing, cleaning, drying, and polishing could be demonstrated. Other school/center machines that are powered by electricity include an electric typewriter. Perhaps the children can experience how easy it is to strike the keys and make letters or numbers. Compare the effort to striking keys of a manual typewriter. What makes the keys go up and down on the manual typewriter? Use the word "manual" for vocabulary study.

Five-year-olds might want to observe how many machines their parents use that evening when they are home. Pictures could be cut from magazines to make a book of machines in the kitchen, basement, or other rooms in the house. Discussion should center on what work these machines do to make it easier for people, and what the source of power is for each of them.

Industrial Machines Perform Tasks

Trips enable children to widen their knowledge of machines and their uses. Visit a site being cleared of trees for building (from a safe distance) or a lumber yard where a clerk can demonstrate the speed and stength of a power saw. Can you do the same work by hand? How do the children know the work is hard? Listen to a power saw. What is the energy supply for a power saw? Another source of energy for machines becomes apparent—the gasoline powered engine.

Once you have introduced fuel-powered engines, the children are ready to look at all types of construction equipment. The large amount of work done in a short time by just one person using a machine can be seen and noted, even if not fully understood. Visits and discussions can involve tractors, harvesters, bulldozers, cranes, cement mixers, and trench diggers as a start. The world is full of examples, and all are invariably of great interest to the young child.

Working With Wood

Margaret McIntyre

WORKING WITH WOOD, or carpentry, is a favorite activity of young children. Have you ever considered the science in this activity? It is easy to set up a woodworking center in your classroom as a science experience rather than for the usual carpentry approach.

Setting up a woodworking station requires advance planning. The appropriate tools, varieties of wood scraps and lengths, and a solid bench or adequate substitute are needed. An old sturdy table is useful. Whenever children work with wood and tools, an adult must be available at all times to supervise.

Wood scraps from a lumberyard or from home building or remodeling are often available for the carrying if only you ask. Select the smoother pieces, such as plywood, and scraps that do not have many obvious defects. Have a variety of hard and soft wood. Small scraps are easier for children to manage than long boards.

When sawing or nailing, attach 10-centimeter (4-inch) C-clamps to the bench. The clamps hold the wood so that children may saw or pound nails easily as well as safely.

Adult-size tools have the weight and sharpness necessary to handle products as heavy as wood. Seven-ounce claw hammers are a good size. Hand crosscut saws of 16 and 11 point are appropriate, as is the coping saw for more intricate projects. A variety of nail sizes will allow children to discover whether they need long or short ones, and to discover what difference nail diameter makes in hammering into soft and hard woods. Nails with substantial heads are easier for the very young child to use, but try finishing nails as an eye-hand coordination task for the children. They respond to the challenge.

Concepts in Wood

Instructional objectives may be useful in structuring the woodworking center to provide opportunities for learning over a period of time. Children can savor these experiences, repeat them, and add to them as they explore the qualities of wood.

1. *Children will classify the scraps of wood by weight, light to heavy, if the wood scraps are approximately the same size.* If they are not, call attention to size as a factor.
2. *Children will classify scraps of wood from soft to hard.* There are several ways children can discover the hardness or softness of the wood with which they are working. For example, can the children scratch the wood with their fingernails? They may also want to see how easy or hard it is to make a mark with a blunt pair of scissors. Let *them* discover ways to solve this problem.
3. *Children will arrange scraps of wood by color if they are painted.* If the scraps are not painted, the order can be light to dark, or by any method they choose that involves inspecting the wood to see likenesses and differences in hue, color, or shade.
4. *Children will communicate to each other or to an adult what sides of wood scraps are smooth and what sides are rough.* (Use wood scraps which do not have splinters.) You may want to question them as to why some sides are rough and some are smooth.
5. *Children will make the rough sides of wood scraps smooth by using sandpaper.* Have a variety of sandpaper from coarse to fine. Let the children feel and label them before they are used. Let the children try to discover which grade of sandpaper is the most effective when the wood is rough. Can the children explain what is happening to the wood when it is sanded? Have the children talk about what happens

Reprinted from *Science and Children,* May 1977, Copyright NSTA.

to the sandpaper when it is rubbed over a long period of time. What is the sensation they feel with their fingers? Collect the material from the sanding process. What is it? How can you tell?

6. *Children will saw wood scraps or pieces of a soft wood such as pine and a hard wood such as oak and tell which is the easier to saw.* Can the children tell you why one is easier to saw? Try out activities done previously in Objective 2. Can the children link these? You may need to explore hardness and softness with other materials.

7. *Children will communicate with each other how the side of the saw feels to the touch before and after sawing wood scraps for a period of time.* You can question why this happens. Are the children able to link this concept to that discovered in sandpapering?

8. Children will sort sawdust from different kinds of wood into piles of the same appearance and texture. You can have children compare sawdust obtained by sawing pine with that by sandpapering pine. Older children can rub sawdust between the thumb and forefinger.

9. *Children will pound nails into wood scraps and order them from easy-to-nail to hard-to-nail.* Many experiences with hard and soft woods will be needed before the child fully understands this concept. Objectives 2 and 6 above are pertinent. Provide the children initially with the same size nails. Then let them experiment with a variety of nail sizes to see if that makes a difference.

10. *Children will pound nails into the sides and ends of wood to find out which is the easier task.* Can the children guess why it is easier to drive nails into the ends of wood?

11. *Children will locate knots in wood scraps and discover what happens when they try to hammer nails into them.* What happens if they try to saw through a knot? This experience could be related to discussion about what wood is and where it comes from. They could examine the grain of various woods.

12. *Children will classify wood scraps by the ease of standing them on end.* This experiment will usually take place naturally when children are working with scraps of wood. Young children tend to label scraps as animals, people, or objects.

Further Activities

These are merely an introduction to the many activities possible with woodworking. Tools used in woodworking all operate on the principles of simple machines.

In the spring, take a field trip to a park or forest. Perhaps the children could see pine, cherry, black walnut, and oak trees. The leaves, general shape of the tree, bark appearance and texture, and branching characteristics could be examined and photographed.

A visit to a lumberyard in your area allows children to see wood from the trees cut into boards, panels, and scraps.

A parent or shop teacher might bring in a small electric saw and sander. Observing power tools from a *safe* distance enables children to see wood cut and sanded with ease. A comparison could be made with how long it takes to do the same work by hand.

Measuring and constructing, as well as concepts about simple machines would logically follow most of these activities; wood is an ideal open-ended material with science as a valuable core.

Discovery Through Sand Play

— Margaret McIntyre —

Young children take a long time to understand the concepts of mathematics that are basic to science. One reason is that children must discover these mathematical relationships for themselves. Another is that repetition is required for children to master the more precise vocabulary needed at this stage of development. Discovery comes first, and practice in the form of play follows. This play is necessary but comes only after children understand what they have discovered.

Teachers must provide children with both the environment and the materials that encourage exploration and

discovery. Time is a factor. Young children do not move easily nor quickly from one task to another. They need blocks of time larger than 15-minute periods. Children do not internalize a concept on the basis of a single experience or an experience repeated over and over in the same way and with the same material. The means must be provided them for extending and deepening the initial discovery.

This article suggests ways to use sand play at many levels—deepening and extending play over a long period of time.

Sand Play

If a sand table is not available, trays and plastic dishpans are ideal containers to use with beach sand. They have the advantage of being portable and make it simple for children to explore both wet and dry sand.

Provide the children with spoons, pails and containers (both metal and plastic) of many sizes, shapes, and volumes. Sieves and funnels of various sizes and shapes are also important. Bring out only a few containers initially; too many choices confuse three- and four-year-olds.

During the introductory period, work with the containers in dry sand and ask the children questions that encourage thinking and science/mathematics vocabulary development. Print the words they come up with on a chart, using sketches for illustration. Such a list might include:

big	deep	straight
small	shallow	curved
thin	full	bigger
thick	empty	biggest
short	few	smaller than
tall	many	huge

Encourage the children to describe what they are doing as they fill and empty containers. Comparisons are natural during discovery play. However, the children can use *bigger, biggest, smaller*

Artwork by Frances Pavlik.

than or *larger than* without understanding the precise meaning. Can anyone grasp the relative meanings of *big* and *bigger*? Here an adult, who can assume a more clinical approach in asking children to explain what they mean, is very important.

Does *bigger* describe height, mass, or volume? The adult can help the child find more precise words: instead of *bigger than* use *longer than* or *taller than* or *heavier than.*

Wet Sand

Wet sand is a perfect material for exploring spatial relationships and shape. Sand pies and other shapes are easy to produce in rows on a shallow tray or pan. Can the children see the relationship between the container's shape and the object produced? Ask each child to produce a row of three or four pies, in diameter from small to large. This is not an easy task. Much time is needed, and only after a great deal of manipulation and comparison will the child be able to select the appropriate containers and arrange them in a sequence from smallest to largest, left to right. Do not push the process or explain how to do it. If you do, the task becomes rote. Extend this experience by supplying square, circular (juice), and rectangular containers.

With five-year-olds, deepen the experience by providing containers whose diameter at the bottom differs from the top, a flower pot, for example. Examine the pot; can the children see the difference? Is this difference visible in the sand object produced? Do children notice the reversal when the flower pot is filled, turned upside down, and emptied? How do they explain this?

Sieves and Funnels

Introduce sieves and funnels into the sand center. There are countless ways for children to explore with these tools. Ask them to comment on the width of sand as it streams through the sieve. How long does it take for 100 mL of sand to pass through a sieve? What about 500 mL? To time the process, have a child count by ones.

Which sieve catches the most stones or debris? Can the children explain why? Observe the size of the mesh openings. Five- and six-year-olds might want to use different size nails to determine which fit into the mesh openings. If two sieves the same size but with different size mesh openings are used, which lets sand through faster? Why? Listen to their comments.

Children can experiment with funnels in a similar way. What shape does the sand take as it goes through the funnel? Is it the same as the container from which it is poured? Predict which funnel will let dry sand through faster —a small or a large funnel? Hold a funnel race to check answers. Can the children explain how to conduct the race or do you have to suggest it? Much depends on the children's maturity and experience level.

Have the children wet the sand. They can experiment to see what hap-

pens when they add too little or too much water. Encourage them to think beyond the present. Why does the sand dry out? Where did the water go?

A Variety of Sand

The children are familiar with the color and texture of beach sand, as well as the sound it makes when they walk on it. To deepen concepts, introduce another sand.

Investigate coarse builder's sand. How does it differ from beach sand? Use it to make sand pies and shapes. Which sand do the children prefer and why? Explore further using sieves and funnels. Is this sand easy or hard to pack? Talk about the differences.

How Much Sand?

Observe children carefully during this discovery play. Often they will count the cups of sand (usually not level) that fit into a pail. Encourage them in this effort. Five-year-olds, who are proud of their counting ability, may enjoy counting up to 20, even if there is a miscount or the count gets ahead of the motor skill required to load, lift, and place sand in a container. It is difficult to do two things at once when you are

just beginning to work on coordination. Allow time to practice.

Once children are interested in "how much," some will discover that more sand in a container relates to greater mass. The children can feel this distinction using their hands like a disconnected balance. A sand-filled pail is hard to hold. It pulls their hand and arm down and makes them tired. Another container rests easily on their hand. Why? Because it is empty!

Introduce a simple balance scale. It provides endless possibilities for discovery and exploration. How does a cup of wet sand differ in mass from a cup of dry? How does the mass differ between like amounts of beach and builder's sand? Older children might measure in cups or half cups. Still others will want to explore the concept of balance. Use the children's comments as indicators of their thinking level and plan appropriate experiences.

Strengthen, extend, and deepen the mathematics/science concepts children have gained by introducing a new material: water, both clear and colored. Through planned discovery and exploration through play, the learning cycle in children goes on.

Reprinted from *Science and Children*,
Nov/Dec 1976, Copyright NSTA.

The Science Learning Center for Preschool

--------------- Margaret McIntyre ---------------

LEARNING CENTERS, so popular today, are imitations and extensions of the corners and interest centers of the traditional nursery school. A science learning center is a specific area of the classroom set aside to provide a planned learning environment for an individual child or a small group of children. At a center, children are free to learn according to their own needs and interests. Science learning centers provide a rich variety of materials with which children can interact at their own level and rate.

Setting up the center is the professional responsibility of the teacher, who must know what materials to provide so that children can "play around" with them. Handling of materials by the child involves observation and investigation of properties of materials, classification by these properties, and even hypothesizing. This approach to learning is not accidental. Much planning and organization goes into the setting up of the centers. Since the typical child under six years of age has limited reading ability, the teacher needs to consider this when setting up a center.

Criteria for Selection of Materials

The following criteria are important in the selection, arrangement, and sequencing of materials:

1. *The use of the materials can be open ended.* The same materials can often be used for more than one purpose, at the children's choice. Water play provides opportunity for measuring and/or flotation study, for example.
2. *The design of the materials encourages action by children.* Children must do something to the materials for something to happen. Dissolving substances such as salt, sugar, and cornstarch in hot and cold water provides comparison results from these actions.
3. *The arrangement of the materials should stimulate conversation among the small group of children involved.* For example, a round table with materials to be used arranged on trays is useful. When dissolving substances as suggested previously, a small tray could hold the substances in separate plastic dishes, with spoons for removal of the dry salt and sugar. Another tray would hold pitchers of water, both hot and cold, as well as spoons and dishes for mixing. The placement of materials causes conversation, and may help children with material use.
4. *There should be a planned variety of material available at a learning center over an extended period.* Centers may last for several days, maybe a week, but at least long enough so that all children should have a chance to use the materials. Some children may visit the center over again. Exposure to a wide variety of materials helps children learn. Not only do they learn about the materials themselves, but they also learn how to learn.
5. *The types of materials used should encourage hypothesizing.* "What if _____?" "Let's try _____." A pan of water with an assortment of plastic and wooden boats, several sizes and types of wood scraps, marbles, toothpicks, a sponge, and plastic foam pieces call children's attention to flotation qualities without a word being said by the teacher.
6. *The choice of materials and activities should be scaled to children's maturity.* Cooking activities such as change in egg appearance and texture from raw to soft-boiled to hard-boiled would be appropriate for older four- and five-year-olds, but inappropriate for two- and three-year-olds because of the hazards of boiling water and hot eggs.
7. *The variety of materials should allow for individual expressions of ability, interest, working pace, and style.* In the flotation experience suggested above, children can consider what floats or what sinks with ease. However, there should be enough variety of objects for some children to consider size as a flotation factor.
8. *The activities with materials should require a minimum of direction.* For the young child, most directions are oral. With three-year-olds and even the young fours, personal directions given by an adult are important. For the older four-and five-year-olds, a cassette recording would be a useful change

of pace. Written picture-type directions are also appropriate for some levels.

9. *The materials should stress process rather than product.* The processes of science are the fundamental skills that the young child will need to use in scientific activities. The processes of observation, classification, prediction, and even inference come naturally from the use of materials. Children will learn basic information as they work with materials, but the prime goal should be competence in the process skills. This comes from working with a wide variety of materials.

In a science learning center for young children, play is the usual initial response to materials, especially if the materials are new to the child. Children need this opportunity to handle materials and to become acquainted with their properties. Yet, there is danger in the adult assuming too passive a role after the initial "playing around." Adults need to be aware of what children are doing to the materials. By listening to children talk (even to themselves) and by watching their actions, adults gain clues as to what conceptual development is taking place. Adults may need to ask questions that stimulate the child to explore materials in a different way or to clarify what children say they are doing. At the same time the adult must be careful to remember that her/his role is that of a facilitator of learning, not the source of it. In learning centers, action explorations should come largely from children's ideas.

Management of Centers

Certain management procedures have to be considered in planning for learning centers. When the centers are running smoothly, the adults are free to observe children and to extend their learning without a continual stream of interruptions from children concerning procedures or location of needed materials. Who does what, and when, and for how long, are questions that must be considered as well as other rather routine procedures such as:

1. *Responsibility for children.* When is this the job of the teacher? the aide? Will responsibility rotate or be the assignment of one person for a stated period of time? The children should know whom to turn to with questions.

2. *Record keeping.* The system should be as simple as possible and increasingly involve children as they gain maturity and experience. Checklists, picture writing, or cassette recording are possibilities. Records help teachers to know what children have had in the way of experiences, as well as when planning further activities and in assessing children's needs as well as strengths.

As an example, with flotation experimentation, a group of pictures could be placed on the lefthand side of a paper, with a float or sink symbol on the other side. The children could check each material. For the youngest in the group, two trays, one with a symbol for "float" and one for "sink" would be appropriate. The child places an item on the appropriate tray after finding out this property.

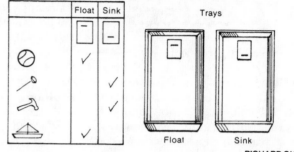

RICHARD GUY

3. *Available options.* What happens if a child is not interested or cannot use materials constructively? Children need to know what else can be done without turning to an adult. Other centers such as art, dramatic play, or language arts should be available as options for this child. Also, be sure children know procedures. Time limits at a center should be clear to both the children and all adults in the room.

6. *Physical arrangement and size of center.* A small center is cozy, but there should be adequate storage space for supplementary items that a child might need in working with the materials. Dishes, plastic glasses, measuring cups and spoons, trays, sponges, soap, and other utility items should be placed consistently in a special area. Science centers that require water must be close to a sink. Window space has possibilities as a plant center. Adequate, non-glare lighting is important. A round table is useful. The floor is also a good space for working; chairs are not always needed. A throw rug might define working space.

5. *Scheduling for use by children.* Is there free choice in using the center? Will the teacher assign children sometimes? This procedure assures that all the children will have initial experiences with all the materials. Will children have a minimum period of time in the center, say ten minutes, and then be rotated to another center after 20 minutes? What should be done if the children are so interested in the materials that they remain indefinitely in the center? Will all centers be free choice or just one or two? Any or all these different approaches could be used at some time during the year.

Teachers will make their own decisions on these management considerations as they assess their children's needs.

Reprinted from *Science and Children*,
May 1980, Copyright NSTA.

Discovery and Exploration Centers

Margaret McIntyre

The total environment of the early childhood classroom has a powerful influence on how and what children learn. Adults working with young children must develop a sensitivity to the physical and psychological appearance of the surroundings. Colors, lighting, and texture all contribute to kinesthetic and sensory awareness. Adults should consider the total visual, spatial, auditory, and psychological messages that children receive from their learning environment.

Take a critical look at the relation of the discovery and exploratory center to the rest of the classroom. The center should provide a stimulating and lively environment, providing a direct impact on all activity taking place within the room. A discovery and exploration center relating to the subject of air, for example, can be prepared using easily located materials which are placed in storage trays in a specified area of the classroom.

Exploring Concepts about Air

"Discovery" implies actions on materials and comments and questions about what is happening. It is not quiet activity, so the discovery center should be away from listening centers, book browsing, and independent work activities. Discovery requires space for a small group of children to work together somewhat apart from other activities. Shelves, a table, and an area rug should be provided to enable children to work without distraction within the space.

The discovery area should have readily accessible materials, carefully arranged within reach. A quality of orderliness that is obvious to children entering the center demonstrates how materials should be left when the children leave the center. Orderliness provides visual attraction and stimulation for children. Brightly colored trays or small dishpans on the shelves are ideal to hold prepared materials for ease in experimentation. Trays or pans can be carried to a rug or table and a group of as many as four children may work as a group, in pairs, or individually.

The ages of the students and the size of the discovery and exploration center determine how many activity trays should be put out each day. Start with two for five-year-olds. Initially, one will do for younger children. The accompanying chart describes five activity trays and explorations to be used in the study of air.

Activity Trays—Exploring Concepts About Air

TRAY	CONTENTS	CONCEPTS TO BE EXPLORED	INTRODUCTION	FURTHER EXPLORATION
1	2-4 each of several sizes and colors of paper bags Box of wire closures	Air can be felt even when it cannot be seen.	Open up bags and look inside. Do you see anything? Fold the bags up again. What do you feel as you do this? Try with several sizes and colors of bags.	How can you make the bag like a balloon? What is the closure used for?
2	12 plastic glasses, water pitcher, plastic drinking straws Red and blue food coloring, liquid soap	Bubbles are really air in water.	See how many different sizes of bubbles you can blow in a glass of water. What else can you do with the bubbles? What happens when you touch them?	Color the water with food coloring. What kinds of bubbles can you make now? What are the bubbles like when liquid soap is added?
3	Colored balloons, string, scissors, and felt-tip pens	Air can be felt even when it cannot be seen. Air makes a noise in some activities.	Blow up balloons. (A small air pump can be used for younger children.) Let the balloons go when they are large enough. What can you hear, feel, and see?	Draw faces and figures on your balloons. How do these change as the balloon is blown up? Tie balloons securely with a string and leave overnight. What changes are apparent the next day? What caused the changes?
4	Several sheets of heavy, colored paper, stapler, and crayons to decorate paper	Air can be moved with a fan.	Fold the colored paper accordion style to make a hand fan. Use a stapler to pull the bottom together. Use the fan to create air movement.	Try moving items from tray 5.
5	Feathers, cloth scraps, small plastic toy cars, plastic animals, packing forms, and cotton balls	Air moves many things.	Try to move these items using your fan. How many small items can you move across a table or floor space?	Try to guess which items will be more difficult to move. Why? Separate items that move easily from those that do not.

Focus on Rug Items for Discovery

Place a flat inner tube and an air pump on the rug to demonstrate the concepts that an air pump is used to put air in an innertube and that air has weight.

Assist children in inflating the tube and sealing with the cap. Children may want to climb and sit on the tube as well as try to lift it to turn it over.

Ask children how air can be let out of the tube. What happens to this air? Pump up the innertube again, and let the children talk about what they see as the air enters the tube. While two children are sitting on the tube, remove the cap. What happens to the children as the air is let out? Timers can be used to see how long it takes to inflate the tube.

Combining Exploration in Two Centers

This activity combines work done in the construction center of the classroom with an activity in the discovery and exploration center. Place on a tray in the construction center small pieces of wood about 15 cm long, dowels in short lengths, sucker sticks, and glue. String, nails, cloth triangles, and heavy paper for sails should be placed on another tray.

The concept to be developed is that moving air moves sailboats, even toy ones. Children can fashion their own sailboats from the materials provided. The finished boats are then taken to a water table set up in the discovery center. If no table is available use a large dishpan or basin. Children can experiment in any way to sail their boats. They may use their breath or a hand fan to make the sailboats sail across the water. Races can be held.

These are just a few suggestions for discovery and learning centers. In each case, an adult has set up a learning environment that invites a child's active participation and further exploration. Within a stimulating, attractive, well-planned, and organized environment, children make use of their own interests and previous experiences to solve problems, to learn new skills, to question and predict, and to work together developing qualities of young scientists.

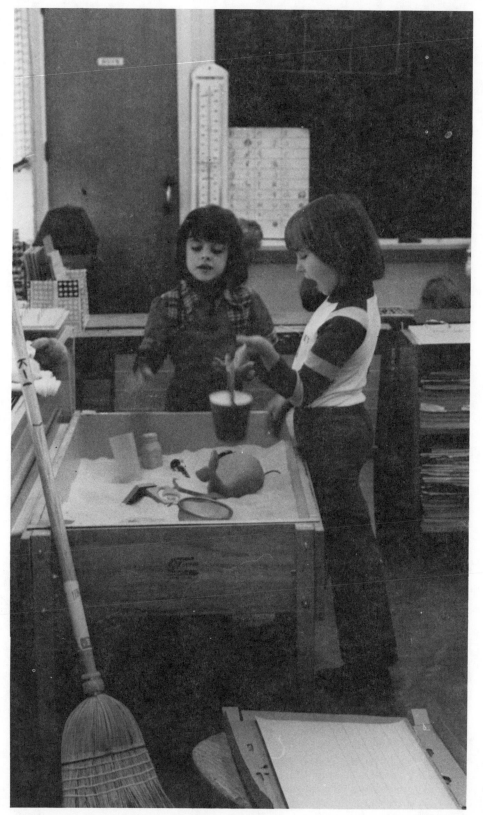

Kinesthetic Tactile Learning

—— Margaret McIntyre ——

Artwork by Katy Kelly

Much of what children learn comes through their skin. Sensitive, active hands, feet, tongues, and tastebuds identify objects by unique characteristics, search for similar objects, and explore three-dimensional representations of shapes, letters, and numerals.

Teachers can plan science experiences to heighten children's tactile-sensory awareness. Children develop observational abilities and, at the same time, language precision—both important skills for budding scientists.

Classroom or schoolyard learning centers set up by imaginative teachers offer the balance of structure and freedom young children need to explore diverse sensory experiences. Depending on children's ages and interests, one or several centers can be made available.

Exploring with Fingers

For this learning center, use several small bags made of smooth, dark fabric thin enough to permit children to feel the lines and edges of objects inside. Initially, place one familiar object inside each bag. Later, after children develop the skill to describe and name objects, place three or four objects in each bag. Children feel the object in the bag, describe what they feel to a friend or an adult, and, if possible, name the object. The child can check a guess immediately by opening the bag.

At first, use common objects dissimilar in shape and outline:

Ping-pong ball	Peg from board
Half-cup measure	One-inch cube
Miniature toy car	Plastic spoon

Later, try objects of similar shapes but different textures, perhaps an apple, a tennis ball, and an orange. In all feeling-bag exercises, emphasize describing the object as a means of encouraging language skills; naming the object is secondary.

Skin Sensing

Set up a learning center where partners explore how materials feel when rubbed gently on each other's arms or hands. All of the materials in this activity should feel pleasant, but press children for precise descriptions of the way things feel.

Try setting out:

Marble	Whole almond
Wide satin ribbon	Rubber eraser
Natural sponge	Feather
Synthetic sponge	Swatch of velvet
Paper towel	Pressure tape
Terry towel	Whole walnut
Foil	One-inch cube
Paper doily	Fine sandpaper

Feel Boxes

At this center, children associate the way fruits and vegetables feel on the outside with the way they taste on the inside. A vegetable-feel box has a hole large enough for children to put their hands in but not see the objects. They feel the vegetables' forms and texture, describe what they feel, then try to name the vegetables. Use a variety of fresh vegetables such as a potato, onion, yam, tomato, carrot, cucumber, small eggplant, and peas.

After the feel-box activity, cut the vegetables into chunks and let the children taste them. How does the vegetable feel in your mouth? What sounds go along with eating it? Describe the vegetable's taste. Here is an excellent opportunity for developing language and exploring nutrition.

A fruit-feel box contains grapes, lemons, oranges, plums, apples, bananas, and peaches. Invite students to explore and describe the fruits as they did the vegetables. These feel-box activities combine sensory awareness and language development with good, healthy snacks.

Barefoot Sensations

Depending on the weather, this activity may be performed indoors or out. Organize small groups led by adults. If you live near a body of water, walk barefoot along the shore. Experience a variety of textures—mud, sand, grass, stones, stones or pebbles, water, twigs. Now walk barefoot on grass, concrete, bricks, a rubber tire with ample tread, an inner tube, fallen leaves, plastic foam, dirt, sand, or through a puddle.

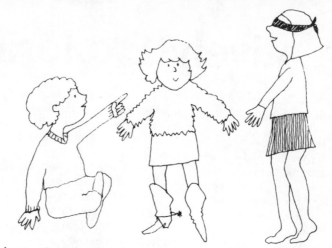

How does it feel to walk on each of these? Although this activity stresses the kinesthetic sense, it encourages rich language sharing, too.

Indoors, prepare a barefoot trail. Try walking on fluffy rugs, bare tile, cork flooring, a beach towel, a pillow, and a window screen. What do you feel through the soles of your feet? Is it the same as feeling with your fingers? Five-year-olds might ask an adult to write down what they feel as they walk over each material. The children can make up stories about their adventures on the indoor trail.

Nature Walk "Feelies"

Children set up this center using natural objects, "feelies," brought back from an outdoor walk. The center changes with the seasons and the natural environment. Leaves, nuts, flowers, bark, soil, pebbles, shells, pine cones, and feathers make good feelies.

Encourage vocabulary precision as the children describe their treasures.

Suggest *bumpy, slippery, sticky, gooey, mushy, hairy,* or *prickly* instead of the overused *hard* and *soft*. Children need to feel the objects very carefully to come up with the best descriptions. What part of each object gives what sensations?

Feeling Patterns

This learning center goes beyond the kinesthetic-tactile sense by focusing on an object's textural pattern. Some of the feelies from the nature walk can be used here, but do not limit the children to those alone.

Start with leaves, whole walnuts, ferns, an ear of corn, and pine cones. What patterns can the children feel and identify in these objects? Ask the children to concentrate on patterns only. Have them close their eyes; visual stimuli detract from concentration.

Next, challenge students to feel the patterns in kitchen utensils—a potato masher, a slotted spoon, meat turner, 'sieve, and flour sifter. Why does each one feel different? Describe what you feel.

Clay Play

Clay, malleable and easy to use, offers both tactile and kinesthetic experiences. If the children close their eyes as they work with the clay, they will concentrate better; peeks are permitted, of course.

Ask the children: Is the clay heavy? Make it lighter. Does it feel dry or wet?

Dip it in water. Smooth the clay. How does it feel now?

Squeeze the clay; squeeze it harder. Make it flat. Pound it with your fist. Feel the clay where you pounded. Describe it. Use your fingernails to mark the clay. Now feel it.

Tear the clay into four pieces. Pick them all up and make a ball. Poke holes in the ball with your fingers. How do the holes feel? Roll the ball into a long, thin snake. Wrap it around your bare arm or hand. How does that feel?

After the children explore the clay with an adult, allow them to work independently. They will be more sensitive to the kinesthetic-tactile possibilities of clay and ready to invent their own activities.

Tactile Detective

Divide the class into groups of three or four. One blindfolded child selected as the Tactile Detective tries to name another child in the group by feeling the child's clothing. To avoid spreading germs, place fresh tissue under the blindfold when changing detectives. Before the game starts, have an adult or child demonstrate gentle exploration.

Assign a child not in the group to answer the detective's guesses so that voices do not reveal identity. This is a tactile game, not a listening one.

If the detective identifies the child correctly, ask how he or she knew. It is important for group members to learn what tactile clues revealed the child's identity. The child whose identity was revealed becomes the new Tactile Detective, and the game continues.

Creatively Exploring Change

Cynthia Sunal
Dennis W. Sunal

Fran and David were stirring substances into water. "My salt is gone. It went into the water. Now I can't see it," said Fran. "Well, my pepper is still in the water. Look, you can see it," David replied. "Stir it with your spoon," Fran told him. "When I stirred my salt it went away into the water." "No, stirring isn't working. The pepper's still there."

The children were talking about the concept of change. Young children know about things dissolving through cooking experiences and through simple actions such as stirring cocoa powder into milk. They know that some objects, such as pebbles, do not readily dissolve. When working with objects alike in texture and size, children may assume that the substances will act the same when mixed with water.

A tray of frozen liquids represents a similar situation in which children are confronted with the different melting rates of various liquids, including oil and water. The experiences led to further questions and continued investigation by the children.

Such experiences can result in unrelated bits of information for the child. Teachers can help in the discovery that a certain action or situation does not always produce the same change. Teachers can offer materials for experimentation that will give children new tools for thinking. By putting experience in context, children will have a basis for understanding other instances of change. This can be the beginning of a conceptual framework which will give greater meaning to future experiences.

Getting Started

Teachers can plan direct experiences with change. Activities within a physical science context—freezing different liquids—may be effective in stimulating an awareness of environmental change. Four questions form a basic framework for the study of change.

- What can you tell or show me about this? (Observing)
- Is there a difference? (Comparing objects and properties)
- Is something changing? (Comparing temporal events)
- What is the cause of the change?

For activities to observe in dissolving, children could experiment with first feeling substances, then with stirring them into cold water. Children can chart which substances dissolve and which do not by putting samples in small plastic bags. Glue or staple the bags into one of two columns, materials that will dissolve and those that will not. Introduce the terms "soluble" and "insoluble." Talk about differences in dissolving and the effects of stirring and not stirring. Repeat the activities using warm water solutions. Dissolving substances in different water temperatures can lead to discussion of factors which speed up the change. The concept that certain conditions promote change is an important one for children to grasp.

As David and Fran were stirring their substances into the water, the teacher could have asked the basic questions. *Is there a difference?* Yes, both children noticed that the salt had "gone" into the

water, but the pepper was still there. *Is something changing?* Yes, the salt. Fran says it went into the water. *What causes the change?* Fran thinks the motions of stirring caused her salt to dissolve. She thinks David should stir his pepper. However, since stirring doesn't work with David's pepper, perhaps something else is the cause. The teacher should offer Fran and David many experiences with stirring and dissolving, using the four basic questions to help them explore changes that occur. The children's reasoning may not agree with the teacher's, but it doesn't have to. Agreement will come later.

Keep It Informal

The questions can also form a pattern of objectives which teachers might have in mind when helping their pupils. We are not suggesting, however, that change be taught formally. Ideas about change are best introduced informally with children being encouraged, in the course of their work, to seek answers for the basic questions. Structured questioning of changes should allow children to develop patterns of thought, allowing them to organize experience. For each question, the number of objects or properties which interact should be kept at two. Offer many examples and trials to help children organize their experiences.

Children's work with change should arise from situations children meet in their world. To guide children to an awareness that something is being investigated, teachers need to plan a sequence of simple activities that have potential for developing awareness. Children need starting points, encouragement, and careful questions to get them started.

The purpose behind a sequence of change experiences should be to focus children's attention on change, to get them to look for change, to question, and not to accept it as inevitable. (1)* Young

Cynthia Sunal is Instructor at the College of Human Resources and Education, West Virginia University, Morgantown, West Virginia. Dennis W. Sunal is an Assistant Professor at the College of Human Resources and Education.

*See References.

Close observation of boiled eggs.

children cannot recognize change without first being guided toward observing differences. (2)

Changes in the Kitchen

The kitchen is an ideal place to begin a sequence of experiences. Much science goes on when something is cooking. We found seven specific processes to yield experiences which teachers could use to build awareness of change. They are heating, cooling, dissolving, washing, soaking, solidifying, and liquefying.

Heating offers a chance to explore changes in the kitchen. Have children put a piece of candle wax in a cup. Add hot water. What happens? Questions such as "What is causing this change?" and "How do things get to be hot?" might be asked. Repeat the questions when the water and wax cool and the wax begins to harden. Children will have seen a sequence of rapid changes. Try putting margarine or egg white on plates above cups of hot water. Children can touch the cups as they are heated by the hot water inside. What changes do they see?

Observation of cooling is the next logical step. Cool hot water in glasses insulated by different materials—fur, wool, cotton, polyesters, paper. Have children help in measuring equal amounts of hot water into plastic glasses. Make sure the water is hot but not scalding to the touch. Use thermometers for exact results. Help the children to concentrate on the water temperature by keeping the colors of the wrapping materials similar. Neutral colors are least distracting. Let children test the temperature of the water throughout the day. Rearrange the glasses in order from hottest to coolest after each testing. Discuss whether the water temperature differs, what is changing, and what the cause of the change is. "If you wanted to keep warm, which material would you choose to wear?"

Washing and soaking are other ways to introduce change. Hand washing can build this concept. Introduce variables such as water temperature, soap or lack thereof. Discuss results. Give children chances to examine and taste dehydrated prunes, apricots, dried peas, and dried soups before and after soaking the foods in water overnight. After soaking, examine and taste. You may want to soak non-dehydrated foods. Use the basic questions to focus discussion.

Making butter is a good way to study solidifying. The quick results appeal to children. Pour a small amount of whipping cream into jars. Cap tightly and shake. A clump of butter will form and float on a watery liquid which is natural buttermilk. Let children taste both. Salt a portion of the butter and taste.

Let children work with liquids that lend themselves to the concept of change. Offer children a variety of liquids to name, touch, and taste. Make a chart for the liquids. Pour them into ice cube trays and freeze overnight. Observe the trays the next day. As children observe and feel first the frozen form, then the melting substances—changes in rate of melting, shape, color, and texture can be discussed. Ask the children to match the frozen substances with samples in their liquid state. Arrange the melting substances according to rate of melting, from most to least melted. Some substances, such as cooking oil, will melt rapidly.

The activities suggested above are common in many early childhood situations. Organization, sequencing, and questioning allow the activities to be used in building awareness of change. When children notice snow melting or holes forming in the tips of tennis shoes, changes are occurring. Teachers can guide children to an awareness of these changes and their causes.

Completing the Cycle

In all activities which explore change emphasize three processes—observing and participating, discussing, and recording. Children are primarily concerned with gathering experience—observing. Natural curiosity about their surroundings motivates exploration. Exploration results in learning with understanding. A study of change and an attempt to build awareness of changes should build on children's natural motivations and should be centered on experiences which invite observation and participation.

Discussion will best occur in heterogeneous groups in which peer interaction is encouraged. Teachers can encourage discussion by calling attention to discrepant events or by creating them as necessary. Ask children to explain or to justify conclusions, predictions, and inferences. "Why do you think this will not change back to the way it was before?" When children have described a change they observed, the teacher can ask for a way to reverse the change. "How can this melted ice be made solid again?"

Encourage students to record observations. They must decide which elements of the experience are important enough to be recorded. Recording observations allows teachers to assess children's experience. Rearranging objects such as jars of warm water cooling at different rates can allow children to produce a three-dimensional record of their experiences. Boxes in which samples of dehydrated and soaked forms of food are glued side by side also produce a three-dimensional recording of experience.

At a learning center children were interviewed before and after studies of change. Before the studies, children predicted that both sugar and pepper would dissolve in a glass of water. Slowness in dissolving could, they felt, be overcome by "mixing it up real fast." They were surprised to see no change in the pepper no matter how fast they stirred. They tasted the solutions and decided that, yes, the sugar was in the water. They also felt the sugar couldn't be made to come back out of the water. No child could name other things that change, nor any process which produces change, although they had observed change produced by stirring sugar into water.

After experiencing the series of activities, the children were again interviewed. They could not define change but gave many examples. Some children discussed the condition of their shoes. Holes were forming in the tips; the shoes were surely changed. Others talked about how snow and ice melted. One child said, "There's lots of changes outside. They happen all the time." The teacher asked, "Will any more changes happen outside?" "Yes. It will get hot. I think we'll get dandelions, because my Dad says the grass looks nice now but it will be a mess later." Another child talked about an orange he found at home. "It had white and green stuff on it and smelled funny."

The children could not list processes causing change such as heating and cooling. They did give examples of such processes. One child talked about making a gelatin dessert. "You put hot water in and mix it and the water melts it and it changes." Another child said that when she steps on bugs, she changes them.

In discussing examples of change and processes causing change, the children correctly predicted whether the change was reversible. Shoes with holes couldn't be returned to their original condition. A melting, soft popsicle could become hard again by being placed in a freezer. After working with the program of activities, the children could name instances of change, processes causing change, and predict reversibility of changes. Finally, teachers found the children were excited about the activities emphasizing change.

Children began to call the teachers' attention to instances of change, discussing changes in objects other than those used to demonstrate the concept. Several months later, teachers reported that children talked about changes they saw in the environment.

References

1. Radford, Don. *Changes: Stages 1 and 2 and Background.* Raintree Children's Books, Milwaukee, Wisconsin. 1977.
2. Mugge, Dorothy J. "Social Studies Beginnings: Piagetian Theory and Sensitive Periods." *The Elementary School Journal* 74:399-407; April 1974.

Reprinted from *Science and Children*, April 1979, Copyright NSTA.

Snack Time Science

Jacqueline Rosenstein

Absent from most early childhood programs is any planned curriculum in science. Impromptu opportunities for presenting science concepts must be determined and elaborated upon by the teacher whenever and however possible. Have you ever considered using snack time to teach some science?

Every child care center or kindergarten has a daily routine where cookies and milk are served, or occasions where special recipes are tested. Eating times encourage relaxation, socialization, and a climate where pleasant learning experiences can take place.

Begin the activity by asking questions that stimulate the children to think—to practice inquiry. Are all of your cookies alike? How does the size (shape, color, texture) of your cookie differ from mine? What happens when you drop a cookie? Spill your milk? What happens when your cookie gets wet? Such questions will stimulate discussion and reports of personal observations and interpretations.

Plan a menu for a "special" snack time with the children. Use this exercise

Jacqueline Rosenstein is Assistant Professor and Coordinator of Child Care at Housatonic Community College in Bridgeport, Connecticut. Photograph by Phyllis Marcuccio.

to practice counting skills. Discuss the number of children who will eat and how much food will be needed. How many dishes, cups, and napkins? Plan amounts and measures. Parents are often willing to contribute and help with these meals.

The purchased grocery containers can be studied for shapes, sizes, heft, labeled ingredients, and textures. The actual preparation of the food can further involve children's comparing, measuring, and observing skills. Try using orange juice and cucumbers.

Materials: Orange juice in different containers—canned, frozen, cartoned, bottled, and carbonated; a liter measuring pitcher, a juice squeezer, and fresh oranges.

Have the children compare the different juice containers. Discuss the sizes, shapes, and materials. How are they different? Is the juice the same from each one? What are some of the reasons for having juice put into so many forms?

Try some comparisons of size and volume. Does each container have the same amount of juice? The children can use the pitcher to measure what each container holds. They can mark the height on the side of the pitcher and compare the amounts with their predictions. The activity of pouring the juice will draw much attention by some students.

Squeeze the juice from one orange, then two, and three. Compare the amount of fresh juice from one orange with the amounts in the various containers. Try some taste tests and record preferences on a chart.

Materials: Three cucumbers of varying lengths with the shortest being the heaviest, and a scale and knife.

Out of the children's view, place the cucumbers in the bag. Have the children feel the contents of the bag from the outside. What do you think is in the bag? How does it feel? Are the objects all the same size? How many are there? When curiosity has peaked, have one child reach into the bag and describe the contents. Repeat until the cucumbers are identified.

Let's take one of the cucumbers out of the bag. Another. The children can count the number. Which cucumber is the longest? The shortest? Compare their lengths. Which cucumber is the heaviest? The lightest? How can we tell? (Use a scale to mass the cucumbers.)

Since the reward of a snack time lesson is eating, you may want to discuss the slicing process as you prepare the "meal." How shall we cut the cucumber? Shall we peel it? What will the slices look like? What's inside? With the amount of handling implicit in this activity, you will want to wash the cucumbers carefully before serving this "snack."

Problem Solving on

————— Rita Swedlow —————

Charles was building a tower with large hollow blocks. It began to wobble. "My building is falling." The teacher asked, "How do you think you can stop it from swaying?" Charles steadied the structure with one hand but couldn't lift the heavy blocks with the other hand. He asked Robert to hold the tower still. That worked fine. Charles built the tower as high as he could reach. The teacher did not tell him what to do but asked the type of question that directed his attention to possible solutions.

Young children can develop problem solving skills at an early age if they are in settings where exploration and discovery are encouraged. A playground can be such a setting if properly arranged and supervised. There is space enough for many activities. Moveable equipment can meet individual needs and interests. The ways in which children learn at three, four, and five years of age are likely to become lifetime habits and patterns of learning, so it is important that activities provide for problem solving.

If children learn to think of themselves as inquirers, this concept is likely to remain with them. The feeling of independence that follows successful explorations builds confidence, leading children to further probing. Children learn to ask questions and on their own, find ways of answering them. Children can state hypotheses and are excited when they prove their statements. When one has been disproved, they try proving other hypotheses. As children, through their own experi-

Rita Swedlow is Assistant Professor of Education at Queens College of City University of New York, Flushing, New York.

ences, arrive at generalizations, their self concepts become increasingly positive. While boys and girls engage in problem solving activities, they have a chance to absorb knowledge. What children learn in this way becomes a part of them, and has greater depth and quality than does rote learning.

No school can teach children all they should know. Children must gain the skills needed to acquire knowledge. Problem solving skills give children freedom to do their own learning.

Burt walked over to the log in the playground. He tried to move it. He tried as hard as he could but it didn't budge. "What can I do? I want to move it. If I get somebody to help me, it'll move." Burt called his friend Saul. "Come here! Help me move this log." Both of them pushing together still

couldn't move it. "We need more people," Burt said. He called to three friends in the sand area. They all pushed hard. The log moved. It was great fun. The children pushed the log to the fence. Burt was very happy. "Saul and me couldn't do it. It took a lot of people." Burt stated the problem—what could he do to move the log? Then he hypothesized—getting his friends to help move the log. Finally Burt generalized from the experience—several people can have more power than one or two.

Children can develop some problem solving skills on their own, but there is a limit to what they can do unless they are in an environment that stimulates problem solving. Here the teacher is crucial. Children will have many problems solving opportunities or few,

the Playground

Reprinted from *Science and Children*,
April 1979, Copyright NSTA.

depending upon the value a teacher places on these processes.

A teacher who wants to encourage exploration will offer open-ended types of equipment—tires, logs, ropes, cable spools, hollow blocks, barrels, planks, sawhorses, aluminum ladders, triangles, water, and sand. If children are to have experiences in defining problems and testing solutions, teachers must let them explore the choices of equipment they will play with and decide how they will use them.

There are times when children can achieve greater depths in exploration if teachers help in selecting and arranging materials. However, depending upon his timing, he can interfere with independent thinking or challenge children to move ahead. A teacher can show how to center a board or an aluminum triangle to make a see-saw for Nathan and Sue, or can let the children discover this for themselves. The teacher's presence can be a form of support, encouraging children to seek their own solutions.

The teacher watched Barbara trying to pour water from a pan into a narrow-necked bottle. Barbara had worked at this for quite some time and was becoming frustrated. Wordlessly, the teacher put a funnel near the water table. Barbara looked up, smiled when she saw it, and took pride in successfully finishing the task she set for herself. In this instance, intervention came when the teacher felt the play was deteriorating and Barbara was losing confidence in herself. The teacher knew of Barbara's frustration because he had been observing, an important teacher practice. While the intervention was silent, introducing the needed equipment helped Barbara find a satisfactory conclusion to her problem. Under other circumstances, the child would have had a right to be annoyed if the teacher offered a suggestion before the child had tried all the possibilities she had in mind.

A teacher can promote problem solving processes or discourage them, depending on the type of intervention. Children can gain independence as they become aware of the problems around them or they can become dependent, fearing to face problems and looking to adults to tell them what to do. In the first instance, problems are a challenge. Many teachers intervene sooner and more often than necessary because of safety factors involved with outdoor play. Observation will help teachers make decisions about changes in selection of materials and in children's behaviors.

Timing questions and offers of help on the playground are important. The same question can extend investigation or restrict it. In some instances, a question encourages a child to continue to search for further answers. Teachers need to know before offering materials or suggestions whether the child has exhausted the possibilities of the equipment already available.

As children solve problems, they are developing the ability to cope with their world. Challenges help children develop a good self concept; then they can establish good relationships with others. They develop a sense of power as they approach a new situation, examine the problems, and know how to try to solve them. When children are engaged in problem solving, they are learning how to learn.

—— **Barry A. VanDeman** ——

S am raised his arms like the outstretched wings of a proud bird and began to soar. His classmates stretched their wings and followed Sam's lead. Around the school's playground they soared in search of updrafts to carry them high above the pavement. After several minutes spent identifying objects below, the flock came to roost upon the playground equipment.

The teacher announced that it was Beth's turn to lead. The children scrambled into line behind Beth, with Sam retreating to the rear. Beth pondered a moment and then crouched over with her arms dangling. Her classmates followed, and soon monkey sounds and laughter filled the school yard.

Sam, Beth, the other children, and the teacher are enjoying a fantasy hike outside on the school grounds. This

Barry A. VanDeman is Coordinator of Instructional Programs, Summit Hill Public School District 161, Frankfort, Illinois. Artwork by Quinton Nalle.

hike encourages them to role play and to go beyond textbook descriptions of animals.

A variety of such hikes is possible. All allow students to apply science-process skills on the school grounds while enjoying the out-of-doors. During hikes, children attend to details they often overlook on walks to and from school.

Twenty-three more hikes are provided here to complement your science curriculum. On some, students can record their observations in words or in sketches. An inexpensive clipboard provides a portable writing surface. To make one, cut masonite or tri-wall cardboard in squares, 35×35 centimeters (cm). Add a bulldog clip to the top of each square for fastening papers. Tape a 50 cm string to a pencil and tie it to the bulldog clip for writing convenience.

Fantasy or Creative Movement Hike

A student leads the group and suggests ways to move. The group follows behind in single file, moving as the leader suggests. The leader then falls to the back of the line, and the next child becomes the leader.

Suggested Movements:
- Waddle like a duck.
- Fly like a jet.
- Hop like a rabbit or squirrel.
- Slither like a snake.
- Sail like a kite.
- Float like a seed or soap bubble.
- Fly like a bee or butterfly.
- Soar like a hawk or crow.
- Walk like an ostrich.
- Hop like a kangaroo.
- Stalk like a lion.
- Crawl like a seal or walrus.
- Move like a dog or cat.

Scent Trail

Using a spray bottle, apply a strong solution of food flavoring such as anise, cinnamon, onion, lemon, or coconut on trees or other objects. The children use their noses to identify the scent and to follow the trail.

Stop, Look, and Listen Hike

Hike for several minutes, or to a designated spot, or for a number of steps. Stop for one minute. Ask students to record all the objects they see and all the sounds they hear.

One Meter Hike

Give each child a piece of string or yarn 1 meter long. The children use the string to lay out micro-trails and look for interesting objects along the way. Later they can take turns leading others along their trails. Use a hand lens to search for stones, insects, or other small objects.

Eyes in the Night

Use a paper punch to punch out circles from reflective tape. Place these circles

Reprinted from *Science and Children*,
April 1982, Copyright NSTA.

on cards to represent the eyes of animals. Position the cards along a trail. With a flashlight, lead the class along the trail at night in search of these eyes.

Alphabet Hike
As students hike, ask them to record an item for each letter of the alphabet. Then classify each item: abiotic (nonliving), biotic (living), or cultural (changed by man).

Bird Hike
Ask children to record the locations and characteristics of birds they see along the hike. Using a resource, can they identify the birds?

Color Hike
As students hike, have them list as many colors as they can spot. Or ask them to choose one color and find objects of a similar color. Distinguish between light and dark colors.

Penny-Flip Hike
To start the hike, flip a penny: heads, go right; tails, go left. Look for unusual objects. At each stopping point, flip the penny to determine a new direction.

Tree Hunt
Pick a leaf and show it to the group. During the hike, students search for a tree that has the same type of leaf.

Identify the tree in a resource.

Centimeter Hike
On the hike, identify things that are a centimeter long, wide, high, or around.

Tracking and Trailing
One group lays out a trail of interesting sights, sounds, or smells. The other group follows it.

Autumn Hike
As you hike, collect fallen leaves. Later classify the leaves according to observable characteristics. Order leaves according to size or shade.

Winter Tracks
After a snowfall, make tracks and have students follow in the tracks. Consult resource books, mimic the tracks of various animals, and ask students to identify them.

Caterpillar Hike
Form a single file or several short lines. Ask students to place their hands on the shoulders of the person in front of them to create a "caterpillar." A leader controls the direction the creature moves.

Shapes and Patterns
As you hike, identify circles, squares, and other shapes in nature, buildings, or playground equipment. Look for patterns: repeated shapes, colors, or textures.

Micro-Trail
Using a hand lens, hold your head near the ground and focus on an object. Crawl along slowly and explore the magnified terrain.

Follow the Ant
Follow the path of an ant for five minutes and attempt to map its path.

Silent Walk
Walk quietly in order to discover how many sounds you can hear. (Blindfolds may heighten the sense of hearing.)

Up, Down, and Around
While hiking, look for objects from one field of view—looking up, for example. On the next hike, change your view.

Texture Hike
Feel for textures in nature and in man-made constructions. Identify contrasting textures: prickly/tickly or smooth/rough, for example.

Litter Patrol
Hike in search of litter. Note the location of the greatest quantity. Any explanation? Collect samples in bags and classify them later in class.

Snow Trail
After a snowfall, provide students with spray bottles containing colored water. Ask each group to lay out a trail by spraying the snow with a color. Trails should lead to points of interest.

But, That's Not Fair!

──────── Nancy Kaplan ────────

Spring is in the air, and it's certainly in the children. As they jump and skip into the science room, these kindergarteners show me that they're already thinking of recess. But I'm ready for them.

Craig is the first to notice. "Why do you have the gym balls here?" he asks.

The children settle down on the rug to hear my answer.

"I borrowed them from the gym because I've seen so many of you using them," I explain. "What do you like to do with balls like these?"

Every child has an answer: "I play baseball." "I play catch with my dad." "We play soccer with that one." "Kickball, too." "Dribbling." "Tossing." "I like bouncing."

"I like bouncing, too," I tell them, "but if I'm going to play a bouncing game, I want to use the best bouncer. Which is it?"

Again, every child has an idea: "The big one." "No, the tennis ball." "The medium one."

"I hear your guesses, but how will I know for sure?" I ask.

"You have to try them," says Margaret.

"You mean we should do an experiment?" I pick up the largest and smallest balls. "Tell me exactly what to do, and I'll test them."

The children explain that I should bounce the two balls at the same time and whichever ball bounces up the highest is the better bouncer. They will watch and judge while I bounce the two balls.

"O.K., I'm ready. But tell me your guesses again. How many think this big ball is the better bouncer?" Some hands

are raised. "How many think this little ball is the better bouncer?" Other hands go up. "Let's experiment to find out."

While every child watches intently, I let the small ball slide off my upturned left hand at the same time as I bounce the large ball down hard with my right hand. Of course, the large ball bounces back up considerably higher than the small ball.

Approximately half the group breaks into a cheer.

"Yay, we were right," they call.

"What do you think?" I ask the whole class. "Do we know which is the better bouncer now?"

Craig is not satisfied. "Mrs. Kaplan," he says, "I don't think that was fair. You bounced the big ball down really hard!"

"I did," I confess. "I like to bounce this one hard."

"But it isn't fair to the little one!"

Several voices now join Craig's, and I revise my experimental design.

"I understand. To make this experiment fair, I have to bounce them down the *same* way. No extra pushes. O.K. I'll do it again. Ready?"

The children watch again as I hold each ball in an upturned hand, the small ball about waist height and the large ball about shoulder height.

"Here we go," I say. "I'll be sure to bounce them both down the *same* way, and then we'll know which one is the better bouncer."

Suddenly a small group calls out, "Wait, it's not fair. You have the big ball up too high."

I look up at it in mock surprise and ask them why that bothers them.

"Because it won't be fair," explains Kim. "The big ball is sort of getting a head start. It's like bouncing it hard."

"I see." I lower the big ball to waist height and raise the small ball to my shoulders.

"No," they all call out, "they have to be the same."

"Ooops! Well which is right, high or low?"

"Both are right, but they have to be the *same*," Tommy tells me.

"O.K., I think I'm ready to try this experiment again," I say. "I'll bounce

both balls down the *same* way, from the *same* height, and then we'll find out if one is a better bouncer. Here we go."

I carefully position myself and drop the balls.

"Oh no!" exclaims James. "The little ball landed on the rug. That's not fair!"

"Why not?" I ask. "I didn't bounce one harder or start one higher."

"But it's like bouncing on grass. It's not fair."

"James, is right," they are all saying. "Do it again, away from the rug. Get both balls on the tile floor."

"Oh, you want that to be the *same*, too. Two different balls bounced the *same* way, from the *same* height, onto the *same* floor. O.K. I think I can do it fairly. Here we go."

This time, as the large ball bounces up higher than the small one, the children know it really is the better bouncer. But some are quick to point out that we haven't even tried the medium-sized ball.

"Tell me how to do it, and we'll compare this medium-sized ball to the big ball, which bounced better in the first experiment."

"Make it fair!" "Bounce them the same way." "Start them at the same height." "Bounce them on the same floor."

Everyone has a piece of advice. And so we experiment again.

Do these children know that they have been designing experiments with controlled variables, critiquing faulty experimental design, hypothesizing and testing hypotheses? Probably not. And there's no reason for kindergarteners to know the technical terminology. But they do need to know and be comfortable with the skills.

Over the next few weeks, we'll conduct "fair" experiments with rolling balls, cars rolling down ramps, maybe even paper airplanes. The critical thinking we have just practiced will become more and more routine. These young children will be on their way to becoming adults who can think intelligently about the scientific issues of their day.

Nancy Kaplan is president of ROGO Educational Consulting Inc., Irvington, New York.

CHAPTER III
Seasonal Activities

Many teachers of young children tie science experiences to the four seasons. This practice is sound if other approaches are used with the seasonal approach.

Possible seasonal science activities are so numerous that teachers need to consider them as they plan activities for the year. Seizing the teachable moment is a useful technique, and teachers should be flexible. However, the best kind of flexibility requires thorough planning so that the objective is always known to the teacher. The activities in this chapter will help teachers plan for the unexpected opportunity to teach the science of seasons.

Fall

In "A Living Science Laboratory," the late summer outdoor environment becomes a natural extension of the classroom. Four weeks of exploration are planned, with latitude for teacher innovation.

In "Learning from Fallen Leaves," nature's recycling process is introduced in ways that allow youngsters to participate actively. Leaf decomposition is observed, felt, and hastened along by the children. Sorting, pressing, and classifying activities with collected leaves are suggested in "Picking Up On Leaves."

Other "Fall Nature Collectibles" include nuts, fall flowers, and vegetable seeds. The labeling of these objects is important to young children, who are bridging the gap from the object to the written symbol.

Fall is also harvest time. Seasonal fruits and vegetables can be materials for learning centers. "Fall Harvest and Science" points out the rich sensory and science potential of snacks. Many can be eaten raw or prepared simply. "Pumpkin Science" presents suggestions for science activities related to measuring, counting, feeling, tasting, smelling, and observing pumpkins. "Taking an Insect View" explores soil organisms in the playground or garden.

Winter

As the holiday season approaches, children become interested in evergreen trees, pine cones, and natural decorations. "Holiday Science" suggests a science learning center using gathered cones and evergreen needles as materials. Edible decorations can be made for a bird's holiday tree or other treats for resident winter birds. Top this off by making "bird pudding," not for children, but for birds. All winter and spring the children can replenish food and become acquainted with the common birds of the area.

"The World in Winter" lays a foundation for understanding seasonal change by observation over a long period of time. Trees, birds, and the weight and restriction of winter clothing are topics to consider. Winter skies for star gazing will need parent cooperation.

"Snow" and "Kindergarten Explorations with Snow, Ice, and Water," by Martha A. Carroll, examines snowstorms and offers suggestions for examining properties of snow. Observations relate to seeing, hearing, and feeling, as well measurement of depth, weight, and temperature variations within snow piles. Children also become nature detectives as they speculate and verify the sources of animal and people tracks.

"A Calendar of Activities" illustrates how you can plan an entire month of science activities using the winter season as the focus.

"Ice Cubes" by Roger Horton provides experiences with freezing and evaporation. A series of open-ended questions promotes inquiry and could be handled as a question-a-day "teaser" for kindergarten children.

Spring

Spring brings a burst of science opportunities as children are eager to be outdoors more. "March Winds Do Blow" highlights a wind walk, describes outdoor activities suitable for the entire month, and a discussion of favorite toys that depend upon the wind for their use. These spring science activities involve art, music, dance, and dramatic play.

"Grasses and Weeds" and "Dandelions" suggest ways to investigate these readily available plants of springtime and early summer.

"Rainy Day Activities" and "When the World Is Puddle-Wonderful" make the most of April. Some activities can be done indoors but plan to don rain gear and go outside when the rain is gentle and friendly. Children are not marshmallows: they do not melt in rain. There is so much to learn while finding out the effect of rain on the environment.

Summer

Many schools are not in session during summer months, but day care centers and summer camps are open. "A Seashore Trip" is an ideal excursion for those children who live close to the shore. The guided observation of water, animals, and plants allows children to become knowledgeable about this unique environment.

"Reading Readiness in Science" is a logical follow-up to the previous article. It demonstrates how shell collections are perfect for using the seven basic skills outlined in Science—A Process Approach (SAPA). Matching a real shell to its picture is a first step in readiness skills for four-and five-year-olds. By adding the common name beneath the picture, another level is added. For young children this pre-reading to reading sequence increases their interest in science as it improves their reading skills. This article is proof of how basic science is to the early childhood curriculum.

Fall

Darshan Bigelson

Picking Up On Leaves

—— Margaret McIntyre ——

Autumn means a deluge of leaves that may or may not be welcomed by adults. For children, though, the fallen leaves are a source of pleasure. Young children gather them just because they enjoy picking things up and having their own collections. Teachers can tap this universal activity to further nature learning and, as a bonus, combine such learning with art. Thus, children can share the beauty of their leaf collections with others during the holiday months of November and December.

Sorting and Classifying

Children can collect leaves almost anywhere they go during the fall—on the school grounds, in their own yards, as they walk around their neighborhoods. Once collections have been assembled, examined, and admired, they can be used to practice classification, with categories based on the children's own observations.

There are many levels of cognitive development at any age, and alert teachers will use open-ended questioning to ascertain the levels of individual children as they sort leaves into various categories. To the usual categories of color, size, and general shape some children will be able to add categories of flat or curled, simple or compound, toothed or lobed. Young children will not use these labels, but a teacher can apply the appropriate terms with older fives and with six-year-olds, who will pick them up with use.

The logical next step is to have the youngsters make outline drawings of various kinds of leaves and use these for classification. Label the drawings, as many five-year-olds will begin to associate the leaf with its name on the label.

The experience of identifying a leaf with its name might lead some children to try to associate a few of the most common leaves with the trees from which they come. Teachers can help children link the general shape of the tree and the color of the bark with the leaf unique to that tree.

All these observing and classifying activities can take place over time and can be used as the beginning of tree study to be pursued during the winter and spring. Thus, children may later be able to add buds, flowers, and fruit to their list of a tree's characteristics.

Card Making

An appropriate artistic application of the leaf-study activities would be the making of holiday cards. Favorite leaves can be chosen to dry and press for this purpose. Insert the selected leaves between several sheets of newspaper for a week or so. Put something heavy, like a board and blocks or books, atop to press the leaves flat.

If some leaves are stiff and would be crushed if flattened in this way, they first can be plunged into hot water for a few minutes. Teachers will need to supervise this activity very closely. If you place the leaf in a handled sieve, you can allow the children to lower it carefully into the water.

During the drying process, children can continue with leaf sorting, outline drawing, and tree walks. They can check the progress of the leaf drying and pressing to note changes from day to day. Older children can make a simple time line or bar graph of the time needed to dry various types of leaves. Observation and discussion are important.

Children can also cut paper for their cards and make envelopes. White and soft pastels are excellent for this.

Use white glue to fasten the dried and pressed leaves to the cards, letting the children arrange the leaves in their own individual ways. Cards can be then pressed under books overnight to make sure the leaves are securely attached.

When the holidays roll around, the children have cards to use. All they have to add is the greeting.

Reprinted from *Science and Children*, Nov/Dec 1982, Copyright NSTA.

A Living Science Laboratory

——— Margaret McIntyre ———

The outdoors tempts young children as they return to schools and centers after a summer break. Why not plan weekly activities that will permit children to use the outdoors as a living science laboratory for the next month?

First, you need to canvass the area to determine what sites are available. Plan how the children will work; the smaller the group, the more personal the learning. Not every child needs to do exactly what everyone else is doing. If you have other adults helping you, consider taking only a very small group of children outside at a time. Another possibility is to have a sufficient number of adults and sites available to permit a group of three or four children to work with an adult when the entire group is outside together.

Collect the permission papers from parents and you are on your way.

The First Week—Plant Exploration

1. Walk around the school to see how many different kinds of plants the children can locate. Naming is not necessary, just keen observation of all growing plants.

2. Children can look for different kinds of grasses in the area. Help the children use a hand lens to examine samples closely. Bring back a few blades of each; the children can identify some of these from sourcebooks. Some grasses are short; others are tall. Why do you think they grow this way?

Phyllis Marcuccio

3. Walk around the sidewalks and areas paved with stone or concrete. What do the children find growing there? What colors are some of the plants? Are all green plants the same color? How could you sort the green plants? How tall are some plants? What could you use to measure them? Try measuring some of the small plants. Are there any plants whose names you know? How do the plants grow in concrete or stone?

The Second Week—Weather Exploration

1. On a day when a brisk wind is blowing, what things can children see that are affected by the wind?

> clouds moving across the sky
> dust and debris blowing
> patterns made in grassy areas
> as the wind blows across

2. On a windy day, the children might lie under a tree. Are the leaves still or moving? What parts of the tree move other than leaves? What sounds do you hear from the leaves or branches? Can you tell in which direction the wind is blowing by looking at the tree and leaves? Show the direction with your body; lean like the tree branches.

3. Take the children on a walk along a fence or a hedgerow on a windy day. What objects have been blown into the hedge? Put the items into bags and carry them back to school. How many items are from nature? How many are made by humans? If you left these items along the fence would any be changed in appearance during the fall and winter? What would happen to them? Talk about stages of rotting or decomposing.

4. On a sunny day, have the children use their hands to determine why some materials feel hot while others are cool. Talk about which of the following are in the sun, or in the shade:

> tree trunk
> metal swing
> window glass
> wooden fence
> bricks on building
> leaves on a tree
> leaves on the ground
> sidewalk
> metal fence

The Science Teacher

Reprinted from *Science and Children*,
September 1980, Copyright NSTA.

5. After a rain look for:
dead worms on the sidewalk
    mud puddles
     rain puddles

Why is one puddle clearer than another?

A hard-soil area such as a playground is ideal for investigating paths of water. Where does the water that makes the path come from? Do little streams of water flow into the larger path(s) of water? Find these streams and trace to the source (gutter, hill, downspout, etc.). Where is the water moving slowly? Why? How can you tell? Where is the water moving very rapidly? Why? Does the water feel cool or warm?

The Third Week—Tree Walks

1. Show the children how to measure trees around the trunk by using hands and arms. If the tree is really old, two or three children may need to join hands.

2. Have youngsters gather leaves from each different tree they see. Mount these on paper or press them between clear contact or waxed paper. How many different kinds of leaves did you find on your walk? What trees are beginning to show different leaf colors?

3. The children can feel the bark on different trees. Describe the feel. Look closely at the bark. What kinds of patterns do you see? How many different colors can you find in the bark? Try a bark rubbing using wax crayons and paper. Look at the bark closely. Do you see any scars? Can you find places where lower branches have fallen off? What happens to the bark at these spots?

4. Have the children lie on their backs around a tree. Let them describe the leaves. Have them look at the trunk to see how it grows. Where are the main limbs? How do they grow? Where are the smaller limbs? How do they grow out from the main limbs?

Tell the youngsters to lie *very* quietly for a few minutes. What birds do you see? Are there bird or squirrel nests? Could there be insects around the tree? Which senses tell you there are? Can you name an insect that you see or hear?

Ellie Snyder

The Fourth Week—A Potpourri of Explorations

1. Observe the activity taking place around an anthill. What kinds of food are the ants carrying? Try to locate where the ants are getting the food. Look in the grass. How does an ant travel in grass? If you were as tiny as an ant, how would a blade of grass look to you?

Are the ants all the same size, kind, and color? Talk about similarities and differences.

2. Take a spiderweb walk along a fence or near low bushes. Where can you find your first spiderweb? What shape is it? What kinds of insects are trapped in the sticky silk? How many? Why are spiders useful to us? Draw a picture of the spiderweb, using a soft pencil. *Do not* put a spider in your hand. Some may bite when they are disturbed.

Spiders weave their webs in different ways, depending upon the type of spider. Can you find a second kind of spider? Talk about the web pattern of this spider. Look at the spider closely to see the difference in this spider from the one that you first saw. Look for small spiders and their silky webs blowing through the air like tiny parachutes.

Take a walk early in the morning. look for webs in the grass. What makes the web of silky substance so easy to spot in the early morning? Look for one with a funnel shape and see if you can locate the spider waiting under the open funnel. You may be lucky enough to see the insect fall in and the spider devour it.

Phyllis Marcuccio

Fall Nature Collectibles

——— Margaret McIntyre ———

Fall is an ideal season for children's walking trips in the neighborhood and in nearby parks and fields to gather nature collectibles. Collecting is fun, and children can use the materials for many science-related activities. Leaves, flowers, seeds, and nuts offer possibilities for both simple and more complex science studies.

Classification

The process of noticing similarities and differences in materials leads to sorting or grouping things that are similar. Have children describe objects they gathered as they classify their collections. Watch and listen to the children as they talk among themselves while grouping their nature finds. Have labels ready for each grouping of similar materials. Question children as to the reason for their groupings. You will gain insight into how they are thinking.

Young children can develop the skill of precise description, the hallmark of a scientist, if given time for practice without fear of having to meet exact criteria. The children have the prerogative to group and to talk about reasons for the grouping. Children might group leaves, for example, by color, shape, degree of freshness of the leaf, texture, smell, edging, or vein pattern. Younger children tend to group on the basis of gross differences; older children use finer differences.

Have children trace leaves and make leaf rubbings. These activities extend knowledge and interest in size, shape, texture, edging, or vein patterns of leaves.

Seriation

Children's experiences extend and deepen, as they slowly begin to perceive gradations in similar materials. The process of comparing and coordinating differences in objects is called seriation. It is an ordering task, arranging objects on the basis of size or any quality that can be graded. Have children, depending on their developmental level, group leaves, flowers, or nuts by size ranging from small to large, in similar or different objects. They might order nuts by texture—smooth to rough.

Labeling is important, especially for older children who are bridging the gap from object knowledge to written symbol representing that object as used in reading. Have older children read labels. Younger children will do so eventually through further experiences with materials.

Centers

Use tables or sets of boxes in classroom centers, extending use of collections. Egg cartons are useful for classifying small objects such as seeds and nuts. Do not merely set up a show-and-tell display table where material is only looked at, but not touched.

You might organize centers by the type of objects collected—seeds, nuts, flowers, or leaves, for example. This arrangement gives a sense of order and permits a continuum of experiences with a set of similar materials. Younger children need this order, as well as limits on the mix of materials.

Naming varieties of nature materials is appropriate, although recall of names does not need to be stressed. Only children's use and understanding of the name as related to the materials will assure that children understand seriation. Children are naturally curious about names, and their normal interest can easily be nourished.

A magnifying glass stool is an excellent tool for observation of nature materials in a center. Children can easily set materials under the magnifying glass for close examination and comparison. Leaf veins, size and shape of seed pods, and flower petals will look different when magnified. Encourage children to talk with each other about what they see as well as with adults.

Seed Center

Set up a center on seeds in the fall. The activities given are based on a seed collection. Classify by fruit or vegetable, size, color, shape, and texture—rough or smooth. Put seeds with a rough texture on paper with a rough texture, put smooth seeds on typing paper.

Use construction paper of different colors for classifying seeds according to color. Match seed shapes to paper cut in round, oblong, or linear shapes. Show seed size by sorting them into small, medium, or large plastic bowls. These activities require little preliminary introduction and permit exploration of seed qualities at different cognitive levels.

Have younger children match flower and vegetable seeds to the plants they come from. Older children can use pictures. Sunflowers, zinnias, asters, and milkweed seeds are readily found in gardens and fields in the fall. Fruits and vegetables such as apple, pear, watermelon, canteloupe, pumpkin, tomato, squash, and grape seeds are available.

Floating and sinking is another possible activity in the seed center. Use pans filled with water to test which seeds float. Have young children put seeds that float in one pan, those that sink in another. Have older children put seeds that float on a paper labeled *float*, indicated by a sailboat on water. Have them put seeds that sink on a plain sheet labeled *sink*. Explain the terms to the children. The float-sink experiment assumes children have had previous experience with the concept of floating and sinking as related to materials in the environment.

Roger Wall

Fall Harvest And Science

———— Margaret McIntyre ————

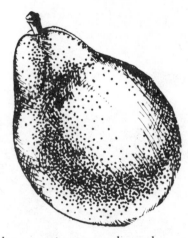

Autumn brings to mind the bounty of vegetables and fruits available from produce stands, home gardens, and supermarkets. It is easy to overlook the science teaching potential in this harvest.

Children need real fruits and vegetables to investigate. Learning variety names is not a principal goal, although adults should identify fruits and vegetables correctly, enabling older children to learn the names as they handle them.

Melons

The most common melons are watermelons, cantaloupes, honeydews, Crenshaws, and casabas, although others such as the Gaylia Hybrid (bred in Israel), or Honey Loupes (a hybrid cross between a cantaloupe and a honeydew) are sometimes available.

That all these melons grow on vines is something children can see for themselves if a visit to a home or market garden is possible. (The average child may believe all fruit grows on trees.) Collect as many varieties as possible. Children need to handle them gently to get some notion of how each one looks, feels, smells, and weighs. Kindergarten children, especially, might want to put them on a scale.

Use a learning center approach. Have a table available with two varieties of melon for four- and five-year-olds—one melon will be enough for younger students. Small groups can take turns going through the center; an adult can act as a consultant. These are probable investigations:

- Color of the skin
- Look and feel of the skin
- Shape of the melon
- Mass—very young children will be unable to lift some melons. How will they handle this problem? Older children can read a scale.
- Mark, indentation, or stem where the melon was attached to the vine
- Odor
- Circumference—fives can use a tape measure, younger children a piece of string or a paper strip. Kindergarten children can make a simple bar graph to compare circumferences.

The best part is yet to come: cutting and eating as part of the snack or lunch. You may have to wait a day or two until the melons fully ripen. If so, the children can watch and smell this ripening—more learning potential.

Do the cutting of large fruits yourself, while talking about cutting in half, in quarters, and in smaller pieces. As the cutting takes place, these questions will beg to be answered:

- What color is the fruit inside? Is it the same as the outside?
- Is the rind thick or thin?
- What's inside the melon? Have children spoon out the pulp and seeds in cantaloupes and similar melons and put them in dishes or on paper towels to examine them. What color and shape are the seeds? How do they feel? Wash and dry the seeds. Some child might want to count them.
- Cut the melon in slices; enjoy and talk about the taste. Does the fruit taste like it smells? How does it feel as you eat it?

Watermelons can be the midget variety, the round, or the long oval. Perhaps you'll have all three during the harvest season. Watermelon seeds can be a problem. After observing with the children that the seeds are not clustered, take them out if young fours and under are going to eat the melon.

Pumpkins

The best known October fruit is, of course, the pumpkin. All the observations previously discussed can be made with pumpkins. Carving a pumpkin will provide access to the inside, so make this activity a pre-Halloween event. Scoop out the meat, fiber, and seeds with a large spoon. Wash the seeds and spread them thinly on paper towels and plates to dry for a few days in a warm, airy place. The dried seeds can be lightly salted and eaten. The pumpkin meat can be cooked and used to make pumpkin bread or cookies. The shell is your Halloween jack-o'-lantern.

Grapes and Pears

Other fruits of fall are grapes and certain varieties of pears. Visits to orchards, gardens, and vineyards will enable children to see how these fruits grow on trees or on vines tied to trellis-like structures. The following observations are possible with grapes:

- Where are the clusters of grapes on the vines?
- Observe the shape of a cluster, the shape of the grapes. Where are most of the grapes in a cluster?
- Observe the color of the grapes.
- Wash the grapes and pop some open to look for seeds. Some may have no seeds.
- Smell the grapes. Taste them. Do they taste like they smell? Give younger children the seedless grapes to try.

Pears have the advantage of being small enough for each child to handle.

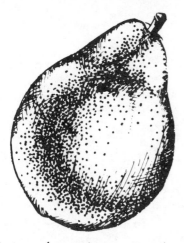

Reprinted from *Science and Children*, October 1982, Copyright NSTA.

Try to take a trip to a pear tree in a garden or orchard. Children can see where the pears grow on the branches and how firmly they are attached. Culled or diseased pears may be lying under the tree. By asking appropriate questions, you can lead children to investigate closely worm holes, scars, bird pecks, and insects. Curious four- and five-year-olds who wonder what eventually happens to this fruit can be led through a discussion of ecology.

If no pear trees are accessible, the supermarket or fruit stand can serve instead. If various kinds of pears are displayed, ask the children to talk about their individual qualities. Then, following the trip, they can have a pear tasting. Cut the pears into small pieces and let the children sample and compare as many varieties as possible.

Squash and Yams

Other fruits and vegetables are less familiar to children but can be used in the same learning center approach. The fall and winter squashes are colorful and vary in shape. Have a selection of at least one of each variety available from home gardens, farms, produce stands, or supermarkets for examination. These fruits keep well and will withstand young children's handling for several days. Butternut, acorn, spaghetti, Hubbard (warted blue), buttercup, and banana squash are varieties usually available. Draw pictures of each and label them to indicate which is which. This is an excellent reading readiness technique.

Squash skins are hard, and squashes are often referred to as hard-shelled. This characteristic enables squash to keep for months in a cool, dry place. The children can feel the outer hardness, but only after cutting can they really appreciate this quality.

All of these squashes can be baked or steamed and eaten. You could use one variety every few days over a period of weeks. The day before you cook the squash, cut it up so children in small groups can examine the inside. These details can then be examined closely:

• Color and texture of the inside
• Stem end where the blossom was
• Location and pattern of the seeds—in the center, all over, or at the blossom end
• Kinds of seeds—shape, color, and size
• Separate seeds or seeds buried in a mass of stringy pulp; moistness or dryness of pulp
• Smell of the squash—cooked and raw

A spaghetti squash can be a real treat when served with spaghetti sauce. Pierce the squash all over with a long knife, then boil it for about an hour. Children will have to rake out the cooked squash to discover that the inside looks like long strands of spaghetti. Other squashes can be lightly seasoned and served as a snack or used as the main ingredient in squash muffins, cake, or bread.

Do not overlook the sweet potatoes and yams harvested in fall. They have interesting shapes, colors, and textures and can be cooked for snacks using a favorite recipe.

How Young Children Learn

There is much potential from this "harvest," but approach such teaching with caution. There is a temptation to teach young children with a heavy hand, and to make claims about the content and concepts mastered that anyone who actually knows young children finds impossible to believe. Didacticism produces the memorization that over-eager parents and teachers presume to be learning.

These activities should take place over a month or more, not in a few days. Allow children the time necessary to savor the many possible learning experiences they can have with a fall harvest of fruits and vegetables.

Young children need time, opportunity, interesting materials, and other children and adults with whom to interact. They need to wonder, investigate, and find out for themselves. These are the *basics* of science that children can master during their early years. Science is fun; learning is fun. It is a perpetual "Look what I've found out." "Look what happened." When this innate enthusiasm is tapped, learning takes place.

Other Articles About Using Fruits and Vegetables in the Classroom

1. McIntyre, Margaret. "Fruits and Seeds." *Science and Children* 15:32-5, May 1978.
2. ———. "Grocery Bag Seeds and Plants." *Science and Children* 16:52-3, April 1979.
3. ———. "Pumpkin Science." *Science and Children* 19:22-3, October 1981.
4. Schafer, Larry E. "Powerful Pumpkin Science." *Science and Children* 14:22-4, October 1976.

Pumpkin Science

——— Margaret McIntyre ———

Reprinted from *Science and Children*,
October 1981, Copyright NSTA.

For young children, Halloween brings the fantasy of jack-o'-lanterns. Why not use pumpkins in your science activities the week before Halloween?

If you are fortunate enough to live where pumpkins are grown, schedule a class trip to buy some. Few things are more satisfying than selecting one's own pumpkin in the field. You can see how far apart the rows are; touch the tangled dry vines and leaves. Choose a pumpkin with just the size, shape, and color you like. If you can't get to a pumpkin patch, make your purchases at a supermarket or farm market. In any case, each child needs a pumpkin.

Back at school with the pumpkins, try these activities before you cut jack-o'-lanterns.

Measuring

Young children can use string or yarn to measure the circumference of a pumpkin. Where is the measurement to be made? Why? The children could make a yarn graph of pumpkin circumferences by thumbtacking the yarn lengths to a bulletin board. Can children guess which pumpkin is the smallest in circumference and which is the largest? Check with the yarn lengths. Do round pumpkins or long pumpkins seem to be bigger around?

Kindergarten children can go a step further. Have them place the yarn along a metric stick to measure the length (even if an adult has to read it). Primary children can easily read the measurement, and draw horizontal bar graphs instead of yarn ones.

Have students measure the pumpkins' height, too. Will children measure from the top of the stem or from the indentation scar where the stem was? There is room for discussion of what the stem is, how it feels, and how large it is. Examining stems may lead primary children to see a relationship between stem size and pumpkin size.

How do you measure the height of something round? Here is an opportunity for investigating, for trying out ideas and finding a solution. Height yarn graphs are possible—using a vertical line graph.

Measuring also involves mass. Children can pick up the pumpkin to feel its weight. They can pick out the heaviest and lightest pumpkin in a group.

Scales make accurate measurement possible. Young children like to weigh pumpkins even if they cannot read the scale or comprehend grams and kilograms. Primary children can begin to do this on their own. Be sure to tape the known mass on the bottom of each pumpkin. Later, when the pumpkins are hollowed out to become jack-o'-lanterns, primary children can note the change in mass.

Ask the children what needs to be done to study change in mass. How will they know what material came from each pumpkin? When will reweighing be done? How can the material from inside the pumpkin be weighed?

What if the mass of the jack-o'-lantern plus the material taken out does not add up to the original mass? Can the children find an explanation? If you keep a jack-o'-lantern and all the material removed from it for a couple of days, does the mass change?

Counting

Help the children count the curved lines along the outside skin of the pumpkin. How many lines are there? For younger children, stick a thumbtack at the top of the first curve as a starting point. Which pumpkin has the most or fewest lines? Older children may link pumpkin size to the number of lines.

After the pumpkin carving, count the seeds. Younger children can arrange seeds in pairs while older children can count them out in fives and tens.

Colors

Observe the skin of the pumpkins. How do they differ in color? Affix the

Measuring

name of each child to his or her pumpkin, and sort the pumpkins by color. What color are the stems or stem scars?

When you carve the pumpkin, what colors do you find inside? Are the stringy fibers a different color than the meat of the pumpkin? Compare the color of the pumpkin's outer skin and inside.

Are all the seeds the same color? Are larger seeds a different color than smaller seeds?

Smelling

Smell the pumpkin before carving. Does it have an odor? Smell the skin and the stem scar. Smell the bottom of the pumpkin, where it rested on the ground. After carving, smell the inside—really put your nose down into it. Smell the pumpkin strings and seeds.

Feeling

Carving the jack-o'-lantern gives children a chance to feel the inside and outside of a pumpkin. The curved lines, bumps, and lumps of the outside contrast with the smooth slickness of the skin. Children will describe these textures imaginatively if you encourage them by questioning.

Inside the pumpkin there are strings and seeds. Quite a different feeling here—almost unpleasant sometimes. Once the inside is cleaned of strings and seeds, the children can rub their hands over the meaty surface and describe that feeling.

Shapes

Carving a jack-o'-lantern is a very individual matter. Using a felt pen to draw a face on the surface helps children carve more accurately. All carving must be *closely* supervised by an adult. Teach the children to carve away from their bodies. Younger children need help in holding and inserting the knife.

Talk about shapes. Will the eyes be squares, triangles, circles, or rectangles? How about the nose? Will the mouth be straight or curved up in a smile or down in a frown? If there are to be teeth, what shape will they be? What is

the difference between making square eyes and square teeth?

Tasting

Any child who wishes may taste a sliver of pumpkin. Ask them to describe how it tastes. Is it soft or crunchy?

If there is an extra pumpkin, children (kindergarten age at the earliest) with adult supervision can cut the meat into chunks for cooking. Once cooked, a teaspoonful topped with a dot of butter and a dash of nutmeg makes a tasty snack. Any remaining meat can be used to make pumpkin bread. Pumpkin also makes wonderful drop cookies, with raisins for eyes, nose, and mouth. Jack-o'-lantern cookies dress up a Halloween party, and provide science experiences in their making.

For another snack, try roasting pumpkin seeds. Children enjoy washing seeds in cold water to remove pulp and stringy matter. Dry the seeds between paper towels, and arrange them in a single layer on a cookie sheet. Put them in an oven set at 350°. (Teachers need to supervise this closely.) Roast seeds 30 to 60 minutes, watching closely. It takes longer if the seeds are large or wet. Why? The seeds will be dry and pale brown when ready to eat. *Cool* before snacking.

Save some unroasted seeds to plant next spring when the ground warms up.

Art by Johanna Vogelsang

Reprinted from *Science and Children*,
October 1975, Copyright NSTA.

Taking an Insect View

———————— Margaret McIntyre ————————

HENRY DAVID THOREAU wrote that "Nature will bear the closest inspection. She invites us to lay our eye level with her smallest leaf, and take an insect view of its plain." How advantageous this viewpoint is for the nursery school child! Not only is a young child physically closer to the ground than adults, but children also gravitate quite naturally to the ground during most of their activities.

Why not help young children observe living things in their unique environment near the ground? Such observation is basic to understanding the emerging science of ecology, which is becoming increasingly significant to the quality of life, and as important for children to be aware of, as for adults.

The fascinating study of ecology is best studied outdoors. As a starter, you need only a plot of ground (hopefully in the school yard), clear plastic beverage glasses in which to place soil samples, a couple of trowels, some plastic hoops about two or three feet in diameter, or lengths of heavy rope if hoops are not available.

Observing the soil first, children can note the color of the bare soil (they might call it mud). Dig some and put a lump of bare soil in one glass and a lump with some vegetation in another. These samples can be used for closer examination right on the spot or taken back to the nursery school. Spread some soil on white paper or old sheeting, and let the children use their fingers to locate twigs, tiny stones, worm castings, seeds, roots, insects, or decayed vegetation. Compare how different soil samples feel.

Children can observe the water-holding capacity of soil samples from different areas of the yard and from other areas. Through the clear plastic, they can see the water permeate the soil. You can introduce potting soil or a humus material from plant containers already in the room. Even the time water takes to permeate the different soils can be checked. Measuring spoons and medicine droppers are best for adding water to the soil.

Plastic hoops make great space definers. The hoops could be placed in different areas of the yard, under trees, in full sunlight, near a sidewalk, and near a dug-up bed of some kind. Children become nature detectives and scout how many living things they can see in the enclosed spaces. While most of the children are taking a close-up insect view, others can be observing air space above the defined areas for insects and flying birds. These observations could be timed to see how many living things one could observe in a given area in one to five minutes. Try to have one observation after a good rain. The children will not be able to name everything they see, but they can note the variety, sameness, and difference in objects and living things observed. They may be able to come up with a very simple classification. It may be time for adults to name living things, and give more information if the children seem interested.

Ant activity in the soil, such as their carrying food, can be a fine conversation topic. If there is morning dew on the ground, let the children feel the wetness as well as note the beauty of the sparkle from the sunlight. Even Spiders might be about. Talk about and observe the patterns of spider webs. Watch for other animal patterns such as the path a slug leaves where it has gone over the sidewalk, or the way a leaf has been turned to lace.

A trip to the woods opens up additional experiences. When you enter the woods, what kind of plants do you see on the ground? Children can locate mosses, fungi of various kinds, weeds, and young trees. As you walk into the woods, what are you walking on? How did it get there? Look for fallen logs. If a piece of bark is loose, lift it up gently to observe any activity there. What kinds of things do you see? What do they look like and what are they doing? Indicate their names, too, and put the bark back so as not to disturb this mini-ecosystem. Try to find a small log to roll over carefully. What do you see under it? It is the same as under the bark? Return the log to its former position. Help the children to see that living things are all workers in a little community of their own that we need to respect.

Woods with evergreen trees provide an additional dimension. What is on the ground under the trees now? Feel the material and describe it. How many different kinds of objects do you have? Help the children with the correct terminology. Does a woods with many evergreens look different from one with largely deciduous trees? This is a good place to gather soil samples here.

Have the children notice how high the branches are on the larger trees. Help the children to see that older branches are closer to the ground, and as the trees grow, the newer, upper branches shut off the light from the older ones. So what happens? Can they see any evidence of this? You could use a light meter in different parts of the woods if the children were made familiar with it before the trip.

Children might want to pick out which are the oldest trees. Can a child put his arms around the trunk of one of these? How many children would it take? Stand in one place and see how many different kinds of trees you can see from that spot. Talk about how they are different by comparing the shape and color of leaves, bark, and shape of trees.

Through many such experiences during the early years, children will become gradually aware of the science of ecology.

Learning from Fallen Leaves

—————— Margaret McIntyre ——————

WHO can forget the acrid smell of leaves burning in the fall? Whether or not leaf burning still occurs where you live, fallen leaves provide the early childhood educator with ways to engage children in activities that will help them grasp concepts of nature's recycling process.

Raking leaves is a good motor activity and could bring out cooperative effort in small groups. If there are no leaves at the school site or center, go to a park or recreation center, or the home of one of the children. Seeing, watching, and touching fallen leaves will give children needed experiences with seasonal change. Each day, the children can watch for changes in color as the leaves slowly decay and disintegrate.

During a leaf walk, there may be many opportunities to see and compare what people do with leaves and what other things happen to leaves after they fall.

After the children make piles of leaves, a compost heap could be a long-term experiment. Use water to wet them down so they will not blow away. There could be a dip in the center of the pile to hold rainfall. A few pailfuls of water could demonstrate why a dip is needed. Such play could be extended to the sand table for further investigation.

Children may have seen adults mixing leaves with soil in the garden. Have the bigger children (or adults) dig a ditch into which the children pile leaves. Mix in the soil after the leaves have had a chance to decompose a little.

The children might make suggestions for putting more or less leaves in the ditch. The children could shovel the dirt in and tamp it down. In the spring, plant flowers on the site.

Children can also bring in bags of fallen leaves, which can be sorted by size or color. Ask questions about leaves under the trees. What happens to leaves when it rains? How can we fix containers of leaves to be wet by rain? What happens to leaves after they are wet for a period of time? How can we find out? Will wet leaves decompose faster than dry ones? What does the word decompose mean to you? How can we find out which leaves decompose faster? Can you guess whether a pile of small leaves will decompose faster than a pile of large leaves? How can we find out? Let the children use the word *experiment* during these activities.

Discuss the leaves outside. What happens to them during the day? During the night? Does the sun have any effect? Leaves can be put in containers in the sun; others in the shade. They can be checked daily to make comparisons and to add water as appropriate. How many days will it take for the leaves to decompose? How can we record this? How can you tell that the leaves have decomposed? Feel the decomposed leaves and compare them with newly fallen leaves. Do dry leaves have an odor? What about the decomposed leaves? Describe the smells. Compare the colors of leaves at various stages from just fallen to fully decomposed. When you hold the container of decomposed leaves, do you notice anything? When do we first feel the heat? *Why do you suppose the leaves are hot?*

What can you do with decomposed leaves? Have you ever heard of the word "mulch"? What does it mean? If there are plants in the room, the children could mulch the plants. Children can thus develop a recycling concept understandable to them about nature's processes.

Winter

The World In Winter

— Margaret McIntyre —

Young children need several years to understand seasonal change. It is easy for them to see that winter follows autumn, but the changes that take place in the environment during winter require observation over a period of time before they can be comprehended. The new year offers a good opportunity to provide such experiences. Even in areas of the United States that have little or no snow, seasonal change does take place.

Evergreens and Holly

If you have not taken the children on a getting-ready-for-winter walk in the fall season, do so now. What signs of winter can be seen in the trees, shrubs, and plants? Ask open-ended questions to elicit children's comments about what they see, and add to these comments by asking related questions.

The senses of seeing, feeling, and smelling are needed to study evergreen and deciduous trees. Some of the latter may still have leaves. How do they look? What is their shape and color? You might name the berries for older four- and five-year-olds. Holly bushes will be especially interesting because they have leaves and berries, and they can also be used to enlarge the children's idea of what an evergreen is. You might see birds eating berries, but, even if you don't, point out that berries are an important winter food for birds.

Children should also observe how winter weather affects plants outdoors. Some children may not be aware of what freezing can do to a plant. Recreate this condition by providing an overgrown or unwanted plant for them to put outdoors overnight when the temperature will dip to below freezing. When the plant is brought inside again, introduce the term "wilt" to describe the condition of the plant's stem, leaves, and flowers. Perhaps some children will want to water the frozen plant and place it in a sunny window. Go along with this: children need to see for themselves, not be told, what will or will not happen.

Snow Birds

During January make a census of birds found around the school or neighborhood. Keep a chart to check during the remaining winter months and to

Katy Kelly

add to in the spring. Fours and fives can learn the names of common birds very easily during daily observation and by checking in bird guides or books about birds. Have photographs and pictures available throughout the winter. The youngest children need photographs rather than drawings of birds, though drawings can provide another level of learning for older four- and five-year-olds.

Extend and deepen the learning by giving children a chance to see what

Reprinted from *Science and Children*, January 1983, Copyright NSTA.

birds eat besides berries. Preschoolers can easily construct simple bird feeders, and even the very young can stuff suet into wire or plastic net containers, put popcorn on string, or place commercial bird food in tray or silo feeders.

When there is snow, help children to become nature detectives by encouraging them to look closely at the tracks on and around the feeders. They should note the number of tracks, their shape, size, and how deep the tracks are. Ask questions to encourage children's thinking about the size and weight of the bird. If possible, take pictures of unfamiliar tracks so the children can look in bird books to find out what birds made the tracks. It's never too early to encourage students to look up answers in books, even when they are not yet reading, and matching tracks is an excellent prereading skill.

Winter Dress-up

Winter's effect on children's clothing is obvious. Children who walk to kindergarten take longer to remove their outer clothing than they did in the fall. Ask them what extra clothes they wear now and of what materials these clothes are made. What about the weight of a winter jacket, snow pants, and boots? Use a scale to weigh a child with and without outer clothing. What is the actual weight? Older children could use a number line to express the increase, while younger children can simply become more aware of the fact that clothes have weight and, therefore, do weigh a person down.

Children might also think about how winter clothing restricts their play. Ask whether they run in heavy coats as easily as in light sweaters? Get them to try. How do they walk in snow? Run? How does snow depth affect the ease with which they walk and run? When it snows, have them find out.

Getting Around in Winter

Cold weather affects the school buses

and the family cars in which children come to school. Discussions with a parent or bus driver can help children think about this and will lead to the subject of winter tires and why they are necessary. Car radiators provide another useful cold weather subject. Is it just water that a parent or gas station attendant pours into the radiator, or is it water with a special chemical added? Get the children to half fill two plastic containers, one with water and one with antifreeze. Mark the fill lines with a felt tip pen, label clearly, cover, and leave overnight in below-freezing weather. Next morning the children can describe what happened. Where are the containers' contents in relation to the fill lines now? Which contents are frozen, which are still liquid? Antifreeze is poisonous, so be sure to caution children not to lick or taste it. Be sure, too, that an adult is always present during this experiment.

On a day following a substantial snowfall, allow plenty of time for the children to talk about their difficulties in getting to school. Outline them on a chart and encourage the children to formulate and answer their own questions about tire chains, parent difficulty in starting the car, shoveling the path and the driveway, snow plows and sand or salt trucks on the streets, and falling down in the snow.

A brief walk around the block could open further discussion. Where are the snow drifts around the school the highest? Where are parked cars the most snowy? Why? Why are chunks of snow and ice stuck under the fenders of vehicles, and why do they drop off in the streets as cars and buses start moving? Ask the custodian to let children sprinkle salt crystals on the sidewalk where snow is packed. Perhaps they can also put sand on packed snow to see what happens.

Watching Winter Skies

Winter is an excellent season for star gazing with young children because stars are visible before their bedtime. In the summer this is probably not the case. Ask them for their ideas about this phenomenon. It will take young children several years to comprehend fully how the length of the day varies with the season.

Kindergarten children might consider making a chart of the times the sun rises and sets each day. This information can usually be found in a local paper, and locating and entering it on the chart would be an assignment that children could take turns in doing. The chart would reveal how the days slowly lengthen as spring approaches.

Winter provides opportunities for science experiences. Take advantage of this season so children can enjoy their learning.

Bulletin Board

Reprinted from *Science and Children*, January 1983, Copyright NSTA.

A Sensible Clown

All children love clowns. And kindergarten children love learning about the five senses with a clown bulletin board.

The clown itself is made from construction paper and cloth, with face, hat, gloves, and shoes made of paper; the body is stuffed fabric. Use scraps of contrasting fabric to cover the arms, legs, and torso and to make a ruff for the neck and a flower for the hat. Add pink shoelaces for a nice finishing touch.

In one hand, the clown holds five bal-

loons (we made ours from wallpaper) to help remind the children there are five senses. Attach the strings to the clown's hand with staples, and fold the fingers over the staples. Use construction paper for the label "5 Senses."

The words *Taste, Hear, Smell, Touch, See* are felt letters decorated with materials evoking the sense they name. For instance, each letter of the word *Taste* can have something sewn or glued on it that children might enjoy eating. (We used popcorn on the *T*, peanuts on the *A*, fruit-flavored cereal on the *S*, candy corn on the *T*, and marshmallows on the *E*.) The other senses can be made vivid by something equally appropriate, such as jingle bells for *Hear*, fabric flowers (perhaps sprayed with cologne) for *Smell*, cotton balls for *Touch*, and foil letters cut to fit inside the felt letters for *See*.

Finally, so the children can see the connection between the sense and the part of the body to which it belongs, attach each word to the appropriate spot on the clown with colored yarn.
Patricia Laney, Instructional Assistant, Fort Bragg School, North Carolina.

Phenomena for Inquiry

"P for I" asks students questions about everyday events and objects to encourage exploration. Send your ideas to column editors Irwin Slesnick, Biology Department and/or John Whitmer, Chemistry Department, Western Washington University, Bellingham, Washington 98225.

Ice Cubes

Reprinted from *Science and Children*, February 1979, Copyright NSTA.

How long will an ice cube last if left on a plate in your classroom?

Will it melt faster if broken up?

Will an ice cube twice as large last twice as long?

Will an ice cube last longer in a glass of water at room temperature or in air?

Does the size of the glass of water make any difference? What about the temperature of the water?

Can you design a container that will keep an ice cube for a long time? What materials would you use for insulation?

Who in your class is the champion "ice cube keeper?" (Putting your container in a freezer doesn't count.)

Would your container also work well for keeping hot things hot? How could you tell?

For further ideas on ice cube activities see the Teacher's Guide for the Elementary Science Study unit on *Ice Cubes.* **Roger Horton**, Holly Area Schools, Holly, Michigan. (Photograph by Roger Wall.)

Eastern Hemlock

Reprinted from *Science and Children*,
Nov/Dec 1981, Copyright NSTA.

Holiday Science

——— Margaret McIntyre ———

November and December are holiday months. Take time to involve children in some of the following science activities related to the holidays.

Evergreen Trees

No Christmas is complete without a tree. Take a trip to a nearby park, tree nursery, forest area, or corner Christmas tree lot. Look at the different kinds of evergreens available. How many different kinds are there? Point to each one and identify it for the children. Ask them to observe how the trees' needles differ from the leaves they gathered in the fall. Explain to them that evergreen trees produce needles and drop them all year long, not just in the fall. Look closely at the needles. What color are they? How do they grow on the tree? Feel the needles. Are they smooth or prickly? If possible, collect some needles from the trees; keep each type separate. Smell the needles. Some have a distinctive scent.

Have the children examine the bark. Does it have long ridges or deep furrows? Touch it with your hands. Ask the children to describe what they see and feel.

Now study the color of the bark. How many trees have bark of the same color? Is the bark on the branches the same color as the bark on the trunk?

Look for cones on the trees. Where on the branches do you find them? Look for cones on the ground; collect some to take back to the classroom.

Tree Shapes

Evergreens have a distinctive shape. Have the children step back a short distance so they can see the entire tree. Then ask:

1. Where do the branches start? From the ground or some distance up the trunk? Measure informally using the height of a child or an adult.

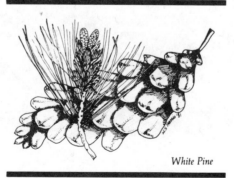
White Pine

2. What tree has branches bending down? (Spruce) Growing straight out? (Pine) Children can point this out on the tree and use their arms to demonstrate how the branches grow.

3. Which tree has thick foliage and is not very wide? (Cedar)

Classroom Collections

Back at school, set up a center for leisurely exploration of the needles and cones. Pine cones can be stored in a basket and brought out on a desk or table top for examination.

1. Describe each cone's appearance. Is it long and slender or short and round? What are the sections of the cone called? (Scales)

2. How are the scales arranged on the cone?

3. Describe the outer edges of the cones. Are they smooth or sharp?

4. Where are the cone's spines in relation to its scales?

5. How big are the cones? Measure with your hands, fingers, or a piece of string.

Now arrange a cone from each kind of tree in two pans. Place one pan in a sunny window or on top of a radiator; the other in the coolest part of the room. Which cones open first? Why? Does the size or the shape of the cone have anything to do with this? Leave the cones out for at least 10 days. (If the cones are not open by then, dry them in an oven—200° for 20-30 minutes.) Push the scales of the cone apart; can you see the seeds?

What color are the seeds? What shape? Are there "wings" on any of the seeds? Why?

Older children can group the seeds with the appropriate cones and label them.

Other Holiday Trees

In warmer regions, some trees have green leaves all year, but are not evergreens. One such tree associated with the holidays is the big-flowered magnolia. Show the children a magnolia. Have them feel the leathery leaves, measure them, and note their glossy green color.

Blue Spruce

Are the leaves dark or light green?

Investigate the American holly, another holiday tree. Visit live trees if possible and ask the children to locate the male and female trees. Which birds do you see eating the berries? Why do birds love the red berries on the female holly?

Describe the texture of holly leaves. Why do you have to be very careful when you pick up a holly leaf? What are the points of the holly leaf called? (Spines) Feel the leaf's mass. Is it light or heavy? Is the leaf glossy or dull? Where do the red leaves grow? Do berries appear singly or in groups?

Edible Decorations

The children can prepare holiday treats for the birds and hang them on trees near the school. The easiest treat is a string of popped corn or cranberries. Children love to pop corn and it is an easy task for five-year-olds. To create a chain, use tapestry needles and nylon thread. Make each string long enough to drape around an evergreen tree. While stringing, children should always be seated and carefully supervised by an adult.

Pine cones can also be used to create bird treats. Mix peanut butter with cornmeal or fat and insert the mixture in the spaces between the cone's scales. Children's fingers or a spoonhandle are best for doing this. As an added treat, mix several raisins or sunflower seeds into the peanut butter mixture. Help

the children tie strong cord around the top of the cone to hang it on the tree.

Put pieces of suet from the butcher into a net bag salvaged from packaged onions or produce. Tie the bag to a tree branch.

Punch holes in the sides of a half-pint milk carton to create a bird feeder. Children can dry squash, pumpkin, and other seeds for this feeder.

When the children eat fresh apples for snacks, have them save the cores and seeds for the feeder. Peanuts or cracked nuts are also tasty treats for the feeder.

Douglas Fir

Bird Pudding

Everyone enjoys holiday puddings—including birds. To make bird pudding from scratch, assemble the following ingredients and equipment. (This pudding is *not* for children to eat. Make a point of this when introducing the project.)

Equipment
Two-quart saucepan
Medium-sized stainless steel bowl
Plastic bag, 30 x 24 cm
Saucer
Stirring spoon
Six empty yogurt cups
Rolling pin

Ingredients
One-half kilo of bacon fat or other fat

One tablespoon honey
Four cups stale cake, bread, biscuits, or crackers
One-half cup oatmeal or cracked wheat
One-half cup wild birdseed

Directions
1. Put stale, dry ingredients in plastic bag and crumble bag with rolling pin. Add oatmeal and birdseed to crumbled ingredients.
2. On low heat, carefully begin to melt fat in saucepan. Add honey.
3. When fat is almost melted, add dry ingredients. There should be signs of fat around the edges of the mixture; if the mixture is too dry, it will crumble.
4. Remove mixture from heat and place in steel bowl. Put a saucer on top and press down. Leave until bowl is cool enough to handle.
5. Press mixture into empty yogurt cups and let stand another day in a cool place.
6. Have adults tie strings around the top of the cups so that the children can hang the bird pudding from tree branches.

One delightful holiday activity remains for the children: watching the birds come to feast on their holiday treats. And that leads to even more science learning.

Kindergarten Explorations With Snow, Ice, and Water

MARTHA A. CARROLL

Kindergarten Teacher
Public Schools
Brookline, Massachusetts

THE UNUSUALLY COLD winter of '77 offered a natural laboratory for my kindergarten students' exploration of snow, ice, and water. Having a classroom with access to the outdoors, I found that our interest in the weather led to a fascinating learning activity for all of us. As the children learned about water, snow, and ice, I learned more about the workings of five-year-old minds.

The activities started when we filled our water table with freshly fallen snow. Throughout the morning, the children enjoyed shaping, holding, and piling it. The longer the snow remained in our warm classroom, the soggier and more compact it became. I joked, "All right, where is it? I filled the water table with snow. Now there's only this mushy mound left. What happened to it?"

The children took me seriously. Solemnly they assured me they hadn't taken any snow, but no one could explain where it had gone.

Melting and Freezing

The next morning I gave the children cups and suggested they fill them with snow. "If you let the snow melt," I asked, "how much water will there be in the cup?" Most were quite sure: A cup of snow will make a cup of water. I suggested they put their cups where they thought the snow would melt quickly. There were cups everywhere—on windowsills, tables, and under radiators. Throughout the morning the children periodically checked their experiments, comparing melting progress. Some moved their cups nearer the radiators as they saw the snow in cups placed there melting most rapidly. It was a surprise to everyone that a cup of snow yielded only about ¼ cup or so of water. The children drew lines on their cups to record the water level.

I reviewed the results of our snow experiment with the children a week later. "Could you reverse the experiment?" I asked. "Take a partly filled cup of water and turn it into snow?" Most children thought this would be possible and developed ideas of how to do it. Many children simply filled their cups with water and put them outside in the below-freezing weather. Others mixed snow and water together, shook the mixture up, and left it outside. One wanted to add bits of ice to his water, so he broke an icicle into his cup. A few children left their cups of water inside.

At noon, everyone checked their experiments. Only the children who had left their water cups inside were disappointed, as nothing had changed. Although they hadn't made snow, others were fascinated with their cakes of ice, ice-covered snow, or ice with icicle bits. They were delighted with their results.

Expansion

We tried an ice demonstration. We filled a tall wine bottle[1] with water, corked it tightly, and put it outside. The next morning, the class was intrigued to see the cork gone, ice spilling out of the neck, and the bottle cracked all over. Why had the bottle cracked? No one had any explanation to suggest.

Next, I gave every child a flexible plastic food container with ridges on the sides and a tight-fitting top. Each child filled their container to the brim with water, put the lid on, and left the container outside. I asked them, "What do you think will happen to the water as it gets colder?" I expected the children to relate it to the bottle demonstration and wonder if there would be room for the ice. But they were operating at another level. One child said, "I think it will become ice." Another said, "Maybe it will become snow." "Snow *and* ice," said a third.

By the next morning the ice had pushed out some of the ridges and raised the tops into domes. However, I found my kindergarteners were not interested in the expansion, but rather attracted by the shapes of the ice pieces as they came out of the containers.

Some children were particularly intrigued by the crystalline designs in the ice, saying, "There's a white porcupine in my ice cube!" Many children enjoyed melting their ice forms in their hands. Others left their ice on trays but checked them often. A few children put their ice

---

[1] Wine bottles are usually thicker than soda bottles.

forms outside so they could take them home intact.

February, with its days of freezing and thawing, became our month for estimating temperature. Rather than concentrate on skills of thermometer reading, each day I asked "Will water freeze today?" At first, the children had different opinions. Four children offered to find out by putting cups of water outside. At noon, they reported their findings to the rest of the class, and we recorded the answer: "Yes."

We checked freezing conditions every day. The children's initial guesses were quite random, even on very cold days. After several freezing days in a row, their guesses were always yes. And after a few days of above-freezing weather, they would all begin to guess no. The day came when we had to write yes and no; the water that a child had placed in the shade was partially frozen, while the three cups left in the sun did not freeze. The next day, with outdoor temperatures bitterly cold, the children's guesses were almost unanimous: Water will freeze in the shade, but not in the sun!

Their predictions seemed to be based on the previous day's findings, rather than on bodily perception of the temperature outside, or on observation of the snow and ice in their neighborhoods and schoolyard. Perhaps with some coaching, the children could have found other clues in their environment for comparing temperatures.

Evaporation

I wiped a section of the chalkboard with a damp sponge. We watched the wet spot grow smaller and smaller and finally disappear. Where did the water go? There were a number of explanations:

"It sank into the chalkboard."

"It dissolved."

"What does 'dissolve' mean?"

"It's like when you put sugar in water and it disappears."

"It went into the air."

"Are you crazy? The water couldn't have gone into the air because if it did it would be raining now!"

I gave each child a clear plastic cup marked with a line about one cm from the top. The children filled their cups to the line with water and placed them on window sills around the room. Every morning they marked the water level with a crayon or grease pencil on the side of the cup.

The water levels kept dropping. Children would show me their cups, and point to the old and new marks. "Where did the water go?" I'd ask.

Some would shrug. "I don't know."

One child used the word "evaporate."

"My mother told me it goes into the air."

"It goes out the bottom of the cup into the radiator."

One child, at five, had become skeptical. When I asked him to check his water experiment and mark the level, he replied, "Why should I? I know after we go home you just go around and dump the water out."

As the evaporation project progressed, the debate narrowed to one question: Can water go into the air?[2]

This unit on water in its many forms was a learning experience for us. While the children carried on some provocative explorations about the nature of water, I learned understandings and perceptions that kindergarten children bring to this kind of study. I was surprised to discover some of the concepts and ideas my children had difficulty grasping, such as:

1. Snow and ice melt to become water.
2. Snow or ice melts when the environment is warm, and the warmer the environment, the faster the rate of melting.

---

[2] Unfortunately, safety regulations prevented us from boiling water in the classroom to see it become steam.

Reprinted from *Science and Children,* January 1978, Copyright NSTA.

3. Water, frozen into a solid, will take on the shape of the container in which it was frozen.
4. A large quantity of snow melts into a small quantity of water.
5. Water can evaporate into the air.

In general, the children struggled with the predictability of events. After finding out that snow melted into a small amount of water, some children still felt a week later that a cup of snow, melted again, would give a cup of water. One experience was not enough to shake a belief that seemed logical to them.

Also, they could not associate how cold the air felt to them with how likely the water was to freeze. If water placed outside froze one day, children were likely to say the next day water would freeze, regardless of the temperature felt. Since they could not figure out any other way of determining what might happen, they evidently relied on the most recent experience.

From this unit, I learned the great advantage of each child having his or her *own* experimental materials—as simple as a cup of water or snow, personalized with their names.

The unit ended, and we put away the plastic cups. I told the children there are always tiny invisible drops of water in the air—more on damp days, but still present even on dry days. I explained the word "evaporation," and related it to our experiment, to clothes drying on a clothesline, to going swimming and drying off in the sun. The children listened quietly.

Now when I sponge off a table and ask where the water goes, the children smile and say, "Into the air." But I'm still not sure if they *really* think so, or if they're humoring someone who thinks you can have water in the air even when it's not raining.

Snow

—————— Margaret McIntyre ——————

February means snowstorms in many parts of the country. Why not take advantage of the season to help children discover some of the properties of snow?

Falling Snow

Go outdoors to listen to the snow falling. What do your hear? Can you see your breath? Why? While outside, have children collect snowflakes on black cloth or paper to study shapes. Why do you need a dark paper? Use a magnifying glass and be prepared for snowflakes to disappear quickly. How many rays or arms of the snowflakes can you count? What do snowflakes look like? Are snowflakes all the same size? Are they all the same shape? How are they different? How are they the same?

Walk around in the snow. Are the snowflakes dry and fluffy, wet, or dry and powdery? How can you tell? At the beginning of a snowfall, walk around the school yard to see where the snow sticks and piles up first. Why does the snow melt at first in some places? Why do some places have no snow at all? How does snow stick on tree branches?

Look for snowplows on the roads. Watch how they remove snow from the road. How? Have children draw pictures of snowplowing when they go indoors. What would happen if the snow were not removed? Watch for cars on the road. What happens to snow as cars go over it? Can you hear cars making a clicking sound as they go by? What makes the sound? Why do people put chains on their wheels for a snowstorm?

After a Snowfall

Take a meter stick outdoors. Measure how deep the snow is in different level areas around the school. Mark the stick with chalk or a felt pen. Why do you think the snow cover varies in depth?

Let all the children use a snow shovel to lift snow. Feel the mass. Is the snow fluffy, wet, or powdery? Take your children outside under different conditions so they can examine different types of snow. Make snowballs. Does some snow make better snowballs?

Make a large snow figure of a person or animal. Use your imagination in decorating it. Use poster paint. Measure the height and width with a string or meter stick. Measure around the middle of the body with a string. Take all measurements again after an hour or a few hours, then the next day. Chart how long it takes the figure to melt. Where did it go?

Talk about the influence of the sun on melting snow. Roofs in the sun and sidewalks in the sun and shade make good places to observe. Talk about the influence of color. Contrast snow melting on the black top of the playground and the cement sidewalk. What do you see?

Pack snow in pans and take them indoors. What happens? Measure the water that results from the melting. Are you surprised at how little there is? Describe the melted snow.

Observe the color of freshly fallen snow. Watch color changes over several days. What happens to the original color? Why? Make two large piles of snow (the same size). Cover one pile with black plastic. Leave the other pile uncovered: Watch the piles for a day or two. Which pile melts faster?

Animals often burrow in snow to keep warm. Have children guess where a snowdrift is coldest. Use a thermometer to measure temperature differences in a snowdrift. Stick the thermometer in a short distance from the top and leave it there a few minutes. Read and record the temperature. Push the thermometer halfway into the drift and repeat. Push the thermometer to the bottom of the drift. Do the children's guesses agree with the results of the experiment? Farmers and gardeners like a deep snow cover. The snow is

like a blanket, protecting plants underneath from bitter winter cold.

Who Goes?

You and your students can also study tracks in the snow. Make footprints in the snow. How can you tell who made a certain footprint? How can you tell in which direction the person was moving? Study animal tracks too. Can you see tracks that are small and look like scratchy lines? These are made by small birds. Are the tracks sunk into the snow or are they on top? Are the birds light or heavy? How can you tell which way the bird was moving across the snow?

Look for paw tracks. Where do they go? If there are squirrels in the area, look for their paw prints and follow them. Can you find a place where the squirrel climbed a tree?

People and Snow

After a storm when the snow is fresh and the sun comes out, what happens to your eyes when you are looking outside? Why? What could you wear over your eyes if you had to stay out in the snow for a long time? Young children may associate sunglasses with summer only. Tell them about snow blindness.

What happens to melted snow during cold nights? How do you walk on ice? What does the school custodian put on ice on the steps and sidewalks outside your building? What happens? On roads, maintenance people use ashes, salt, or sand and dirt on hills, at intersections, lights, and on icy stretches of roads. Have children look for these places. Why are these materials used?

Take a trip to a garage to see the differences in the tread of snow tires, radial tires, and regular tires. Use the word "tread." Let children feel the tread. Measure the tread and the width of the tires. Talk about why tires with deep tread work better in the snow.

Snow offers many chances to practice observational skills. All you need are a few warmly dressed students and snow.

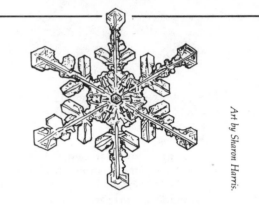

Reprinted from *Science and Children*, February 1982, Copyright NSTA.

Margaret McIntyre

February is the shortest and, in many states, coldest month of the year. As winter activities begin to pall, try these to add zest to your program.

February 1

Take the children to observe a nearby tree. Ask them to describe its appearance. Take a picture to compare with one you take later in the year.

February 2

Read aloud *Keeping Your Body Alive and Well* (Joy Wilt, Word Incorporated, Waco, TX, $4.95). It describes the physical needs of kindergarten children, emphasizing the body's value and care.

February 3

Bake banana date cookies with the children. Use fresh dates so that the children can examine the whole fruit. Carefully crack walnuts in the shell. Discuss the nutrition in bananas, walnuts, and oatmeal. Try this easy recipe:

79 mL oil
1 mL salt
3 bananas, mashed
237 mL chopped dates
118 mL chopped walnuts
474 mL oatmeal

Mix the ingredients together. Drop by teaspoonfuls on a greased cookie sheet. Bake at 350° F until light brown.

February 4

Read aloud *Animals Should Definitely Not Wear Clothing* (Judi and Ron Barrett, Atheneum Press, New York, NY). The children will chuckle at the absurd situations into which the animals get themselves. Discuss appropriate clothing for people.

February 5

Set up a center to measure liquids. Cut off the top of a half-gallon milk carton. Let the children guess how many cups of water are needed to fill the container. They can verify their guesses by counting or printing a line tally during an actual filling. Repeat the action using smaller cups. How many cups are needed? Repeat the whole process using larger and larger cups. Cups can range from doll-sized to demitasse to large coffee mugs. Older children might want to experiment with a range of measuring containers.

February 8

Take advantage of freezing temperatures. Fill an ice cube tray with tap water. Then fill another with a salt-water solution. Put both trays outdoors or, if necessary, into a freezer. Ask the children to guess which tray will freeze first. Why? Later check to see which tray is frozen. (Keep the ice cubes made from tap water.)

February 9

Take yesterday's ice cubes and divide them equally in four bowls. Cover one set with sand, one with sawdust, another with dirt, and the last with salt. Set the bowls aside. Ask the children periodically to check on them. Under which substance is the ice melting fastest?

Find an icy patch outdoors. Have the children sprinkle salt on the ice and describe what happens. While waiting, discuss the safety precautions children should follow on icy surfaces.

February 10

Pour water into a wide-mouth, plastic glass until it is almost full. Carefully add a large ice cube. Be sure that the cube floats freely. Using a medicine dropper, carefully and slowly add water. What happens to the ice cube's position as water is added? When the ice cube melts, what happens to the water level?

February 11

Read the first part of *Everything Moves* (Seymour Simon, Walker and Company, New York, NY) to a small group of children. Try rapping a spoon against the floor as Simon suggests. Feel the vibration? Use a triangle from the rhythm band. After hitting the triangle, quickly place the striker in a cup of water. What happens? Why? Do the same thing with a spoon after rapping it against the floor.

February 12

Since this is the last school day before Valentine's Day, read the children the material in Simon's book about how blood flows to the heart. Teach them how to find their pulse points. If they

f Activities

lie on their left sides on a hard surface, can they hear their heartbeat? Allow them to listen to one another's heartbeat with a stethoscope.

February 15
What birds live around your school this time of year? Take the children on a bird walk to see how many they can identify and list. Repeat the walk every two or three weeks until school ends. Discuss how the list of birds changes and why.

February 16
Help the children build a simple bird feeder on an outside window. Fill the feeder with cracked corn, bread crumbs, raisins, peanuts, suet, apple slices, and wheat. Make a chart showing what birds come, when, and the food each eats. Be patient. It may take a while for the birds to find the feeder and to feel comfortable using it.

February 17
If the ground is soft enough, take the children outdoors to dig up a 30 centimeter (cm) square of dirt, 13 to 16 cm deep. Put the dirt in a sturdy box, covered with clear, plastic wrap. While the box's contents warm up over several days, ask the children to observe them. Any signs of life? Why are these changes happening?

February 18
Locate a copy of *Zoos Without Cages* (The National Geographic Society, Washington, DC). Students will pore over the book's lifelike illustrations for hours. Read aloud the astounding list of foods the animals eat daily. This behind-the-scenes introduction to animals and their lifestyles might spark interest in a winter visit to a zoo.

February 19
In mid-to-late February, in some areas, pussy willow may be getting ready to bloom. The children can locate bushes in their yards and bring a branch or two into school. Keep the branches in a water-filled, glass container near the light. Watch the pussy emerge from its dark brown shell. Feel the buds. Talk about color. Draw pictures. Direct the children's attention to how the buds are arranged. Watch the roots grow— in what direction? In the spring, plant the cuttings in the school yard for observation next year.

February 22
Use balloons to show the children how air contracts when cold and expands when warm. Blow up a balloon for each child. Trace the outline of the balloon onto paper. Put the balloons outdoors or in a freezer. Thirty minutes later, retrieve the balloons and compare their sizes with the outlines. What happened? Listen carefully to each child's explanation. Feel the balloons. Describe their appearance. Leave the balloons in a warm room for an hour or so. Again compare their sizes. Discuss what has happened. (*See "Investigation of Air" article in this issue.*)

February 23
If it is snowing, bundle up and go outside. Catch snowflakes on dark wool cloth or black paper. Observe the flakes' intricate six-sided designs through a magnifying glass. Notice how the designs differ. Count the sides. Describe

the sound of snow falling. What other noises do you hear? Are they loud or soft? Name their sources.

Later try making paper snowflakes. Cut out circles at least 15 cm in diameter. Fold the circles in half, then in thirds. Carefully cut designs along the top and sides; unfold a snowflake design. Have the children arrange the results on a bulletin board.

February 24
Take a small group of children outdoors to record street sounds. A child can narrate the date and time of observation. Back indoors, have other children listen to the tape and identify the noises. Discuss the sounds with them. Are they quiet/noisy? Pleasant/unpleasant? Repeat this activity later in the year to discover how outdoor noises change.

February 25
Bring in an alarm clock (spring driven with a loud tick-tock) or a small portable radio. Ask the children to discover ways to muffle or diminish the sound. Provide them with boxes, towels, plastic packing material, and newspaper. What material works best? If a small radio is used, vary the intensity of its sound. How much material is needed to muffle different sounds?

February 26
Spring is less than a month away. Force some Forsythia or other blossoms to bloom by putting branches in water. Watch for changes daily. Keep a chart. Why do the branches bloom indoors before outdoors?

Spring

March Winds Do Blow

Artwork by Doreen Curtin

Reprinted from *Science and Children*, March 1981, Copyright NSTA.

———— **Margaret McIntyre** ————

Winds blow every month of the year, but in northern areas of our country, folklore associates March in particular with wind. Why not use March winds as a focus to initiate the concept of wind as an energy source? The concomitant concept of energy producing motion is a difficult one for young children to understand. Nevertheless, we can provide activities in which children may grasp some connection between wind's variable force and energy.

Preparation from the Classroom

Observing from classroom windows is one way to sensitize children to movements resulting from a brisk wind. Children can be asked to look outside and identify what they see moving at *first* glance, then describe the movement of the various objects, describe how the wind is moving the objects, and enumerate what they see moving when they take a *longer* look. Perhaps an adult can record the children's observations on the board or a chart.

Beginning Wind Walk

Take a small group of children outside on the playground on a windy day. Before leaving the classroom, give each child a small stick to which a cloth streamer or an old nylon stocking has been tied. This activity needs to be carefully supervised with four- and five-year-olds. As they go outside, ask the children to notice what happens to the cloth. Can they point in the direction in which the cloth is pointing? Does the cloth point in the same direction all the time? If the children walk to a different spot outdoors, what happens to the position of the cloth?

Collect the sticks, leave them in a safe place, and begin the wind walk. The area covered should include the space outside the classroom viewing window. Now that they are out in the wind, can the children identify even more objects the wind is moving?

Allow plenty of time for the children to comment on how they feel in the wind. What does wind do to them? Try walking in different directions so that the wind makes it hard to walk or easy to walk. Use the words "with" and "against" the wind to expand the children's language. Can they find a way to stand so that the wind pushes against them? What places are available to get away from the full force of the wind and yet stay outdoors? Why does the wind feel less strong in these places?

Ask the children to close their eyes and stand still. How can they tell the wind is blowing? Do they hear the wind? What sounds does the wind produce? Have them repeat these sounds for others to hear, then listen again. What does blowing wind do to their clothes and hair? Have the children describe the sensations they feel. When they open their eyes, have them verify the descriptions they have given. Can they figure out what is causing the sounds of the wind?

Take a walk around the block in the city or around the school yard in a rural area. Look for more signs of wind movement. Encourage children to look up in the air and down along the ground. Use questions to enable children to extend the list of objects or signs of wind blowing. Are clouds racing across the sky or barely moving? What about smoke from chimneys? Is smoke being blown in a certain direction? Ask the children to point in the direction the smoke is being blown.

Outdoor Activities in the Wind

What materials seem to blow around the easiest outdoors in the wind? Put a piece of paper on the ground. Where does the wind blow it? Ask the children to run and see if they can catch the paper before it blows again.

Try doing the same with a small cardboard carton. Does this move as far as a piece of paper? Can the children tell why? Have the children arrange a race between the paper and the carton. The children could measure informally how far both go by counting the steps they take to reach both objects.

If you have saved milkweed seeds from an autumn walk, have the children guess how far the seeds might travel in the wind. Then throw them, one at a time, into the wind. How far *do* they travel? Can they guess how high they go into the air? Was their movement slow or fast?

Before reentering the building, check the school flags outdoors. Listen carefully. What sound do the flags make? How are they flying? In what direction? Have the children use their hands to indicate this. Checking the flag every day is a method to observe firsthand the effect of wind force on how the flag flies and what sound it makes.

These activities can be done over several days. Ideally, brief walks can be taken during a period of weeks. This exposure permits the child to develop a growing awareness of variability in the force of wind. At times the wind is barely felt. Observations under such conditions need to be made repeatedly by the child. At other times, the wind is very strong, perhaps strong enough to present a danger to children outdoors. Watching the force of wind from a window on such a day could lead to a discussion of the dangers of walking with an opened umbrella against the wind, being under a tree when branches fall, or getting dirt or sand blown in your eyes. Children can see what happens in strong winds and describe what is taking place.

Toys that Use Wind

Wind also moves or activates many toys young children enjoy using. Simple kites can be made in school, or parents can be encouraged to make them with children at home. Some five-year-olds can handle kite flying, but younger children are often frustrated by the experience. Older siblings and parents could help a five-year-old get the kite elevated and share the thrill of the wind's moving the kite. Younger children enjoy watching a kite fly. How much wind does it take to fly a kite? Which is better—a strong wind or a gentle breeze?

Pinwheels and windmills made from milk cartons are toys that children can easily construct. Children can move the wheels with their fingers, run with them, or blow on them. Give the children plenty of opportunity to experiment at will and to talk about what they are doing.

Once outdoors the children can see what effect the wind has on their pinwheels/windmills. Go out on several days when the wind is blowing at different strengths to give children an opportunity to work through the concept that the pinwheel turns slowly or rapidly, depending on the strength of the wind. Allow the children to experience this themselves.

Integrating Experiences with Wind

After several personal experiences with the effects of wind on themselves, the outdoor environment, and their toys, children may be ready to explore in more than words what they feel about the wind. Art, music, dance, and dramatic play provide opportunities to integrate what they have learned. Children need only time, space, and teachers who provide materials and encouragement. Scarves, for example, allow children to run and move as the wind, with varying strengths or as gusts. Appropriate rhythm instruments can be used by some children to express their knowledge and feelings about the force of wind.

Gifted children can make up chants appropriate to the wind's movements/sounds. These often lead to songs, with creative movement and instrumentation. Why not free your children to express their knowledge, impressions, and even concerns about the force of wind?

DaNDeLIONS

How long does it take a yellow flower to change into a seed head?

Suppose that the plant that would grow from this seed produced an average number of seeds. (About how many is that?) And suppose that all these seeds produced plants that made seeds and grew into plants. What would be the population of dandelion descendants during the fourth generation?

How long would it take dandelion seeds to germinate if placed in a closed jar with wet paper towelling? Do they all germinate at the same time?

In what kind of soils do you find the longest dandelion roots?

This dandelion has five leaves. Can you find any dandelions with six or more leaves?

Is the latex (milk) that appears when you break open a root useful as a glue? How is rubber made of latex?

Reprinted from *Science and Children*, March 1972, Copyright NSTA.

From the "Phenomena for Inquiry" column by Irwin Slesnick and John Whitmer of Western Washington State College, Bellingham, Washington.

Grasses and Weeds

——————— Margaret McIntyre ———————

SPRING must be the perfect season to take young children out of doors to investigate the common but fascinating living subjects, grasses and weeds. Often adults overlook such unspectacular materials readily available because they are so familiar and ubiquitous.

There should be no problem in finding a location in your area for a grass and weed hunting expedition. Grasses and weeds grow in the sidewalk cracks of urban areas as well as in school yards, parks, lawns, and farmland.

A group of four or five children exploring with each adult is best for safety. The children will need collection bags; adults can carry trowels and a dandelion weeder. A good hand lens would be useful both on the outdoor expedition and in the classroom learning center that will be set up after the exploration and finding of materials.

Adults can involve the children in their groups with decision making about the quantity to be picked and reasons why grasses and weeds are permitted to be picked in particular locations.

Size of plants makes for interesting comparisons. In an unmowed area, both tall and short grasses and weeds can be picked. Perhaps children can find large and small versions of the same plant growing in different sites. Why are some short and some tall? Length and width of the blades of grass, as well as vein patterns, are good for close observation. Use the hand lens to make the pattern easier to see.

Dandelions

The children will see that the dandelion stem is different from some other weeds and grasses. What does the stem look like, in their own words? When the children break the stem what do they see and feel? Try to find a large dandelion plant. Have the children describe the leaves and show where they grow on the plant in relation to the stem.

Let the children pick dandelions. The stem of the flower is thick enough to peel. What happens then? Stems may be split to make dandelion chains or bracelets to wear. Some flower heads may have gone to seed. What is the purpose of the "parachute" that holds the seed? It is always fun to blow the seeds away, then be a detective to locate where they have blown. Be sure the children really examine the seeds carefully to locate the lumps along the sides of the seed and to feel the pointed end. They may be able to suggest functions of these seed characteristics.

Large dandelion plants will have unopened flower buds as well as open flowers. Children need to have a chance to locate where these are on the plant and to feel them. Let them break open a green bract to see what this

RICHARD GUY

looks like. Some children might have had some experience with watching buds open. They would be able to tell which ones would open first. The feel of the unopened dandelion can be compared with that of the one in bloom and the one that has gone to seed. Colors can be noted.

Dandelions can be dug up to allow children to see the type of root and to locate root hairs. It's fun to touch the root and root hairs. Have the children describe the sensation and tell you what roots and root hairs do for the plant.

Let a child hold a dandelion flower under another's chin. What do you see? What is your explanation?

Plantains

Plantain, a common roadside and lawn plant, can be compared with the more familiar dandelion. Encourage children to look carefully at the sizes and shape of the leaves. Feel the edges of the leaves. Put leaves on top of one another to compare.

Chickweed and clover are often found in grassy areas. The children can count the leaves. They may discover that finding a four-leaf clover is not easy. Has anyone seen a five-leaf clover? Compare the feel of the leaves of the two plants. You may be lucky and locate two types of chickweed, smooth and hairy. Where is the hair? If there are blossoms, describe these in terms of color, size, and type of blossom. Is there any fragrance to these? What is the fragrance if there are no blossoms? Look closely at the stems of clover and chickweed. What do you see?

Oxalic, at first glance, may look like clover. Heart-shaped leaflets distinguish the oxalic plant. Children will recognize the shape as that of a valentine. Compare the flower of the oxalic with that of the clover, and look closely at the stems too. By digging up plants of clover and oxalic, the children may see the root systems and compare them with the root systems of the dandelion.

Reprinted from *Science and Children*, April 1977, Copyright NSTA.

Fescue

Some grasses such as the clumpy, coarse fescues look very distinctive. The foxtail one is bushy, giving rise to its name. Perhaps you could find some of them. Goosegrass is another choice grass to find on an expedition, even if homeowners do all in their power to discourage its entrance into the lawn bed. It has a large seedhead that bears close examination. (The distinctive straight green line down the middle of the long slender seedhead resembles a closed zipper). See how creative the children can be describing what they think it resembles. The growth pattern of goosegrass is unique, similar to the spokes of a wheel.

A learning center on grasses and weeds could be set up in the classroom as a result of this expedition. Other specimens could be added to it. Plants could be matched at first. Later, they could be classified by size and shape of leaf, by general appearance while growing, or by the feel of leaves of stems. Classification by root systems is possible. Size or color of flowers as well as seed sizes could provide other systems of classification. It would be interesting to compare the stems of all specimens.

One or two of the more familiar grasses or weeds could be called by name so that all children would know them. However, learning names by rote is not the purpose of this learning center. Children may want to draw or paint dandelions and clover since these are familiar. Children could make booklets of grasses and weeds that they know. Labels on specimens could be used with older fives and sixes, as they might be interested in how the names look.

Some children might ask about how grasses grow. Planting grass seed in a barren area would be a useful exercise, involving preparing the seed bed, planting the seed, watering, and mulching the growing grass to protect its new growth. Early spring is the ideal time for this. (Planting grass inside in containers is possible, but seems inappropriate.)

What shape is the rain when it hits the sidewalk?
How high does the rain splash?

Rainy Day Activities ———————— **Margaret McIntyre** ————————

RAIN CAN stimulate indoor and outdoor science activities. Watching rain fall on windows can be an individual or a small group activity. What is a raindrop's shape? Are all drops the same size? What color are they? Which drops seem to be separate? Which drops seem to move the fastest? Which drops join together? What do they make when joined? Encourage children to point out and match the raindrop pattern on the outside of the window with their fingers. Two children at a window encourages conversation. One often helps the other watch and describe what is happening to the raindrops. Let children draw the patterns they see. If a window is screened, compare the raindrops that hit the window under the screen with those hitting an unscreened window. Is there a difference?

What does rain hitting a window sound like? Do this activity many times during rainy days to help children observe and listen to light, heavy, pouring rain, and rain driven by the wind against windows.

There may be no rain on the window, yet it is raining. What is the reason for this? Are there windows in the building where the rain is hitting? Why does this happen?

While in the classroom, have children make observations on the effect of rain outside. Then go outside and look for:

1. Areas where raindrops make the biggest splash.
2. Areas where there are puddles.
3. Areas where there seems to be the biggest puddles.
4. Areas where there are the deepest puddles.
5. Areas where water seems to be running fastest.

Have children look at the sky while rain is falling. What color are the clouds? Is the sun shining? How fast are the clouds moving? In what direction? (towards or away from landmarks rather than compass directions.) Can they predict when the rain will stop? During the inspection outdoors, use the terms *light, heavy,* or *pouring* often so children can make the association with the volume of rain they see, hear, and feel. What does it smell like outside?

Let children talk about why the biggest puddle is where it is. Why is it so big? Where is the water coming from that makes it the biggest? Is it the deepest puddle? Encourage children to use sticks or their feet (in boots) to find the deepest puddle.

Look for the muddiest puddle. Where is it? What makes it this way? Collect some water in a clear plastic cups to take indoors to let the dirt settle. Let children strain out the dirt eventually. Look for the clearest puddle. Why is it this way? Have children catch rain in plastic bags or cups. Why is it clear? Compare the rain to the water in both puddles. What do they see?

While it's raining, have children walk (with boots) on the grass. What sound do they hear? Walk on a sidewalk or driveway. Is the sound different? Jump on the wet grass. What happen? Jump in a puddle on the sidewalk. What happens to the water? Which jump makes the bigger splash?

Watch rain coming down on a sidewalk or road. Does it come straight down? Can you see individual drops of rain? When you tilt back your head to look at falling rain what do you see? Watch the rain as it hits the side-

Reprinted from *Science and Children,*
Nov/Dec 1978, Copyright NSTA.

walk. What shape is the rain when it hits the sidewalk? How high does the rain splash? If the rain is light, does it splash as high as when it is a heavy rain or a downpour? Indoors, have children talk more about this, make up experience stories, or draw what they saw.

Effects of Rain

During a light rain, let children see drainage of rain water from the roof, from the playground area, from the streets. If there are hills, look at drainage there. Have them observe the volume of water being drained away. Where does all the water go? If there is a nearby stream, let children locate run-off areas. What does the stream look like before and after a rain? Exercise caution near streams.

Walk under trees during a light rain to see if branches and/or leaves stop the rain. Look at a sidewalk that is dry under a tree while it is raining. Why is this? Look at rain falling on flowers, grass, bushes, or leaves. Look again after the rain has stopped. What happens to the raindrops when children shake a bush?

During several walks in the rain during the year, children could put out large shallow pans to catch the rain. Use a mark of paint or nail polish to show how full the pans become during each rain. While these are not accurate rain gauges, they lay a foundation for measuring rainfall. Use the rainwater for watering plants.

In winter, rain may be mixed with snow. Can children tell the difference between the two? Catch the snow mixture in a cupped hand. What does it feel like? Watch what happens. Why? Look at the snow as it falls on a sleeve or dark paper. What do you see?

In summer, rain often steams off hot roads, sidewalks, or grassy areas. Have children observe this. Walk through it to feel the moist heat. Explain that the cool rain hitting the hot surfaces produces the steam.

Absorption

Have a bag full of samples to test reactions to rain or soft snow. Use foil, wax paper, tissue paper, newspaper, cardboard, tongue depressors, paper towels, plastic cups, egg cartons, for example. Have children sort materials into those that absorb water and those that shed water. With five-year-olds, use *absorption* and *non-absorption*. An extension of this activity might involve using various cloth samples, including fabrics used in raincoats (ask for samples of some fabrics at a dry cleaners or tailor shop). Include synthetics and wool.

COURTESY SCHOLASTIC PHOTOGRAPHY AWARDS SPONSORED BY EASTMAN KODAK COMPANY

When the World Is Puddle-Wonderful

Margaret McIntyre

April is an eagerly awaited month in schools and day-care centers. Spring is *really* here, and with it comes the chance to go outdoors again without bundling up in all those mufflers and mittens. Frequent spring showers also provide many opportunities for special rainy-day walks and playground activities. Water fascinates young children, so use these "puddle-wonderful"* days for some firsthand scientific investigation.

Water, Water Everywhere

Once the children have donned their raingear, go with them on a puddle hunt. Where do most of the puddles seem to be? Are some deeper than others? How is it possible to tell? If it's still raining, the children might notice that the raindrops make a pattern on a puddle's surface. Or, if the Sun is shining, they might use the puddles as mirrors. Can they see their reflections easily? Encourage them to talk about differences between nature's mirror and the one they use at home.

Have them drop pebbles, twigs, and other objects into a puddle, one at a time, and ask them to observe the ripples that appear. Can they see any changes in ripple patterns as they drop in various objects? The children might remember some of the patterns they see and want to paint them when they return to the classroom.

Next, you might get the children to try some fancy footwork. What happens when someone wearing rubber boots steps gently into a puddle with just one foot? Two feet? What if he or she jumps in? Encourage the children to compare these ripple patterns with those they made earlier using pebbles and twigs. What happens to the water level in a puddle after all that jumping? This question is going to take lots of experimenting, which is great fun when the weather is warm and the children are dressed appropriately.

More Rainy Research

Walk around to see where you can find water running in a steady stream. Look carefully at the slides, swings, and other playground equipment; they're good sources of running water during a rain shower. Have the children place a bucket at the end of the slide, putting it close enough to catch the water that's running off. Leave the bucket and return after you've finished other rainy-day activities. How much water has run into the bucket? Return again after the rain has stopped and see if the bucket is full, or even if it has overflowed. While looking for running

*See e.e. cummings' poem, "In Just—."

water, take the time to examine water flow patterns in the mud, on hillsides, and in the street.

Don't overlook the trees in the playground or around the schoolyard, either. Look closely at deciduous trees (water will run down their sides, too). If the rain has stopped, then where is this water coming from? Examine shrubs and low tree branches for water droplets. Older children can count the droplets falling from a short branch; others can watch how the drops fall when you shake the branches, gently at first and then more vigorously.

Check evergreen branches for raindrops, too. Do evergreen branches have fewer or more drops than deciduous trees? (In many areas of the country, deciduous trees are not yet leafed out in April.) Older children could explore this whole concept in a fairly detailed scientific manner while younger children can simply locate where the water droplets form. This is easy to do after a shower if the Sun is shining brightly—or even peeking through clouds.

Indoor Waterplay

Continue your investigations indoors. Few things are more satisfying to a young child than filling and emptying containers with water. Capitalize on this fascination, and begin to introduce the children to some basic scientific concepts. Collect a variety of safe, waterproof containers in different shapes and sizes. Choose some containers with large openings and others with smaller ones, and make sure to include containers made of different materials (plastic, waxed cardboard, or metal, for example). To begin, have the children pour water into several containers of different shapes. This is a good way to show them that water will assume the same shape as the vessel that contains it. Or, introduce the children to the idea that different-sized containers will hold different quantities of water. Preschoolers are too young to understand the idea of scientific measurement. But four- and five-year-olds can begin to count how many containers it takes to fill one large one, and some kindergarteners can even reverse the process with surprising accuracy.

Focus their attention on the way water sounds. While you were walking outside, your students may have noticed that rain makes one sound when it falls on their hats and umbrellas and another when it's rushing from a downspout. How does water sound when children empty it from one container into another in the classroom? To find out, pour the water slowly, letting just a little bit drip out at a time. Pour it more quickly, and then simply overturn the container and let the water rush out. Ask the children to describe the sounds they hear. Or pour the water slowly into a metal pan. Does the sound change as the pan fills? Fill a soda bottle and a wide-mouthed bucket with water, and slowly begin pouring the contents into a sink or another container. The water in the soda bottle will bubble out at first and make a gurgling sound as air replaces the water leaving the bottle. The water in the bucket, however, will flow smoothly. Have the children describe the differences in the sounds they hear.

During all these rainy-day or water activities, make a point to tell parents or guardians what you are doing by means of a simple newsletter. Encourage them to follow through on what is being done at school. Short family walks, during or after the rain, and bathtub or kitchen activities with water enlarge the child's experience and demonstrate the parents' interest in what is being learned at school. Who knows? Parents may even enjoy a little puddling around themselves.

Summer

Reprinted from *Science and Children,*
October 1980, Copyright NSTA.

A Seashore Trip

———— Margaret McIntyre ————

The seashore, where saltwater and land come together, is one of the most interesting places children can visit. It provides an environment in which birds, fish, and hundreds of small animals and plants live together. For children who live close to the shore, a field trip is essential.

Each child should dress appropriately and carry a plastic shopping bag for collecting pebbles, shells, feathers, small pieces of driftwood, and other specimens washed up on the beach. Allow plenty of time for play, digging, and building, especially after the bus or car trip. Bring along enough adults to assure safety and to give children someone with whom they can share the treasures discovered along the beach.

Adults should be able to discuss the names of common marine life, sea birds, shells, and fish indigenous to their locality. A field guide to shells, marine plants, and animals is useful for onsite identification, and gives children the experience of using resource books.

The beach offers much to observe. Alert adults to what children first will want to see and to what is a teachable opportunity. It helps to focus on some flora and fauna in advance. By thinking through what one could see, adults can use every opportunity to help children closely observe what is happening on the beach. Depending upon your locale, try the following observation questions at the beach.

Water

Watch waves rolling in, cresting, and breaking. Estimate the area of white-caps to the rest of the wave. What is the height of the waves? Do the shapes of waves change as they break? Is the white foam left on the sand and rocks? Describe the color of the sea close to the sand, the color of the shallow water beyond the surf, and the color of the water far out. What is the direction of the tide, coming in and going out? Measure the temperature of the water by the shore. If you have a fishing line try measuring water away from the shore. Throw a piece of wood into the water and watch where a wave tosses it.

Animals

Gulls: Watch how gulls soar in the air currents and how they swoop down into the water to catch food. Is there a central place where gulls congregate to catch food? How many gather in one place? Imitate the distinctive sounds they make. When do they make these sounds? How do gulls sit on the rocks and sand? How do they walk on the beach? How deep are the tracks they make in wet sand? How do they escape from children?

Sandpipers: Where do sandpipers look for food? How do they use their long bills in finding food? What do they eat? How do they keep from getting wet when the waves come in? Notice their size and the length of their legs. Do these features affect how they walk along the beach? How do sandpipers rest?

Starfish: How many arms or rays does each starfish have? Notice the tube feet on the underside and the pattern of the starfish. How do they move along the sand? When do you know whether starfish are alive or dead?

Sand dollars: Notice the pattern on the underside and the upperside of a sand dollar. What color are sand dollars? Are they easy to find? Do the thinness and the flatness of their shell help them hide?

Clams: Count the different kinds of clams you find. What are the differences in the shapes of the different kinds? Do they move differently? Where do you see live clams? Look for tiny jets of water made by a clam digging itself into sand. Try digging for a clam. How does a clam dig into the sand for safety and protection? Do you find clam shells with no clams inside?

Horseshoe crabs: How does a horseshoe crab compare with other crabs? Notice its long spine and tail. Can a horseshoe crab easily flip itself over? How many eyes do they have? Where are they located? What is the size of the horseshoe crabs? Do you find mostly live crabs or discarded skeletons?

Mussels: Notice the distinctive blue-black color of mussels. To what type of material do mussels anchor themselves? Look for anchor threads that hold them to the rocks and wood. Feel them and try to dislodge one from a rock. Why are they hard to dislodge? How do they open? Have an adult open the gills so children can watch water going through their gills. Where is the mussel's mouth? Why is it hard to find? Find some baby mussels. How do they compare in size to adult mussels? What are the different heights of their humps.

Plants

Seaweed: How many different kinds of seaweed are there along the beach or in the water? What are the different colors, smells, and feel of the different varieties of seaweed? What is the difference between live and dried-up seaweed? Where do you find the seaweed?

Driftwood: What different kinds of driftwood can you find along the beach? Notice the color of wood that has been in the water a long time. Feel wood that is silvery gray. How many different sizes and shapes of wood can you find along the beach? Where did the wood come from?

Vegetation along the beach: Count the number of different kinds of grasses or plants in or near the water. Next locate the types of shrubs on banks near the sea or estuaries. Notice the different colors of the grasses and plants and textures of the stalks and leaves. How high is the vegetation? What kinds of trees grow near the beach?

Reading Readiness In Science

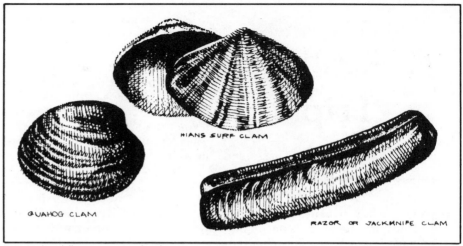

Different clam shells—razor, surf, and quahog.

——— Margaret McIntyre ———

Early childhood teachers need to be aware of the value of science experiences *as* reading readiness rather than as a separate content area. The concepts of space, number, color, and condition are integral parts of science investigation and reading readiness. Also, children sharpen their listening and thinking skills of predicting, locating, remembering, organizing, and evaluating in science investigation. These skills are an important part of reading readiness.

A Shell Collection: Prereading

Many children enjoy collecting shells. Teachers of young children can use shell collections to show how language development and reading readiness skills are interrelated with science. The seven basic skills outlined in Science—A Process Approach (SAPA) are principal steps in this exploration and are equally applicable to reading readiness. They are observing, classifying, measuring, communicating, inferring, recognizing number relations, and predicting.

Place shells on a large tray or in a basket so each child in a group of three to four will have a collection. Visual discrimination of these shells leads to more precise observation.

Allow children time to look, feel, shake, and decide on their own classification system. Ask the children their reasons for classification. With five-year-olds, a great deal of communication will take place among the group members. Encourage this.

The younger the child, the simpler they will group and arrange the shells. Size, color, and mass may be the sorting factors. The youngest children quickly discriminate between shells that are grossly different, while five-year-olds discriminate between shells that differ only by minute characteristics. Grouping of shells that are the same follows the same developmental pattern. If children recognize oyster shells, grouping large and small ones together requires precise observation and making an inference. It is more difficult to group shells that differ by more than one variable.

There are many types of clam shells— ribbed, razor, surf, and quahog. It is unlikely that young children would group these together unless they knew and remembered the names or unless you show how the entire group is a bivalve. If the two halves remain attached in some shells, children can open and close them. They can observe the inside of unattached bivalve shells to locate the muscles that draw the two halves together.

Children need to look at the space relationships of clam shells to compare the outside with the inside. Encourage discussion and questions as children make their discoveries and comments, appropriate to their language ability and experience.

The oyster group is interesting because of the contrast between the inside and outside of the shells. Children can feel the roughness and describe the out-side shell. Encourage them to use their own words to describe the smooth feeling and the pearly shading inside the shell. Have the children search their clothing for buttons that might be made from the inside layer of oyster shells.

The scallop group of bivalves is noteworthy because the shell halves are not the same. The upper half may be *curved*, while the lower is *flat*. The colors vary greatly from colorful to dull blacks and browns to white. The color pattern of the shells could be a grouping characteristic also. Scallops have valves that are different from those of clams and oysters. Either valve has one or two ears or wings, which stick out near the hinge. Ask children if they can detect the difference in valves.

Another large group of shells is called gastropods or single shells. Snail shells are gastropods. This group usually has a pointed head, an opening, and look as if they were coiled around a central core.

A moon snail is a gastropod.

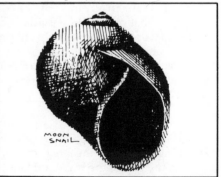

Artwork by Darshan K. Bigelson.

These offer numerous classification possibilities—smoothness or roughness, spiney or spineless, cone or auger, right or left-handed in upward growth spiral, and color.

Some shells resemble objects children know. Such shells are canoe, mandarin hat, angel wings, turkey wing, screw, coffee bean, volcano, and bleeding tooth. Label these so children can link the shell name and the object for which it is named.

The sculpture (ornament) of shells is another basis for classifying. The smooth cowries and olives are one kind of sculpture, but most shells have growth lines or surface irregularities such as spines and bristles. The gastropods have ribs regularly spaced all around the whorls. Ask children to observe and describe shell sculptures.

Color patterns can consist of a single or many colors. Locate snail or scallop shells which show wide color variation and have children describe them. What patterns are made up of dots, rectangles, triangles, rings, or wavy lines?

A Shell Collection: Prereading to Reading

For late four- and five-year-olds, matching shells is a beginning reading readiness skill. The next level is matching a real shell to a picture of it. Pictures mounted on cardboard or illustrated in books without much print to distract the child are ideal. Children can use yarn to link shells and their pictures. Print common names beneath the picture of the shell for the language value of a visual letter picture. Do not force the children to learn names. Children inclined to learn will do so.

Next, place on a tray half a dozen shells with named pictures and isolated printed name cards of the shells. Children can link the named picture to a shell and put the name card beneath the shell. Use lower case letters for the name cards. Though children will be matching pictures and names with the shell, some will want the names spoken to learn the names as well as the written word symbol. This step toward reading includes visual memory as well as discrimination. After practice, some children will be able to link name cards to the shells without using the picture. These children use labeling as a reading process.

Science activities provided teachers with a way of linking science with reading readiness. This technique not only increases science learning and reading skills, but removes reading-readiness from the traditional program of paper and pencil activities.

Reprinted from *Science and Children*, Nov/Dec 1980, Copyright NSTA.

Ann Zane

CHAPTER IV
Using Science Content Areas, A-Z

The entire spectrum of science is exploration material to young children, from agronomy to zoology. Youngsters prefer to learn a little about a lot of subjects and don't need information in depth right away. You need only provide the investigative materials. The children will do their own discovering in their own way and on their own schedule. Listen to their comments, ask questions to clarify their thinking, and you will lead them into further investigation. When a child asks why, you can always say, "Let's find out." You will learn together. Science topics and the science investigations they stimulate are presented in this chapter.

Young children enjoy digging in dirt. Marilyn J. Atyeo's article, "Learning About Dirt," suggests activities that tie into ecology, botany, conservation, and zoology. Through observation, exploration, and planting in various types of soil, children lay a foundation for an understanding of agronomy.

The sky is a source of fascination for children. "First Steps in Astronomy" outlines the roles that both the teacher and the parent play in children's initial celestial observations. Children need to develop an awareness of the Earth, the Sun, the Moon, stars, and outer space. Parents play a crucial role since they accept responsibility to provide observations of the evening skies. They provide feedback to the teacher about their child's reactions and comments about various experiences. Discussion in school permits children to share experiences and learn how others perceive the same experience.

"Grocery Bag Seeds and Plants" focuses on the use of fresh fruits and vegetables to learn about plants and seeds. Grasses and onions are grown, allowing key concepts to emerge—seeds differ in size, shape, color, and texture; each seed grows into a specific type of plant; and many types of seeds and plants exist.

"Wheels—Simple Machines" combines explorations in energy with construction techniques. Children use their engineering talents as they design pulleys for lifting and small wheel toys for moving with building toys.

Young children are born collectors, and rocks and stones for collections are available everywhere. In "Many Children Are Budding Geologists," you will learn how to use these resources to develop learning centers. Field trip suggestions invite children to several environments where they can look at, describe, and compare rocks. "Some Environmental Observations for Young Children" delineates approaches to help children develop awareness of their impact on the environment. "Human Ecology" is not too sophisticated a topic for children to explore. This article introduces concepts related to climate, clean air, personal space, and noise level, all geared toward children.

Measurement is an integral part of science, and to understand it children need time and opportunity to work concretely using nonstandard measuring units. "As Long As Three Brooms" lays the foundation for the use of standard measurement by first showing how to use nonstandard.

"Cloud Watching" suggests outdoor observations, sky watching, and plotting cloud patterns to show weather changes. Follow-up activities involve poetry, measurement, and physics.

"Dust Off Those Magnifiers" details the use of magnifiers and microscopes to see the world in a new way. Children are encouraged to discuss observations and note changes. Generally, microscopes require too much physical dexterity for young children and are not useful in preschool.

Most nutrition habits are formed during the early childhood period. "Of Seeds, Nuts, Fruits, and Grains" and "Soup to Science" deal with the food we eat. Different breads and dairy products are some of the foods investigated in these activities.

"Wet Spots" is another activity designed to promote investigation and creative research at the child's level of understanding.

"Water, Water Everywhere" and "Water Concepts" are a young child's dream. Water allows experimentation with depth, size, texture, and quantity. Thirteen basic concepts about water are outlined, with suggested activities for each. A selected trade book bibliography is of special interest to primary-grade teachers.

When children think of water, they may think of bubbles. "Bubbles and Brainwork" by Margie Mayfield and Michael Padilla is a blueprint for investigation of them. Soap bubbles are a way for children to make discoveries about behavior of materials, the properties they possess, and their different uses. Oral and written expression along with creative movement activities integrate with science experimentation.

"Exploring Concepts About Air" gets teachers off to an easy start by using familiar materials. Children slowly work to understand principles of air by using paper bags, balloons, inner tubes, fans, and toy sailboats. The previously cited bubble blowing is reintroduced with a different emphasis.

"Light and Shadow" introduces yet another physical science area that fascinates youngsters. A flashlight provides the impetus for a series of activities including prisms and shadow play that develop the concepts of transparency and translucency.

"Learning to Observe Animals" is full of questions that will help a child to observe animals. This first level of learning about animals introduces an important science skill. Three-year-olds start to develop observational skills essential to inquiry. Pets, farm animals and even worms provide opportunities for children to handle animals. Teachers need to constantly reinforce a respect for the living things that are an integral part of our earth ecology.

Learning About Dirt

MARILYN J. ATYEO

Child Development Specialist
Athens-Clarke County Community
Coordinated Child Care, Inc. (4-C)
Athens, Georgia

THE foundation for any environmental study should start when children are young and possess a keen curiosity about the world in which they live. One segment of the environment, the soil, seems to easily attract the interest of young children. In a playful manner they explore sand, rocks, and dirt whenever possible. Unfortunately, instead of taking advantage of this natural curiosity about the soil to develop a better understanding and appreciation of it, adults in supervisory roles often react in horror to the sight of children with dirty hands or clothes!

The following collection of activities utilizes a child's interest in playing in and with the dirt. The activities are appropriate throughout the school year in either preschool or early primary grades. The objective of this study is that through pleasant play experiences children will begin to realize a fundamental ecological truth—*Even the soil on our earth requires respect, care, and attention!*

The first activity will provide the opportunity for children to observe several types of soil and define their characteristics.

Materials

Three buckets filled with soil samples:
  Bucket A—Rich organic garden soil
  Bucket B—Hard-packed clay
  Bucket C—Sandy soil from a drainage area
Three square plastic sheets (approximately one square meter) and labeled A, B, and C
Three large sheets of drawing paper similarly labeled attached to a low bulletin board
Spoons, sticks, or small sand shovels
Three pans, also labeled with letters

Activities

Present the three buckets of soil samples to the class for observation. When you ask the children to define the material in the buckets, the initial response will probably be "dirt." Through discussion lead them to extend definitions to include little rocks, sand, clay, or soil.

Dump the three buckets of soil samples onto the corresponding sheets of plastic. Invite the children to explore the dirt with their fingers. Encourage close examination by asking questions such as:

—Have you seen soil which has a texture like this before? Where?
—Are all the samples of soil the same color?
—Do the three samples feel alike as you move your fingers through the soil?
—Let the dirt sift through your fingers. Does each sample sift the same as the other?
—Squeeze a handful of each sample, then

I. Looking At The Dirt

observe what happens. Does the soil stay in a ball or fall apart once you release your grip?

Take a sample from each pile of soil and place in a pan with the corresponding label. Slowly add water to each sample. Observe what happens to the water and how the soil feels.

If you have enough soil for everyone to do it, have the children make mud pies.

—Which dirt works the best?
—Why is one kind better than another?

Provide each child with a spoon, stick, or other tool for digging (use the remaining dry soil here). Use the tools to discover any other forms of material which might be hiding in the soil. (Be sure the garden soil has a few earthworms, insects both alive and dead, leaves, sticks, bark, and small rocks). As children discover a hidden object they may record their findings on the charts provided. When the observations are completed, compare the charts A, B, and C.

—Which soil sample had many different things hidden?

Return the soil samples to the original buckets and save for later experiments.

II. Exploring The Dirt

The purpose of this field trip is to discover different types of soil in a natural setting, develop awareness to the many kinds of plants and animals which live in the soil, to have creative opportunities for expression of understanding, and to experience enjoyment in working and playing in the dirt. The concepts learned can be developed and extended through the use of stories, films, and filmstrips.

Materials

The schoolyard or neighborhood park
Digging tools and small cartons or pails for each child
Earthworms
Earthworm farm
Language art materials

Outdoor Activities

Explain to the class that the trip outdoors will be for the purpose of exploring the soil around the schoolyard or in the park nearby.

Observe the difference in the textures of soil found in the schoolyard. Children should be able to find areas where the clay is packed and hard, perhaps on a driveway or path. The baseball field will have areas where the soil is loose and dusty. Under low shrubs the soil is likely to be loose, crumbly, and damp. An anthill, with its grainy and loose soil, may also be discovered. Encourage children to discuss and compare the different soils found. Samples can be collected for classroom study.

Revisit the same areas after a shower. If the weather is warm, suggest children go barefoot so they can discover how the soil feels with their feet. Notice how the different soil types change when wet.

—How does the hard-packed soil on the pathway feel as you walk on it?

—Does the loose soil on the baseball field squish between your toes?
—What happens to loose sandy soil after a rain?

Observe the many types of plant life which live in the soil. Children may name flowers, grass, trees, bushes, vegetables, and weeds. Pull up several weeds and observe the root system which extended into the soil. Ask children to suggest reasons why the roots of plants extend into the soil.

Look for holes in the soil. What made the holes? Children may suggest small holes were made by worms, insects, moles, or little snakes. Others may recall from stories or films that larger holes are homes or hiding places for rabbits, chipmunks, or prairie dogs. Perhaps children would like to dig and see how far a hole extends into the ground. Hopefully someone will find an earthworm as he digs. Classmates may react by displaying interest but there may be some who express fear and a wish to destroy these small creatures. Explain that earthworms are important because they help to maintain the soil.

Indoor Activities

Use several soil samples collected from various areas around the schoolyard to explore the texture differences in soil. A magnifying glass or child's microscope will be helpful in discovering differences.

Earthworm Farm

Collect several earthworms from a garden or buy a supply from a bait shop. An earthworm farm can be provided by using the commercial ant farm which has had dark paper added to the back, or a simple one may be constructed by covering the outside of a wide-mouthed jar with dark construction paper. Add gravel to the bottom of the jar and then fill the jar with loosely packed, slightly damp soil which contains an ample amount of humus (decaying plant and animal material).

Feed the earthworms cereals or small portions of lettuce, oatmeal, or plants. Each day add enough water so soil continues to be slightly damp. Carefully observe the earthworms building tunnels in the soil. Children may note that the worms literally eat their way through the soil. Develop the idea that the worms are cultivating the soil by keeping it loose.

Carefully take an earthworm out of the farm and place it on a piece of construction paper. Use a magnifying glass to observe the features of the long body. Watch to see how the body moves. Darken the room, then turn on a flashlight near the earthworm. Does the earthworm move toward or away from the light? Pour a portion of dirt on the paper near the earthworm. Does it try to hide in the soil?

Creative Activities

After observing how the earthworm moves, invite the children to mimic the movements. Appropriate music may be provided with the piano or a record. Children may enjoy creating a musical background by the use of rubbing two sand blocks against each other or by rubbing a stick over a ridged wood block.

Encourage activities such as creating stories, songs, and poems about experiences and observations. If the children have not learned to print yet, their comments can be printed on the page by their teacher. The children may then paint or draw pictures. Display this creative work for parents and other children in the building to see.

Captions for pictures may be similar to these:

—I found a worm and watched him squirm.
—I felt the dirt squish between my toes after the rain.
—Look at me dig a hole in the dirt!
—I saw an anthill where little ants live and work.

A group story may result in everyone cooperating and enjoying the results. The sequences of the story can also be illustrated by the children. A group story may also be presented in the form of a play for another classroom or for parents. Individual stories can be duplicated and sent home for parents to enjoy also.

III. Growing Things In The Dirt

By playing in the soil for fun and exercise, the children will have experiences that develop understanding that the soil can and should be improved. They will also observe the results of building soil by planting and tending a garden.

Materials

Two areas of the schoolyard designated for vegetable and flower gardens

A volunteer with a Rota-tiller to turn the soil in garden areas. (Ask fathers, custodian, or perhaps older boys in school to help)

Tools for digging in the soil

Soil samples from buckets A, B, and C which were left over from the first lesson, "Looking at the Dirt"

Activities

Fill containers with soil taken from samples A, B, or C. (Plastic milk cartons or cottage cheese containers are adequate.) Be sure the containers are labeled. Plant seeds such as marigolds, beans, or radishes. Water all seeds at the same time and keep variables such as light and heat similar. Observe how the seeds grow in the different soils when other conditions are similar.

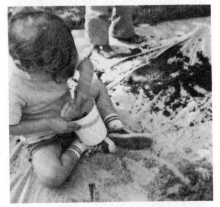

The Garden

In early fall have the soil turned and loosened with a Rota-tiller in one garden site. Designate another garden area but do not disturb the soil at this time.

Encourage children to dig and play in the garden area much as they would in a sand pile. Provide digging tools, sifters, containers, and small plastic jars. Encourage children to bury sand, pine needles, bark, leaves, grass, twigs, and insects in the garden area. Scraps from the kitchen such as coffee grounds, vegetable peelings, or cereals may be added also. Be sure a shovel is available and organic materials are covered adequately, to discourage rodents which may be attracted to the area. Add several earthworms to the soil. If not otherwise available, these can be obtained from a bait shop.

Along with the organic materials, have the children bury plastic spoons, cups, metal cans, and similar objects to dig up later. Discuss the reasons why some of the things disappear completely, while others only partially decompose (and still others do not change).

During the winter months cover the loose garden soil with a layer of straw. Children may continue to add kitchen scraps to the soil when the ground is thawed enough for digging.

In the early spring again loosen the soil with the aid of a Rota-tiller. Turn the soil in a second garden area also. Invite children to work and play in both garden areas as they did in the fall.

Send a soil sample from the original garden plot in to your county agent (U.S. Department of Agriculture) for analysis. Just before planting, lime and fertilizer may be added if the analysis indicates they are needed. The use of these materials by the children is **strongly** discouraged. As the teacher uses them, there should be a discussion about why the soil needs such materials.

In both garden plots plant radishes, lettuce, peas, beans, onions, or easy-to-grow flowers such as marigolds or zinnias. Observe the growth of plants in both gardens. Which garden area seems to have more plants growing? Measure to see if there is a different growth rate in the plants from the two areas. See that the original garden plot is regularly weeded and soil is kept loose by careful hoeing.

When the vegetables are ready to eat invite parents or other children to a vegetable party. As the children enjoy the results of their labor, encourage discussion about the experiences of working with the soil during the year.

Various individuals or groups in the classroom may want to serve as garden guides. Suggest they take other children or parents on a tour to see the vegetables and flowers in the garden.

Through these activities, the children are not expected to know all the answers as to why one soil is better than the others. However, the experiences of observing and working with the soil should develop clues which will be remembered and used later.

Creative activities have a place in an environmental science unit. Young children need to express in many ways the things they observe and question. Music, art, and language arts provide the child an opportunity to imprint new ideas more firmly in his mind and create an appreciation for the interrelatedness of things.

References

1. Fiedler, Jean. *The Green Thumb Story*. E. M. Hale & Company, Publishers, Eau Claire, Wisconsin. 1957.

2. Hogner, Dorothy C. *Earthworms*. Thomas Y. Crowell Company, New York City. 1953.

3. Kessler, Leonard. *The Worm, The Bird and You*. Dodd Mead & Company, New York City. 1962.

4. Klein, Leonore. *Mud, Mud, Mud*. Alfred A. Knopf, Inc., New York City. 1962.

5. Krauss, Ruth. *The Carrot Seed*. Harper & Row, Publishers, New York City. 1945.

6. Schoenknecht, Charles A. *Ants*. Follett Publishing Company, Chicago, Illinois. 1961.

First Steps In Astronomy

———— Margaret McIntyre ————

Space travel intrigues young children, even though they cannot comprehend the vastness of space nor the time element involved. Space travel draws attention to our solar system and beyond. Yet, how much of this subject can a young child understand?

Children amaze adults by their very adult-like vocabulary and comments about space. Most of this is rote memorization, however, with little understanding of basic concepts. Nevertheless, some concepts can be understood and integrated into the child's thinking about space.

We Live on the Earth

Ask the children to look out the window as far as possible and describe what they see. Take them to any intersection and ask what they can see if they look first to the north, then to the south, east, and west. Use these directional terms. What do they see near them, and very far away? How can they see even more from a particular position? One way is to go to a nearby hill, or even a short rise in elevation. Looking from the top of a tall building would present a wider view. Even a second-story window helps children to see their space on Earth. Some children could talk about an airplane ride, as they remember looking out the window and seeing how tiny the houses and cars appeared.

These activities help children think about space on the planet Earth. You may tell them that Earth is one of the smaller planets, but it will be several years before this fact is integrated into their knowledge of the solar system.

Children talk about how far they have traveled in a car, train, or airplane, but do not understand the magnitude of the Earth's space. Once children have a rudimentary feeling for space on Earth, we can extend their sights into space. The most obvious large body they can see is the sun.

The Sun Gives Light and Heat

The sun is the most observable and sense-stimulating feature of the planetary system that children see. What can young children learn about the sun?

On a clear day, what do you see shining? (CAUTION: warn children not to look directly at the sun). What side of the classroom does the sun shine in during the morning, during the afternoon? How can you tell the sun is shining, even when you do not see it directly? How does the sun change the way the classroom looks?

Walk around the building in the morning, at noon, and in the afternoon to see where the sun's rays hit the building. Make a chart to show the changes. Why do the directions of the rays change?

Experiment in casting shadows in the early morning, at lunch time, and just before going home. Use chalk to outline one child's shadow at each of these times. Talk about the sizes of the shadows. Do this several days so children can really see when their bodies make longer shadows. Where is the sun then? What is the sun's position when the shadow is very small?

Try casting shadows on a cloudy day. What happens? Where is the sun on an overcast day? Watch the shadows come and go when the sun is covered briefly by a cloud.

Talk about the color of the sun. Ask parents to have children watch sunset and sunrise and describe the colors they see. Parents can help children contrast the sun's position in rising and setting in relation to their own houses.

After observing and talking about the sun, the children can concentrate on another object easily seen in the sky. Can children guess what the name of this object is?

The Moon Shines in the Night Sky

The moon is not as familiar to young children as the sun. Parents need to help provide viewing experiences in the early morning and evening.

The moon's color is a good starting point. What color is it? Is it the same color every night? How can you find out? Is there a color difference between early and late evening? When is it easier to see? Why?

When the moon can be seen in the daytime sky, make sure that you take the children outdoors to locate it. Often young children believe that the moon goes to bed when the sun gets up. Seeing both moon and sun in the sky during the day will help dispel such thinking. Talk about the moon's color and position during the daylight hours. Allow plenty of time for observation before eliciting any general statement.

The shape of the moon during observation over a month or two is discernibly different from that of the sun. The full moon is a good starting point for observation. Every day in class talk about the shape that the children saw the previous evening with parents, or with classmates during the day. Keep a class moon calendar of the phases of the moon. The children can draw the shapes and may even want to record their own calendar. Use the terms full, half, and quarter moon to label the shape changes during the month. Many four-year-olds can relate to size terminology if these terms have been used previously in science or math play activities.

Ask the children to tell you how large or small they think the moon is. Listen to their replies. Ask how they think the astronauts who went to the moon would answer that question. Posters of the moon walk are useful at this point. Children know men walked on the moon, but how was it different from a walk to school? Talk about the surface, the dust, the craters, and the lack of air

Reprinted from *Science and Children*, January 1981, Copyright NSTA.

on the moon. On the posters have children look for the air hoses attached to the astronauts for breathing.

The sun and moon are not the only objects children see in space. There are planets and stars.

Stars Shine in the Evening Sky

Take children to a planetarium, or have an adult take them out in the evenings to view planets and stars. "Twinkle, twinkle little star" describes the stars. There are larger and brighter objects that shine, but do not twinkle. These are called planets.

Experience the brightness of the sky with children on a clear evening from an uncrowded, relatively unlit area such as a park or an athletic field, as well as from their own backyards. Viewing from a shopping center lets five- and six-year-olds notice the difficulty in seeing stars from a lighted area.

The nearness and farness of stars is another concept that needs developing.

If parents take children outdoors or to a planetarium to observe an evening sky, Mars and Venus are easy to spot. Which is higher in the sky? What color does each seem to be? Telescopes for viewing may be available at local high schools. Primary-age children can handle these with supervision. The ability to see many stars in a given spot is more fascinating to children than seeing a few stars.

Children see stars at night when the sky is dark, but where are the stars during the day? It is unlikely that children will transfer the concept of the moon being visible in the day to the characteristics of stars. The stars are always present, but the sun makes the sky too bright in the day for us to see them.

Stars seem to move across the sky. Primary-age children can locate a certain bright star at a stated hour. By walking around the area, a child could spot this star just above the chimney or telephone pole. Leave a marker to indicate where

the child stood. An hour or so later, return to this spot. Where is the star now? It looks as if the stars have moved.

It is not the stars though, but the Earth which is turning so slowly we are not aware of it. Perhaps older primary-age children might understand this example. If you drive in a car past a street light, the light appears first ahead of you, then beside you, then behind you, yet it is the car in which you are riding that has moved, not the street light.

In observing stars in the evening sky, have children locate stars that seem brighter than others. Where are they? This could lead to naming a *very few* stars, such as the North Star. Primary-age children could locate, with adult help, the Big Dipper, if they know what a dipper looks like.

Astronomy is an area of study that children can pursue for years. With young children, a perceptual awareness is our goal, an awareness that will serve as the basis for more fascinating studies.

Helpful Hints

Reprinted from *Science and Children*, January 1981, Copyright NSTA.

Another Way To Make A Diver

The Cartesian Diver has intrigued children for many generations. One way of constructing this device is stretching a piece of rubber balloon over the mouth of a widemouth jar after first floating a glass medicine dropper on the surface of the water. However, it is difficult to keep the rubber balloon in place while youngsters press down on its surface.

An alternative is using a plastic soft drink bottle which is readily available and solves the assembly and maintenance problems. First balance the glass medicine dropper so that the rubber end of the dropper just breaks the surface tension of the water. Carefully insert the dropper into the mouth of a two-liter plastic soft drink bottle nearly full of water. Be sure that the water temperature in the bottle and the water temperature in which the dropper was balanced are the same. Ideally, they should be at room temperature before assembly. Tighten the cap and squeeze the sides of the container. The assembly is inexpensive and safe enough for a child or pair of children to make one.

Direct students to make observations during each "squeezing" and write or describe their explanations for the phenomena they observe. This provides an excellent opportunity for students to learn about air pressure, the distribution of pressure in a closed system, buoyancy, and the inquiry process. **Robert K. James,** College of Education, Kansas State University, Manhattan, Kansas.

Artwork by Amelia Bellows

Grocery Bag Seeds And Plants

—— Margaret McIntyre ——

Children enjoy planting seeds and spring bulbs, and making cuttings for planting. If your classroom has a sunny window, you can extend space for pot gardens by using a table or large blocks and boards. Children can build a simulated greenhouse of plastic.

Fresh fruit often provides a seed bonus. After eating the fruit observe and touch the fruit's pits and seeds. Compare size, texture, shape, and color of the seeds. Have children plant these seeds.

Avocado

Wash an avocado pit in warm water. Put three toothpicks in the sides of the pit so it will rest suspended in a jar, broad end in the water. Cover only about one centimeter of seed with warm water. Put the jar in a warm place but not in direct sunlight. Watch for roots in two to six weeks. A plant will start to grow. When the plant is about 20 cm high, cut off the top half of the plant to make it branch out.

When the roots and leaves are well developed, plant the seed in a large pot filled with potting soil. Leave half the seed exposed. The pot should have good drainage. Put the plant in a warm sunny place.

Oranges, Lemons, and Grapefruit

Soak seeds overnight in warm water. Plant the seeds in a pot in a mixture of sphagnum peat and potting soil. Keep in a warm place out of direct sunlight until sprouts appear. This takes about three weeks. Keep the soil damp but not wet.

Dates

Use unpasteurized date seeds. Soak them overnight in warm water. Plant in a large container—date palms need room. Use a mixture of sphagnum peat and potting soil. Plant three or four seeds in each pot because not all the seeds will germinate.

Pineapple

Your pineapple already has green leaves. Cut off a 2.5 cm section of fruit below the leaves, with the leaves still attached. Put this in a dish containing water. When roots develop, carefully put the plant in potting soil and cover both the pot and plant with a clear plastic bag. Keep it warm, but not in direct sunlight, for three weeks. Remove the bag and observe the small cactus-like plant. Water the plant and move it into the sun. In six to twelve months, tiny pineapples may develop.

Dish Garden Root Vegetables

Your grocery bag may also contain fresh vegetables. These vegetables also make attractive dish gardens. Cut off the top cm of carrots, beets, radishes, or white turnips. Keep the stubby tops. Set the pieces in dishes with water. New shoots will appear in a week to ten days. Keep the sections in water while you watch the shoots grow. Children can identify the vegetable from the foliage.

Sweet Potato or Yam

Suspend a fresh sweet potato or yam, tapered end down, in a vase or small-mouthed jar filled with water. A sweet potato with "whiskers" roots more easily. You may have to insert three toothpicks as with the avocado, so that only one-third of the vegetable is in the water. Put the jar in a sunny window. Sprouts appear in about two weeks. Make a string trellis on which the foliage can climb. Keep the water level constant. Children can chart the number of days it takes roots and foliage to grow, and note changes in root and foliage growth.

Using Potato "Eyes"

Old potatoes often have "eyes" or sprouts. Children can use a vegetable peeler to dig out the eyes from the potato. Be sure there is adult supervision. Use good potting soil to plant the eyes. Water, and place in a sunny window until the plant is several cm tall. Plant in a garden or in a very deep pot (if you are keeping the plant in the classroom). Dig up the developing potatoes. Sometimes urban children are surprised to learn that potatoes grow underground.

Onion Sets

Yellow and white onions are easy to grow from onion sets sold in the spring planting season. Discuss size, shape, and odor while planting the sets in deep clay pots about 15 cm apart. Water and put in the sun. Watch for the green tops to appear. It will take several weeks for the onions to be large enough to pull. Plant enough onion sets so that onions can be pulled every week after the first two weeks. Children can then see the size change in the bulb. They can measure the size of the plant using either standard or nonstandard measurement.

Grass Seed

Eggshells can be recycled as containers for growing grass seed. Young

Reprinted from *Science and Children*,
April 1979, Copyright NSTA.

children can paint or decorate the shells first, perhaps with faces. Fill the eggshells with soil. Scatter grass seed on top. Keep moist. Put the eggshells in the sun. You can use the egg carton as a holder for the eggshells. As the grass grows, it becomes green "hair" for the face. Children can cut the grass to keep it at the height they like. Measure the grass every two or three days. Chart how fast the grass grows. Data about appearance, grass growth in sun and shade, roots, and growth when watered and unwatered can be gathered through experiments.

Children in rural areas may have access to old corn cobs. These make novel grass containers. Soak the cobs in water overnight. Sprinkle the wet cobs with grass seed. The green grass will look like a hedge and can also be cut with shears.

Vegetable and Flower Seeds

Vegetables and flowers such as corn, beans, radishes, and nasturtiums have a short germination time, making them ideal for young children to plant. Use small cans or milk cartons that have a hole punched in the bottom for drainage. Experiment with the size of the hole so children can see what happens if the hole is too large. Put a layer of pebbles in the bottom. Add potting soil. Plant the seed and water thoroughly. Children can put their names on their own pots and be responsible for them. What seeds produced what plants? Send the plants home to be put in the garden when the plants are big enough.

Key Concepts

There are many key concepts you can develop through the activities:

Seeds differ in size, shape, color, and texture.

Each seed grows into a specific kind of plant.

There are many types of seeds— seeds that grow inside fruits, seeds we can eat, seeds that grow into flowers, seeds that grow into shrubs, and seeds that grow into foods we eat.

Resources

Branley, Franklyn M. *Roots Are Food Finders.* (A Let's Read & Find Out Book) Thomas Y. Crowell Company, Publishers, New York City. 1975.

Jordan, Helene J. *Seeds By Wind and Water.* (A Let's Read & Find Out Book) Thomas Y. Crowell Company, Publishers, New York City. 1962.

Phyllis Marcuccio

Some Environmental Observations for Young Children

———————— Margaret McIntyre ————————

TO young children the surrounding environment has a real fascination, which adults who live hectic lives have quite forgotten. Pause long enough to try to grasp the child's perception of awe, wonder, and excitement of the world around him. Young children are natural scientists. They are eager to look, poke, touch gingerly or squeeze, taste, and smell almost everything and anything in sight. This is how children acquire an understanding of the concepts of environmental education that will enter into more formal learning later in life.

You start by asking lots of questions and listening intently to the answers, encouraging the children to hypothesize, guess, ask questions of you. Ask questions about materials in their habitat. Take these slowly, pacing to the child's interest level. Piaget tells us that young children learn by doing, thinking about what they have done, and discussing this with others. This verbal interaction is essential; it is through the exchange of ideas that the child organizes and reorganizes his thinking, and thereby learns. The preoperational child (ages 2-7) cannot perform operations mentally. He must *do* them. What can the adult help him to do?

The Trash Basket

Empty the trash basket in the room. What is in it? Can you sort the trash? What are the child's categories? Are there any papers in it that could be used again? What is paper made from? Why are trees important other than for paper? Why is it important to conserve paper? What does conserve mean? How can we conserve paper here at school, day-care center, or home? What happens to the trash after it leaves here? How can we find out? Does it cost money to have the trash disposed of? Who do you think pays for all this? Why does it cost money? Do not expect answers from all the children, especially the three year olds. Just ask questions so that they can start wondering.

Trash in Other Areas

Visit the school cafeteria or kitchen. What is in the trash basket there? How is it different from trash in the other room? Does the trash in the kitchen have an odor? Why? What can we do to make less trash in the cafeteria or kitchen?

Walk to the play area or take a short walk around the block. The children can carry small bags in which to collect trash they see. What kinds of trash do we see? What kinds of trash should children leave for adults to pick up? Why? Empty the trash into big bags. How many do we have? Can we classify it? What do we call people who do not throw trash in proper containers? What can we do to cut down on the amount of trash that we see? Why is it important to pick up trash?

Visit a local store or business establishment to find out what kinds of trash they have. What do they do with it? Do they try to cut down on the trash they accumulate? Are they using materials over and over if possible, and recycling? Do you know what recycling means? How can we recycle paper?

Make a visit to the local gasoline service station. What are the kinds of trash that they have? How is it different from other trash we have seen? What do they do with all the oil drained from cars? Is it reused? How? What do you think they do with old tires?

Water

Turn on the faucet. Where does the water come from? Where does the city, village, or farmhouse get its water? Why do you know it is safe to drink? Is there an abundance of water available around this city or village? How do you know? Class trips may be needed to get answers to some of these questions. Do we drink rainwater? Is it safe to drink? How can we conserve water? Why is this important? Why is water important? What do we use water for in the nursery school or kindergarten? What do you use water for at home?

An Aquarium

What animals live in the aquarium? Why do they need water? What do they eat? How often? How much? What happens to the food if they do not eat it? Why are there green plants? Look for the snails. What are they doing there? Why does the water not stay at

Reprinted from *Science and Children*, April 1975, Copyright NSTA.

the same level? How can you tell that the water level changed? Why do we need to add water from time to time? Why is the aquarium in the light or have a light over it? What might happen if it were kept in the dark?

Air Pollution

Have any of you heard of air pollution? Where have you heard this? What is polluted air? Is there any air pollution in this area right now? How can we find out? Taking a walk may be helpful. Can you see any dirt being spewed into the air? Look at cars and trucks. Do you see any dirt coming from their exhaust pipes? Where is the exhaust pipe? The children may need to see where these pipes are located on cars. A visit to the service station might locate some trucks so the children can see where exhausts are on the trucks. What happens to all the gases and smoke that are being put into the air? How does this affect the air we breathe? You could introduce five year olds to the concept of emission controls and what these are trying to do.

If the area is suburban and the weather cold, children could look at house chimneys. In areas close to commercial buildings and factories, smokestacks and chimneys could be looked at. Is there dirt coming from

Pace questions to the child's interest level.

these? Is there an odor? Why are states and communities requiring factories to have filters and convertors on smokestacks? What does a filter do? Have you ever seen any? Where? If smog is located in any of these areas, the idea of what smog is, how it is formed, and how dangerous it is to human beings, can be brought out.

Conclusion

Arouse children's concern for the environment by involving them in finding answers to the questions. The adult is free to develop the environmental problem under discussion to the extent of the children's interest and understanding. The questions suggested here will lead to others and are open to amplification.

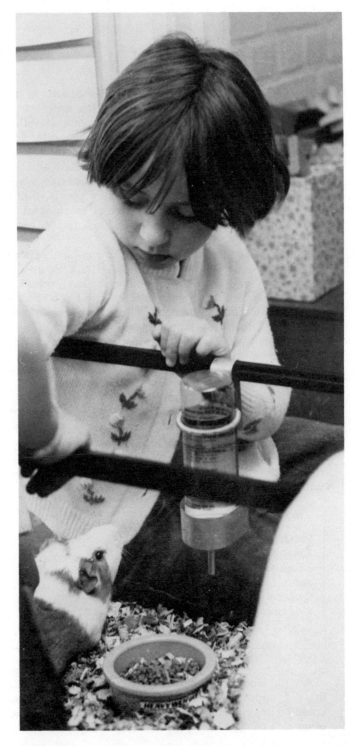

Human Ecology

———————— Margaret McIntyre ————————

HUMAN ECOLOGY may be a sophisticated area of investigation for young children. The teacher must introduce this comprehensive concept at the child's level of understanding, in small segments, and over an extended period of time. Human ecology is defined, for this article, as a study of the interrelationships between man and the various forces within his environment. Since ecology will assume growing importance in the coming years, young citizens need to be involved in activities meaningful to them and suitable as a foundation for their further comprehension and understanding.

Teachers can plan and provide those first-hand experiences in several ways. Possibilities include clean air, clean water, sunlight, an acceptable noise level, personal space, liquid and solid waste disposal, and a favorable climate both indoors and out. This article will be limited to climate, clean air, personal space, and noise level.

Teachers can develop concepts concerning bodily adaptation to different climates by using the environment of the children themselves. A long-term weather book could be written daily by children, on a rotating basis. By using a spiral or loose-leaf binder, each day would be in sequence, and the months could be tagged. Such a book could have large pages, possibly 18 by 24 inches. Each page would be headed by the month, day, and year, with identical items to be filled in each day by the children, even if they have to copy the data from an adult model.

```
                    January 2, 1976
Temperature outdoors.............................
Temperature indoors..............................
Precipitation (using pictures or symbols for rain, snow, and
sleet.)
Sun factor (using picture drawings of sun or clouds)
Wind factor (gentle breeze............... drawing a kite
             gusty or strong.......... leaves on the ground)
```

A child would then draw a picture of him or herself, dressed appropriately for the weather outdoors. This could be drawn below the weather data or placed on the other side of the sheet. Another child could draw a pic-

ture of someone dressed for the school indoor climate, if desired. These pages done by the children would provide a year-long look at weather, allowing a wide variety of discussion. The chart would be available for all children to "read."

Another option would be dressing cardboard figures of a boy and/or girl in appropriate clothing, as in a large paper-doll wardrobe, at the same time naming the item and explaining the reason for selection. Both activities could be used in small groups or as a total group activity, depending on children's age, group size, and classroom management philosophy of the program. In any case, the children should do the explaining, with the adult role limited to asking the right question to probe a child's level of understanding or to support him if hesitant.

Physiological aspects of human ecology would quite naturally be integrated into the above activities. When you feel cold, why do you think you shiver? What happens when you are too hot? How many ways can you think of to cool off? When playing outdoors, in what season do you most easily get thirsty? Plan a drink for snack after taking a walk in cold weather. What drink would you like after a walk in hot weather?

After the children have been outdoors in cold windy weather, let the children look at their lips. Describe how they look and feel. What will protect them? When you go to the beach in summer how do you protect your lips and skin from the sun? If children regularly go to a pool, they can describe what lifeguards put on their noses. How do they protect their eyes from the bright sunlight? Why?

Air Pollution

Clean air is directly observable both indoors and out. The center's custodian can be enlisted to show children the furnace and/or air conditioning equipment; giving attention to the filters, preferably when they need cleaning or changing. Permanent filters can be washed in a tub to enable youngsters to see how dirty the water becomes. The children can hypothesize where the dirt comes from. The children may need to see the vents to know why the filters are needed.

Five-year-olds could ask their parents to show them where filters are used in the home. Humidifiers, clothes dryers, vacuum cleaners, and stove hoods are likely places. Young children need many opportunities to integrate and consolidate center activities with those in the home.

To help children relate filtered air to the air they breathe daily, have them breathe in and out while standing to demonstrate chest expansion. Air passageways in the respiratory organs are efficient in filtering out dust particles, but if the air is always dirty, the passageways may become clogged, making it difficult to breathe.

Campfires, burning trash, and chimney smoke in both residential and commercial areas of the community demonstrate air pollution. Even buildings near smoking chimneys look different.

Vehicle exhaust from school and city buses, trucks, and cars is noticeable. Children can describe the colors from the various exhausts. Murals and drawings can show what children observed. Five-year-olds might be interested in learning about air pollution monitors working in many communities. These individuals track down polluters and advise them to cease, citing environmental protection laws.

Such observations and discussions help children become pollution-conscious as they walk and drive around with their families. They gain an understanding of pollution controls and why they are important. The awareness may spread throughout their own families.

Snow provides a good subject for related activities. Children could take pictures of the dazzling whiteness of freshly-fallen snow and a couple of days later take another picture to compare with the first. Talk about the differences. (It helps to have an instant-development camera.) Snow looks clean, but is it? If snow starts to fall while children are in the center, put a clean coffee can outdoors to collect snow. When there is an inch or more, bring the can (covered) inside and let the snow melt. Take a piece of clean filter paper or paper toweling. Put it in a funnel and pour the melted snow through it into a clean jar. Then use a hand lens to look at the filter paper.

Living Space

The role of affective education can also be brought into the concern for human ecology. The amount of space a person has affects how he feels. Also, people make varying responses to these feelings. Children can talk about their feelings while enjoying unlimited space or being crowded together.

Most playgrounds have plenty of space. Let the children run out and use all that space. Later, inside, crowd

Reprinted from *Science and Children,*
April 1976, Copyright NSTA.

the children around you while you show them some pictures. What happens? Another day place three students in the playhouse. Then add three more. The children will react differently. Help the children to talk about their feelings.

Noise

Play a record with the volume turned up high while the children are trying to listen to a story. Observe their behavior for a few minutes, and also ask the children to explain their reactions to this.

Talk about noise that is fun. Children can tear pictures of noise makers from magazines to make charts. Excursions with a tape recorder could help children be aware of the noise level in a park, on the playground, and in business districts of the town or city in which they live.

Walk around different rooms in the building, describing the differing noise levels. Tape record noise in the hall at the beginning of the session. Compare with that at another time. What activities contribute to the most noise? the least noise? Charts with illustrations could be made to reinforce this.

Have the children make similar observations at home. What is the noisiest room in the house and why? What is the loudest machine in the kitchen? Have them bring in their loudest toy. Another day, the quietest. Which toys do they play with the most?

The quality of life in the future may well depend upon beginning early to understand how each person is an integral part of the ecology of his own community. Even nursery school youngsters can begin to understand the importance of keeping the environment as pollution-free and favorable as possible.

Margaret McIntyre

Reprinted from *Science and Children*, Nov/Dec 1975, Copyright NSTA.

As Long as Three Brooms

WHEN YOUNG children ask questions such as "How long is it?" or "How big is it?" they provide adults with an opportunity to introduce measurement at a level the child will understand. Piaget has observed that linear measurement involves two operations that preschoolers are not yet able to handle at their stage of development. The first operation is dividing the unit to be measured into subunits of similar length, and the second is substituting one part of the measuring unit on the object being measured the appropriate number of times. This does not mean that adults working with young children should wait until they are seven or eight, and supposedly able to handle linear measurement. The child should have opportunity and time to freely explore and to use concrete materials in a hierarchical progression designed to develop an eventual understanding of this concept.

The ability to measure follows the understanding of number as a concept. To understand number, there first must be all kinds of experiences in classifying, comparing, and ordering. The children should be familiar with the terminology of *as many as, more than, the same as,* and *as long as.* Not only must they understand, but they must also be comfortable with the use of the words.

Children need to work in the area of nonstandard measurement when they are very young. One of the first things you must remember is that the answer to the question "How long is it?" requires an answer saying "As long as . . . . . ." There always has to be something to compare it with. Show the children how you can determine the length of a table by measuring it with your outstretched palm. The children, perhaps with help from adults and other children, can count the seven outstretched palm lengths. Let individual children do the same thing. How many of their palms does it take? Can they move the little finger to the thumb to hold a place when measuring? Can they see why there are differences in the number of outstretched hand units required? If children have problems in perceiving this, have them match their outstretched palms against an adult's.

Suggest measuring the width of the room. The children may have several ideas for using their bodies to measure this. They could use the length of their bodies, the number of strides in walking, or the number of their own foot lengths putting one in front of the other. Allow many opportunities for children to measure distances using their bodies. Some discussion is necessary, as they will only gradually understand that a measurement unit can be anything you want it to be as long as you *name* the unit and measure *only* with that unit. Since children love to use their bodies, this initial physical approach to measurement is ideal.

Next, the children can use materials as nonstandard units of measurement. Start with long units to lessen the numbers involved in measuring large tables, room lengths, etc. Some fine units are jump ropes, a broom, dustmop, the largest unit block in a set, walking boards, or even a chair laid on the floor. Eventually, some child is going to want to measure something that is smaller than the unit of measurement being used. This frustration makes an opportunity to have a small group discussion to see what solutions the children will come up with.

Shorter nonstandard units of measurement can be equally creative: paperclips, erasers, pencils, crayons, cuisenaire rods, small unit blocks, children's shoes, gloves, lunch boxes, hair ribbons, and pieces of paper. Books can be measured using units of crayons or large paperclips. Does the size of the book make a difference in units used? Measurements with young children are always approximate. Don't attempt to be precise, as the children are not yet ready for this. Encourage verbalizing of approximations such as the book is two and a little more pencils long. The table may be three and one-half hair ribbons long. Ages five and six may be familiar with the concept of one-half at least verbally; they can fold the ribbon in half and actually see it.

Children love to compare heights, usually to see who is the tallest (or the biggest, as they are more apt to say). Children with books on their heads can stand against a wall against a piece of wrapping paper or wallpaper. A child or an adult pencils a line on the paper along the underside of the book. By looking at the marked lines, with names printed on each, children can compare heights generally. By cutting a length of string from the marked line to the floor, children experience another measurement concept. The child lies on the floor, head against the wall. Another child can put down the string next to him. Is the child the same length lying down as standing up? Keep the paper with heights marked so that another measurement some months later would show how much the children have grown.

Many children of kindergarten age want to know their height in inches or centimeters. Adults may use yard or meter sticks to measure and tell the child what the standard measurement is. When the children repeat this measurement, remember that they are merely verbalizing in a rote manner. Children of this age, as Piaget says, are not yet ready to understand the concept of measuring in inches or centimeters.

——— Margaret McIntyre ———

Wheels—Simple Machines

Reprinted from *Science and Children*, May 1975, Copyright NSTA.

YOUNG children become acquainted with machines early in their lives—through their toys, their families, appliances, automobiles, and all sorts of equipment that operate the modern, mechanized world about them.

In the classroom, some children will show an interest in moving large blocks and cardboard boxes around the room. What power makes these objects move? A few races with the children pushing boxes will demonstrate to them that the power is the muscles of each child involved. When the children become tired, ask them how they think the task could be made easier. Have some large dowels available, long enough to go under the boxes. Provide round thick pencils and some small boxes for the other children to use.

What other ways can the boxes be moved? Sooner or later someone will suggest using a truck. Try it. What part of the truck makes the job an easy one? When the children understand that wheels help the truck move, you are ready to explore the wheel in more depth as a machine.

Examine the wheel toys in the classroom. What is the shape of the wheel? Are wheels always this shape? The children should try making all the wheels turn. Perhaps someone will suggest making a wheel of another shape. Have him or her try out their design in paper or cardboard. Investigate enough wheels in the classroom so that children notice that there are varying diameters to wheels, varying lengths and diameters of axles, and varying materials of construction, but that all wheels function in the same basic way.

If a wheel comes off a tricycle, the children will have an opportunity to examine the axle and perhaps even the ball bearing. Tinkertoys can be available for children to make their own wheel machines. Even very young children can construct simple framelike wheels and axles as a beginning of a vehicle. Small boxes might fit on top of these, a string can be attached, and the "vehicles" pulled around the room. The new large-size Tinkertoy sets provide more possibilities for this use. A group of children might want to walk around the inside of the school looking for other uses of wheels. A walk around the block could reveal still other uses. The children could discuss these uses and demonstrate them with wheels they make in the classroom.

Children can make their own wheel toys if there is a workbench. Sliced spools make fine wheels. Mounting wheels on a wooden block so that the wheels turn may take some time to figure out. There probably won't be a complete axle made at this age, but the children will have to use a modified axle before the wheel turns. You can help with this.

What about kinds of machines that employ wheels? Since pulleys make use of the wheel, demonstrate the flagpole pulley in the school yard. After viewing the raising and lowering of the flag, go back into the classroom and make your own pulley. It could be used to raise, lower, or otherwise move a bucket or box in connection with a large block construction project. When operating the pulley, the child will see which part of the pulley moves to move the weight. The class might visit a construction site to see large pulleys in operation, hauling up bricks, steel beams, or buckets of cement. Children can look for pulleys at home and share their information with others.

The wheel is only one of many simple machine examples that can become the focus of a science exploration. There will be ample opportunities for such investigations throughout the school year. The children should have them occasionally and should be encouraged to take advantage of any when they occur spontaneously.

Reprinted from *Science and Children*,
May 1976, Copyright NSTA.

Many Children Are Budding Geologists

———————— Margaret McIntyre ————————

YOUNG children are born collectors. Rocks of every size, shape, and description are favorite items, since they can be found almost everywhere. A teacher can use rocks in a variety of ways to help young children gain understandings basic to the later mastery of concepts and principles in the field of geology. The teacher helps children initiate their experiences by a series of observations built around the rocks brought into the classroom by children on their own initiative, through field trips, or by the teacher's own interest in rocks collected on various trips. As children look at, describe, and compare their rocks, these experiences provide built-in language development.

Children can devise their own classification schemes. The younger ones will notice color and size first. Rocks can also be classified by how they feel to the touch. How many words can they use to describe the feel—slippery, smooth, bumpy, rough, sharp, pebbly?

The general shape of rocks could be another means of classification. Are some rocks more round than others? Are some jagged and angular? Are some flat? Can you tell the top or the bottom of the rocks? What other questions could you ask?

More investigation might bring about an awareness of the hardness or softness of rocks. How can the child distinguish relative hardness? Try scratching rocks with the fingernail. Are there some that can be scratched or powdered in this way? Are there other materials available to use for scratching? Use a roofing nail or a penny as geologists do to determine hardness. (Be sure to use the terms "geology" and "geologist." Children may not remember these words, but the correct labeling is important.)

Some stones look dirty. Provide a dishpan for washing rocks. Children can compare the rocks when wet and dry. What differences do they notice?

Let the children take some rocks outdoors to see which ones can be used to draw streaks or lines on the (dry) sidewalk. If the rocks are soft enough, the children may be able to make distinctive colored streaks with them. What colors are the streaks? Can the children relate the colors on the sidewalk to the colors of the rocks?

Some child is sure to want to know about what is inside a piece of rock. Take a long look at the rock and describe it. Several children may want to help do this. Then put the rock in a cloth bag or wrap it in an old towel and hit it with a hammer. Talk about the reason for wrapping the rock if the children have not done this before. Unwrap and see if the pieces are all the same shape, color, or size. How many pieces of the rock are there now? Can you put the pieces back together again as a form? Let the children investigate all the pieces thoroughly and describe the inside appearance of the rock. Is there a difference in comparison with the outside of the rock?

Excursions to gather rocks can develop additional ideas about rocks and their formation. If the children are near a lake or the ocean, this would be a fine place to see some smooth stones. A walk along the beach to pick up rocks is a natural for young children. Children can have their own heavy paper sacks or empty coffee cans in which to carry their treasures. Stop to watch the wave action on pebbles on the beach. As they are tossed against the sand all the time, what is happening? Can the children relate the smoothness of rocks to their own use of sandpaper on wood at the carpentry bench?

A trip to a stream bank is another learning opportunity. Here you often find many kinds of rocks all together, especially if the stream has a little current. Many city parks have such streams. The children can see how water moves small rocks over small waterfalls, or smaller rocks are pieces of large ones. While young children are not primarily interested in learning the names of rocks, they can grasp the understanding that small pieces of sandstone come from larger pieces of the rock.

A trip to a local gravel pit, with supervision, is a chance to see gravel scooped up, washed, and perhaps even sorted by size. Words such as coarse, medium, and fine describe the sizes. Loading and storage facilities for the different varieties would be interesting to see. The children can obtain a bucket of gravel to take back to the center. There the gravel can be washed, sorted, and explored. Weighing scales can be used in conjunction with this experimentation. Questions such as which type of gravel weighs the most in a given quantity can be answered by the children's play with the gravel.

In some localities there are rock quarries that small groups of children could visit, and see slabs for patios, walks, and home building. If there are no quarries or gravel pits, a trip to the local home building center will let children see patio stones, gravel, sand, slate, and even the ground limestone the home gardener uses.

By holding rocks up in a strong light such as sunshine,

the children can compare the shine or luster of various rocks. Indoors, a small lamp will serve the same purpose. Are there any rocks that shine almost like silver, that sparkle, or that shine like glass?

Some rocks contain fossils, the remains or imprints of plants and animals that lived millions of years ago. Fossils always fascinate children. You may want to provide a magnifying glass to see more of the detail. Magnifying glasses are useful in centers when children are examining rocks. They may want to draw pictures of what they see through the lens.

Rocks do belong in the early childhood center, even though the children are not ready for formal and scientific classification. The teacher can provide many opportunities during the course of the year for young children to explore this area of physical science.

Helpful Hints

Recycled Apples

Now's the time to think about putting to use the apples that your kindergarten children will probably have left in the bottom of their trick-or-treat bags. Make them the center of a science lesson that teaches children how to observe and describe.

Ask every child to bring an apple from home, and then invite them to compare sizes, shapes, colors. Get them to notice the apple's firmness to the touch, its smooth and shiny skin. (They might rub the apple skins against their own and discuss why fruit, and people, have skins.)

Point out the stem and get the children to talk about its function. (Why do apples need stems?)

After the outside has been thoroughly examined, children can, with appropriate assistance, cut the apples into halves and then into quarters. Not only will they see that two halves—or four quarters—make a whole, they will also become aware of a whole new set of things about their apples. Get the children to smell the apples and taste them, and again to compare apples. Invite them to comment on their apple's sweetness, tartness, juiciness, crunchiness. Point out the apple skin again so they can appreciate how thin yet strong it is.

This will probably be as much knowledge from the apple as kindergarten children can absorb in one lesson, but subsequent lessons might include discussion of the apple seeds (Do all apples have them?) and the planting of some seeds. The apples can also be presented in another form—as applesauce. While the children enjoy a taste of the sauce, encourage them to talk about exactly how the apples have changed. The shape, yes, but what about the texture and the taste? What's happened to the skins, cores, and seeds? What brought about this change?

It is also possible to expand the science lessons into a unit which includes creating an apple poem, drawing apples (and then perhaps "selling" them at the "supermarket" during playtime), and playing an apple counting game. **Helen Laufer**, volunteer kindergarten teacher, Tommie Barfield School, Marco, Florida.

Reprinted from *Science and Children* October 1982, Copyright NSTA.

Artwork by Doreen Curtin

Cloud Watching

Margaret McIntyre

YOUNG CHILDREN, like adults, talk about weather. "It's wet, I'm soaked." a child might say, running in from the rain. "Whew, I'm hot," or "I want a drink," children announce as they enter classrooms on hot days. While the customary kindergarten weather charts symbolize this awareness of weather, teachers can do more to both deepen and extend a child's interest in weather beyond mere communication of the obvious.

Clouds, of interest because they are directly observable, present one possibility for expanding children's natural curiosity about the weather. Over a period of days or weeks children can focus on the concept that cloud types and patterns are constantly changing. A bright sunny day in the month of October, when there are many cumulus clouds, is a good time to make some observations.

Take the children outdoors. Have them lie on their backs, in such a way that they will not look into the sun. Encourage them to discuss the general sky color. Have them look at the clouds and describe them to each other. What color are the clouds? Look at the shape of the bottom of the clouds. Describe this. Now look at the top of the clouds. How does this differ in shape?

Have the children select and focus on their own special cloud for a few minutes. What happens to it as you are watching? Does it change in shape? Does it appear to move? Call attention to the fact that the sun is shining. How does the sunshine feel? When the clouds block the sun, how does the shade feel? Where is the sun then? Have any of the children taken an airplane ride in the daytime on a cloudy day? What did they see?

What shapes can they imagine in the cumulus clouds? Some may see clouds that suggest animals or scenes. Encourage children to tell their classmates what they see.

Young children could learn to label the floating "whipped cream" clouds as cumulus. If enough observations were made over an extended time, the concept that cumulus clouds are generally fair weather clouds might be associated.

Be sure to have additional observations on overcast and cloudy days when dark gray clouds are present. Of course, severe weather days should be viewed from shelter. Ask the children to look at the general sky color. It is bright blue or gray?

RICHARD GUY

To reinforce the concept of winds moving the clouds, do a "cloud watch" on calm days as well as windy days. A young child naturally believes that a cloud is animate and is free to move at its own will around the sky. Through many observations and discussions about direction, speed, and changes in wind movements, a young child can gradually build the concept that air in motion is moving the clouds.

Follow-Up Actitivites

Some children might like to share their cloud watching experiences by painting a sunny or cloudy day "cloudscape." For others who might prefer more motor activity, creative movement offers all kinds of possibilities. Have the children move as if they were cumulus clouds in a blue sky on a day when there was just a gentle breeze. Now, the sky changes to a light gray color, and the wind blows a little harder. How will clouds move now? Climax this activity by having them move as storm clouds in a dark gray sky, and the wind blowing with greater force.

A short action story as a drama activity could involve much of the same movement, with children assuming roles of wind, trees, clouds, sun, paper on the ground, etc. Five-year-olds would appreciate this challenge. They are becoming quite verbal, and many children welcome the opportunity to make up their own dialogue and actions with little adult prompting. By describing their experiences in cloud watching, the children are beginning to integrate those experiences into learnings and concepts they are able to understand.

Some children would question what clouds are made of. A cloud forms when water vapor is condensed in the air. To make this definition more meaningful, some children might be interested in producing a "cloud" of their own in the classroom. Bring water in a teakettle to a full, rolling boil, so the youngsters can see the water vapor from the teakettle leave the spout, and the hot steam condensing in the cooler room air to form a "cloud." Be sure to observe safety precautions when the children are near the heat source and the steam. What happens to the "clouds" after they leave the spout?

Poetry would be appropriate either as an introduction to cloud watching or as a follow-up activity. There are many poems about clouds. This brief verse is very appropriate for even the youngest child.

The Sky
> Today
> The Sky is very far away,
> So blue
> It is; and, soft as squirrels' tails,
> Float over it, like little sails,
> Small clouds.*

M. Bardwell

---

*Dorothy Knippel, Compiler. *Poems for the Very Young Child*. Whitman Publishing Company, Racine, Wisconsin, 1932. P. 85.

Dust Off Those Magnifiers

— Margaret McIntyre —

Child development expert Jean Piaget noted that assimilation and accomodation are basic cognitive processes used by young children. Assimilation occurs as children gradually incorporate elements in the environment into their understanding. These elements are usually oversimplified. Accomodation occurs as children begin to modify their responses to these initial experiences. The magnifying glass can be used effectively to enhance the assimilation/accomodation process in children.

Even children as young as two can use a magnifying glass to see that objects placed under it appear bigger. *Bigger* is a word to which young children respond positively; they wish they were bigger. But bigger also implies change. A child looks at an object with the naked eye and sees one thing; with a magnifying glass, he or she sees the object differently. A two-year-old may recognize that the object seems larger; a four or five-year-old has the ability to see greater detail.

Variety of Magnifiers

Magnifying glasses come in many sizes and shapes. Make more than one type available for children to use. Very young children enjoy the jumbo-sized magnifier mounted on a three-legged stand. Nothing needs to be held and objects of different sizes and heights can be placed easily under the lens. An entire plant can be examined at once. Children can place the magnifier on the floor and kneel to adjust their view.

Another type of magnifier resembles a gooseneck lamp. Its adaptability allows children to move either the object or the magnifying lens for easy viewing. Since the gooseneck magnifier requires some adjustment, it is more suitable for four and five-year-olds.

A hand magnifier with an unbreakable acrylic lens and handle is perfect for children of all ages. This magnifier has the advantage of being small, mobile, and inexpensive—children can have their own to use whenever they choose. Such hand magnifiers, available in several diameters and a variety of shapes, are ideal for field trips and outdoor activities.

Powers of magnification differ among hand lenses. Even toddlers are able to observe these differences; ask older children to examine objects closely and compare the way the same object looks under a variety of magnifying lenses.

An interesting variation to the hand magnifier is a small box measuring 2½ × 2½ × 1½ centimeters with a 4x magnifying lens as a cover. The box is ideal for observing live insects. Make certain insects are gently caught, carefully observed, then released to their own environment without injury. This activity encourages both scientific observation

A child looks at a the naked ey thing glass

and humaneness, important qualities for young children to develop. Naturally, the box will hold any small object a child treasures and wants to examine.

Reprinted from *Science and Children,*
May 1982, Copyright NSTA.

Also available for viewing use is a 3-D Magnascope: a circular box with a recessed compartment and a removable cap. Its principle is the same as that of

> bject with
> nd sees one
> with a magnifying
> ne or she sees
> he object differently.

the small box, but its magnifier is larger. Place a small leaf, creature, or other object inside the box for children to examine. Because the object to be viewed is contained inside the box, even young children can use the box safely. Exercise some caution with older toddlers as they may try to remove the cap.

Adjusting microscopes requires more dexterity than most young children possess. But a magnifier exists that is a bridge to microscopes—the tripod magnifier. This tool is small, works well on a table, and is an excellent way for children to study very small objects. The focus adjusts and magnifies to a set limit.

Let Children Do It

When introducing magnifying glasses in the classroom, let the children use the instruments on their own. Too often adults are tempted to list what they see, not what the children view. Children may *look* at the same object, but do not *see* in the same way as the adult. The adult has experienced years of assimilation/accomodation; the child has not.

Plan viewing opportunities that permit children to observe objects in different ways—with the naked eye, magnified, and magnified under different powers.

The big question children need to consider is: Why does the same object appear different through a magnifying glass? Encourage children to follow their own interests in answering this question, but help them by providing background materials or asking questions that encourage precise description. Record children's observations, or make a class picture book of children's experiences with magnifiers.

Initiating Experiences

As children get used to the magnifiers, provide them with time, opportunities, and greater challenges. Allow them to examine what they wish and to describe what they observe when examining an object under a magnifier. Suggest these activities to the children:

—Examine your clothes from shirts to shoes.

—Examine the cooking center in the classroom from chopping board to strainer.

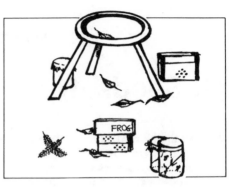

—Examine black-and-white newspaper pictures; then examine color photos from the Sunday advertisements or magazines.

—Go outdoors and observe a patch of grass. Circumscribe your own patch with a piece of yarn.

—Examine some of your friend's hair.

—Borrow a magnifier to take home; examine the coat of your dog or cat.

—Find a snail, if possible, and observe its foot movements and that of its feelers. Snails leave a trail; examine this.

—Locate a spiderweb; use your magnifier to observe its construction.

—Examine your snack or lunch under a magnifier.

Some children are bound to be curious about the magnifying glass itself. Explain that this is a lens. Four and five-year-olds might want to study the appearance and feel of different magnifying lenses. Encourage them to do this. Some children will notice that the lens appears curved and is thicker in the middle than around the edges. Explain that this construction makes the magnifier work as it does. Leave it at that.

During the early childhood years opportunities abound for children to discover that objects appear larger and clearer under a magnifying glass. Children also find out that magnification reveals details unseen with the naked eye. Above all, children are using the processes of assimilation and accomodation to learn about the world around them.

———— Margaret McIntyre ————

Of Seeds, Nuts, Fruits, Grains . . . .

NUTRITION HABITS are being formed in the early childhood years. Often TV advertising gives the child specific food messages that are not based on good nutrition concepts. Young children need to become knowledgeable not only about wholesome food but about so-called junk foods and non-foods as well.

The study of vegetable stems, instead of the usual leaf and root vegetables, might be an interesting starting point. Children can decide what a stem is, what it is used for in a plant, and which stems are good to eat—the latter requiring naming the vegetables. A visit to a supermarket or farmer's market is a must, where perhaps celery, asparagus, and *cultivated* mushrooms could be purchased. Celery can be stuffed with peanut butter or cheese, asparagus can be cooked for a taste or made into a cream soup, while the mushroom tops can be stuffed with cream cheese and mixed with the chopped stems. Washing and preparing these stem vegetables present opportunities for health discussions, as well as the experience of the raw versus the cooked taste of vegetables.

Fruits can be investigated for shape, color, size, smell, feel, taste, and texture. The sounds of eating a banana would differ from eating a firm apple. Parts of the fruit such as skin, stem, core, pulp, and blossom can be noted and discussed. Differences and similarities in the various citrus fruits can be seen and tasted. Fruits are nutritional snacks and are also used in salads and desserts. Help children to see the value of fruit over cookies and candy.

An investigation of dairy products could include different types of cheeses. If there is a cheese shop nearby, be sure to take the children as most have no idea of the wide variety available, from this country and abroad. The source of cheese can be discussed, remembering that goat's milk is used in many cheeses. Children can compare cheeses as to color, shape, and appearance as well as taste and smell. Have them examine the rinds of some cheeses as well as the wax coverings of others. Grate hard cheeses and use them on bread for a taste. Both small and large curd cottage cheese can be sampled with a touch of paprika to give it color or with a topping of grated carrots. Compare swiss and cheddar cheeses, then melt both and compare the products. Make a rare-

bit of processed cheese, and serve as a snack on a quarter of a piece of whole wheat toast. Add crushed pineapple to cream cheese and serve on crackers. Tell the children that milk and milk products provide protein, calcium, and vitamins necessary for growth and well-being. Refer to calcium as building strong bones and teeth and explain the importance of protein in their diet.

Many other sources of protein can be listed such as poultry, meat, fish, and vegetable products. A visit to a food locker or butcher might help children relate the meat with which they are familiar, to the animal from which it comes. Picture games could reinforce this food source knowledge. Meat can be broken down into categories such as beef, pork, and lamb. Questions about what the animals eat might lead to a farm visit or slides and movies to illustrate the idea of converting vegetable matter (grain and plants) into animal protein.

Vegetable proteins include peas, beans, lentils, and peanuts. Explore the size, shape, color, and feel of such dried legumes as navy, mung, pinto, lima, soy, kidney, black, pea, and cranberry beans. Or the characteristics of chick peas, split peas, and lentils. Children can soak them and note the expansion. Why are the beans fatter? Where did all the water go? How do they feel now? By marking the level of the beans before and after soaking, children can see how much more space the legumes take in the pan. Try a Piaget-adapted conservation test. How many beans are there after soaking? (Do not be surprised at the answer.) Can the children tell the reason for soaking? What can you do with the soaked beans? Besides cooking appetizing main dishes, mung and soybeans may be sprouted to use in sandwiches.

Nuts, another source of protein, come in many varieties. They are not only tasty eating but are good for nutrition if not overly salted or oiled. First, look at the nuts in their shells. Brazil nuts, almonds, peanuts, pecans, black and English walnuts, butternuts, hazel, hickory, and pistachio nuts can be included. Children can describe size, shape, color, and texture of shell. Do the nuts have different smells? Nuts can be sorted by variety. From what kind of a plant did they come? Pictures will be needed for many unless they are grown in your area. Can the children crack the shells with nut-

Reprinted from *Science and Children*,
February 1976, Copyright NSTA.

crackers? Which nuts open easiest? Which takes the most force? Look at the nuts extracted from the shells. Talk about the differences in kernels. Did they come out whole or in pieces? Why? Can you eat them as they come from the shell? What happens to nuts when they are cooked as in cookies or bread? Try a recipe using nuts.

Seeds are also a source of protein, and health stores have a wide variety. Some seeds, such as pumpkin seeds from the Jack-o-lantern of Halloween, can be prepared by the children themselves. Sesame seeds taste better when they are lightly toasted in the oven. Caraway and poppy seeds can be sprinkled on bread or cookies. Sunflower seeds make a good snack. In examining seeds, the taste, hardness, color, and size can be compared. Remind the children about the protein and vitamins that are necessary for good health, and how seeds provide some of them. Stress the value of seeds and nuts for snacks instead of candy or sweet cakes.

The grains from which cereals and breads are made may not be familiar to children. Most will not know what the grains look like or even the names of the grains. Wheat, oats, barley, rice, corn, millet, and buckwheat are grains to acquaint them with, and children can match the cereals they eat to the grain source. Pictures of the growing grains are no substitute for the real thing but they may have to be used. Talk about the natural grain cereals. Use the term "whole grain cereal" so that children will gradually become aware of the fact that these cereals have all available nutrients present, with none removed. Mention that cereals are high in carbohydrates for needed energy. Cereals also contain some fiber, fat, and vitamins that keep us healthy. Have the children become aware of the cereals that are colored artificially or sprayed with sugar.

Flour and meals made from grains can easily be studied, too. Most children have seen only the bleached white flour. Talk about bleaching and compare to the fading of cloth in the sun, so they understand the term. Bring in rye and graham flour as well as unbleached white flour. You can even plan to bake bread. This would bring in the use of yeast and its part in the rising process. What other ingredients go into bread? Compare your own whole wheat bread with the store bread. Is it crustier? Be sure to eat the bread while it's warm from the oven so the children can see the butter or margarine melt.

Quick breads can be made with flour and meal. Where does corn meal come from? How is it made? What about the color? Make corn sticks or muffins. Pancakes made in an electric frypan or griddle would provide the taste of buckwheat or the mixed group grains in some pancake flour. Pancakes make a fine climax to a maple sugaring, if you live in a part of the country where it's common.

A visit to a bakery could provide a bread-tasting party that includes the childrens' favorite cheeses. Compare the texture, smell, taste, and appearance of rye, oatmeal, whole wheat, cracked wheat, soy, and some of the health breads that contain a variety of grains and seeds. Which ones do they like best? Examine bread for the many shapes in which it is baked. Try sourdough and French breads. If you are in a multicultural area, the varieties of bread, a universal food, are endless.

Reprinted from *Science and Children,*
May 1983, Copyright NSTA.

From Soup To Science

—————— Margaret McIntyre ——————

Children enjoy preparing food, and they enjoy eating the food they prepare. As they practice kitchen techniques, they also develop ideas about measurement and mass, and they get a chance to observe physical and chemical changes in the food being prepared. Using food preparation as a classroom activity also allows teachers to instruct children in important health and safety procedures, explain where various foods come from, and discuss the value of good nutrition. With summer approaching, it is useful to focus on food activities that children can repeat with their parents during vacation. The following recipes and accompanying questions and activities are designed to help both teachers and parents as they explore science and cooking with children.

Before You Begin

Success and safety in doing the activities described below depend on following some simple guidelines:

• Make certain that children wash their hands before preparing and eating food.

• *Closely* supervise any activity that calls for cooking or baking.

• Adapt the activities to the age group involved. Three-year-olds cannot slice an apple in half; they can, however, mash a soft fruit, stir, or turn a food mill.

• Supervise the use of an electric blender. Although children can prepare ingredients to put into the container, they should not plug in or disengage the cord, nor should they operate the machine on their own.

• Make sure children understand that tasting means using individual spoons, dishes, and glasses—not licking the spoon that is being used for stirring, or poking a finger into what's being prepared.

Take the time to discuss these guidelines with the children.

The First Course

Fruits are a good food to begin with because you can find them in such variety at your grocery store or at nearby fruit and vegetable stands throughout the spring and summer. They're a good "first course," too, since young children can handle them easily. Before you begin any cooking, have the children taste and smell the fruits and observe their size, shape, mass, and color. Children will probably also like to compare the various skin coverings. Give your novice cooks plenty of time to engage in all these activities.

For your first recipe consider a somewhat unusual first course—a cold fruit soup. Children are unlikely to associate fruit with soup, and even less likely to think of soup as a cold dish. Introduce them to this idea by preparing a soup made with a familiar fruit, the orange.

Orange Soup

1. Gently heat 2 cups (475 milliliters [mL])* orange juice in a saucepan. (Using freshly squeezed orange juice gives children a chance to learn about extracting the juice, but juice made from frozen concentrate will do. To measure the juice, use whole-unit cups for very young children and half-unit cups for kindergarten children, who would enjoy this challenge.)

2. Add 1 teaspoon (5 mL) cornstarch mixed with 2 tablespoons (30 mL) cold water, and cook slowly over medium heat until mixture is clear. (Measuring spoons may be new to some children, and they will need to experiment with the spoons before beginning to cook. Cornstarch is wonderful to the touch. Have extra available so all the children can feel it between their fingers and describe the sensation. Children can also watch the juice change color as the cornstarch is added and as the mixture cooks.)

3. Add a scant ¼ cup (60 mL) sugar. Stir well, remove from heat, and chill. (Kindergarteners could use a candy thermometer to check the temperature when the sugar is added and again after the soup has chilled.)

4. Vary the recipe using cherry, cranberry, apple, or pineapple juice.

---

*Metric conversion of cups in these recipes is based on the standard U.S. measuring cup (237 mL) rounded to the nearest 5 mL.

Fruit Shakes

Children often get thirsty in warm weather and clamor for soft drinks or shakes to quench their thirst. Introduce them to the fruit shake, a drink that's more wholesome than any fast-food shake or carbonated beverage. As you make these shakes, take the time to emphasize the fact that synthetic drinks contain too much sugar and too many artificial flavorings and preservatives to be considered healthy.

Begin by preparing a fruit juice to act as the flavoring. You can use canned or frozen juice, but it's also fun to have the children squeeze their own lemons, limes, oranges, or grapefruits to make the drinks. This way they can observe the fruit pulp, which accounts for much of the fruit's nutritional value. The orange milk shake is simple and basic.

Phyllis Marcuccio

Orange Milk Shake

1. Dissolve 1½ cups (355 mL) powdered skim milk in 3 cups (750 mL) cold water. (Powdered milk may be new to children. Let them make some to drink first. What does it look and taste like? How do you get the powder to dissolve in the water?)
2. Mix in 1 cup (235 mL) orange juice. (How does the appearance of the milk change when the orange juice is added?)
3. Add a few ice cubes, and whirl in a blender or shake vigorously in a large container. (How does this affect the liquid's appearance? Discuss the frothiness of the mixture and the increase in volume. If you're preparing the shake with older children, have them measure the increase. Let the shake sit a few minutes. What happens to it?)

Experiment further by using 1 cup (235 mL) crushed pineapple or some pureed fruit—peaches, fresh strawberries, or raspberries, for example. Sweeten lightly if necessary. Or, for a quick shake, mash a ripe banana with a fork. Stir in 1 cup (235 mL) plain yogurt. Put the mixture in a glass. Can the children explain why the mixture is best eaten with a spoon rather than a straw? Use the same ingredients, but whirl the mixture in a blender. Is the shake different? What causes the change?

Making Yogurt?

For most children, yogurt is probably something that comes out of a little paper or plastic cup with a lid, and the idea of making it themselves is sure to be a hit. The process is easy, and you don't need a yogurt maker.

Yogurt

1. Heat 1 quart (1 L) milk in a scrupulously clean, stainless steel pan until bubbles appear around the edge. (The temperature will be just below boiling. Kindergarten children could use a candy thermometer to test it.)
2. Let milk cool to lukewarm. (How do you know when it's ready?)
3. Add ½ cup (120 mL) fresh, *plain* yogurt from the grocery store.

(Check the label to make sure that no sugar, gelatin, or flavorings have been added.)
4. Cover and put in a warm place for 8 hours or more, until thickened. (A closet or shelf of a cabinet is a good place—and some recipes even suggest wrapping the yogurt container in a blanket to keep it warm. The point is to maintain the heat of the milk so the yogurt culture can develop.) Once you have settled the mixture in its warm place, do not move it or your yogurt may not set.
5. When thickened, store in refrigerator until ready to use.

Children can flavor their yogurt with chopped nuts, shredded coconut, honey, applesauce, raisins, fresh fruit, or other tasty toppings. You might limit very young children to two choices. (Two- and three-year-olds have a difficult time choosing.) Kindergarten children would be comfortable making three or four choices.

Although science is often fun, it isn't usually tasty as well. And these warm weather activities have the added advantage of introducing the concept of good nutrition. So why not get out your apron and end the school science year on a delicious note!

Reprinted from *Science and Children*,
September 1975, Copyright NSTA.

———— Margaret McIntyre ————

Water, Water Everywhere

THE EASE of access to water may account for its under-use in early childhood situations as an investigative, manipulative, and highly sensory science resource for young children. Water has the advantage of eliciting a variety and increasing complexity of responses to its physical properties. A wise teacher plans for these responses by gradually introducing materials such as funnels, different-sized containers and spoons, tubing, siphons, sponges, floating materials of many kinds, and sieves. These can be used in a sink, plastic baby bath, dishpan, or metal tub, indoors or outdoors, on tables or on the floor.

Why not use water for developing a sense of touch? Water is soft, slippery, and usually cool. Water gives objects a different feel. Play with a dry and a wet rubber doll when bathing the doll. Feel a wooden boat when dry and after being in the water. The word *slippery* will then have significance.

After children play in the water a while, have them look at their hands. What made them look like this? How do they feel? Why?

Putting out containers of different sizes and shapes invites pouring from one to the other. Volume and size can be talked about. Investigate other aspects of pouring. Is it easier to fill a wide- or a narrow-mouthed container? How can you make it easier? What happens when you use a funnel? Does the size make any difference? Does using a funnel take longer? Why?

Later on, tubing or siphons can be provided for investigation. What can you do with them? How can we empty a pan full of water without carrying it over to the sink? (This would be a good activity to try outdoors on a warm day.) Siphons provide many opportunities for dramatic play that will enhance the science experiences inherent in the activity.

If you have no access to sieves, make your own with foil pans of differing sizes and shapes. Punch the holes with large and small nails to provide further research opportunities. Do the children see the relationship between the size of the hole and the stream of water? Can they notice the size of the resultant streams and the patterns they make, and relate these patterns to the size and shape of the sieve itself?

Adding food coloring to water will add interest and provoke more learning. The primary colors can be mixed to make orange, purple, and green. When the water is colored, volume differences are more noticeable. Children can use felt pens to show heights on containers after pouring a certain number of measures into them. Comparisons can be made between tall, thin and short, fat containers that have the same amounts in each.

Soap adds another dimension to water play. The different feel of water with and without soap is quite distinctive. Doll clothes can be washed using soap and using plain water. Are there differences? Compare swishing liquid soap into water with dissolving soap flakes or beads. A child can use an egg beater to make bubbles and a cover of suds. If you poke your fingers into the suds, what happens? Can you guess why? Blowing soap bubbles might be a natural next step. What is a soap bubble? Why does it pop? Who can make the biggest, the most? (Try catching bubbles!)

Have available all kinds of floating and non-floating objects. What floats? Children have the opportunity to test *big* corks and little marbles. Sorting out what effect size and shape have on floating becomes apparent through repeated play.

Provide marbles and stones for children to drop into containers of water that are not full. What happens? Perhaps adults can help children count the number it takes to make water overflow. Use different sizes so young children can use large stones, making it easier to count. Why does the water spill out? Older children might want to catch and measure what spills.

Water play is soothing; it gives children the added bonus of achievement, because they control what they do to water. If it spills, one can wipe it up. If a can is too full, one can pour it out. This natural, familiar material makes possible concrete experiences, in depth, size, texture, quantity, principles of measurement, ordination, seriation, parts and whole, and relationships between shapes and sizes for the young child.

Reprinted from *Science and Children*,
May 1979, Copyright NSTA.

Water Concepts

—————— **Margaret McIntyre** ——————

Water can be an excellent medium for developing science concepts. Many concepts about water are useful to teachers in planning activities for young children.

Water is needed to maintain most plant life. Observe what happens to two plants, one watered and one not.

Water can dissolve some substances. The result is called a solution. Stir 15 mL of sugar, salt, dried milk, and instant chocolate drink powder into a cup of cold water. What happens.?

Do the experiment again, this time use hot—not boiling—water. What happens? Do the substances dissolve faster? Does it take more or less stirring in hot water to dissolve ingredients?

Water cannot dissolve some substances. The result is called a mixture. Stir 15 mL of sand into a cup of cold water. Add hot—not boiling—water. What happens now?

Water has mass. Compare the "feel" of a cup filled with water and one that is empty (filled with air). Which one feels heavier? Observe the differences in mass of the two cups on a balance scale.

Water evaporates. Observe two containers full of water, one placed in the sun or on a radiator, the other not in direct sunlight. Observe evaporation of rain on the wet pavement when the sun comes out. Paint a sidewalk or your chalkboard with water. Watch the drying process. Teachers could time how long it takes the water to evaporate.

Water can be clear or contain dis-

Roger Wall

solved solids. Take a trip to a pond or stream. Collect 4 L of water. In the classroom pour 1 L into clear plastic glasses. Observe the color. Pour some of this water from the glasses through a cheesecloth strainer. What is in the cheesecloth? Where did this come from? Observe the color of the water poured through the cheesecloth. Compare the color with the original water sample.

Observe what happens when you use another filter system. Half fill a small funnel with small stones or gravel. Cover the gravel with clean sand. Put the funnel in the top of a clear plastic container. Pour some of the pond or stream water you collected into the funnel. Watch the water as it passes through the stones and sand. Examine the filtered water. Compare the color of the filtered water with that of the pond water.

Take some of the water strained through the cheesecloth. Pour the water through the funnel filter. Compare the color of this water with that of the water filtered through the cheesecloth.

Water comes to schools and homes from many sources. Trace the pipes that bring the water into your room as far as you can. You may be able to take a trip to the source.

Water varies in hardness. Observe the amount of suds made from one capful of liquid soap in rain or distilled water, tap water, and tap water in which you have dissolved salt. Have children "feel" the different kinds of water by rubbing their thumb and forefinger together in the water, both before and after adding soap. What differences do they note?

Some materials float in water. Observe an ice cube floating in water. How much of the ice cube shows above the water's surface? Watch the ice cube as it melts. What do you see? Observe what happens to a sponge, a small rock, a plastic straw, a piece of wood, a strip of foil, and a thread spool. What floats, what does not?

Water expands when frozen. Fill a plastic glass half full of water. Circle the water line with a felt-tip pen. Freeze the water, then circle the frozen water line with a felt-tip pen. Compare the two circles. Let the frozen water melt in the sun. Where is the water line?

Drinking water can have many tastes. Taste spring water, mineral water, and tap water. What are the differences in taste? (Warn children not to sample every kind of water they find.)

Water mixes with some liquids, but not with others. What happens when 60 mL of salad oil are added to 240 mL of water in a jar and then shaken? What happens to the oil?

Add 60 mL of milk to 240 mL of water. Shake the mixture. What happens? Let both jars sit for an hour. Now what do you see? Has there been a change in either jar?

Have students bring in juice can labels or buy some canned fruit juices and drinks. Find the word *water* in the label. Which juices contain mostly water? mostly fruit juices? Which is easier to carry home, a can of frozen apple juice concentrate or a bottle of apple juice? Why? Which takes less room in the grocery bag?

Water soaks into some materials, but not in others. (This process is called absorption.) Observe absorption of water by pieces of blotting paper, waxed paper, aluminum foil, terry cloth, and plastic.

Bibliography

Bloome, Enid P. *Water We Drink.* Double-day & Company, Inc., New York City. 1971.

Cartwright, Sally. *Water Is Wet.* Coward, McCann & Geoghegan, Inc., New York City. 1973.

Goldin, Augusta. *Ducks Don't Get Wet* (A-Let's-Read-&-Find-Out Science Bk.), Thomas Y. Crowell Company, Inc., New York City. 1965.

Lefkowitz, R.J. *Water For Today & Tomorrow* (Finding-Out Books for Science & Social Studies, Grades 1-4), Parents' Magazine Press, New York City. 1973.

WET SPOTS

Reprinted from *Science and Children*,
April 1972, Copyright NSTA.

From the "Phenomena for Inquiry"
column by Irwin Slesnick and John Whitmer
of Western Washington State
College, Bellingham, Washington.

? Do wet spots on opposite sides of the blackboard take the same time to evaporate? What about wet spots on different days?

? Do water wet spots evaporate faster than salt water wet spots? How about hot water wet spots?

? Who can make his wet spot disappear fastest without touching it?

? How can you preserve a wet spot for a long time?

Which part of a wet spot dries first; the top, middle, or bottom? Or does a wet spot dry uniformly?

? What patterns of drying can one find by drawing chalk lines around the receding "shore" of wet spots?

Worms

—— **Margaret McIntyre** ——

Children like to be outdoors especially when the weather is pleasant. You offer science explorations to your children that enhance this natural desire. The earthworm is an excellent means to discovery, observation, and learning.

Spring showers often drive earthworms to the surface of the ground. Take children on a walk to observe them. If rain has been heavy, children may even find dead worms on the grass and in gardens. Let children examine the earthworms, both live and dead. Have them feel the worms. (Don't squeeze the live ones!) Ask children to observe size differences in length and circumference, and coloration characteristics. Can they find the holes in the ground that indicate the earthworms' burrows? Can the children find worm casts, the finely ground waste that passes through the worm's digestive tract?

Many birds eat earthworms, and you may have the chance to watch birds, especially robins, catching them. Ask the children to stand quietly to watch the bird find a worm and pull it from the ground. The children can look at the worms again and find the parts that have hard materials or bristles. The worm uses these bristles to cling to the sides of its burrow's walls. What does the bird do to find worms under the ground? Children will have to make several observations of birds catching worms to notice a pattern.

Catching live worms to keep in the classroom can be your next step. Earthworms are often called night crawlers. If the children's parents are sport fishing enthusiasts, the children will know how night crawlers are caught. They will be only too happy to explain the routine. The very name suggests the time when worms crawl from their burrows. A collaborative parent-child expedition to locate night crawlers for the class could be pleasant for everyone.

Live worms are often found, any time of day, under woodpiles, old tree limbs in the woods, or old boards. Lift these carefully, and have a container ready with moistened garden soil in which to put the worms. It is easier to find them on a dark cloudy day.

Another alternative for catching worms is to dig for them. A garden plot is ideal for easy digging. Dig down about 30 cm. Have an old sheet or white plastic bag ready on which to put the clumps of soil. Children can then carefully separate the soil with their hands. Have the children notice any other animals present as they pick through the earth—ants, sow bugs, beetles, larvae. Put the worms in a container that has some damp grass and a wet leaf or two.

Now, back in the classroom, put the worms in an aquarium or large plastic or glass jar half-filled with good garden soil mixed with a little sand. Be sure to keep the soil moist, but not soaked. Six

to eight earthworms are the ideal number for a large container; they need plenty of space in which to crawl.

Earthworms burrow deep into the soil to keep moist and cool, so keep their home cool and slightly damp. *Never* put the habitat in the sun or near heat. If the earthworms burrow deep in the soil, ask the children how they think the worm's habitat could be kept dark. You can cover the habitat on all sides with black paper, if you lack a small dark closet.

What do earthworms eat? If the worms lived in a vegetable garden, what leaves could they eat? Try celery leaves, carrot tops, lettuce, cabbage, or beet tops. If worms live in lawn areas surrounded by trees, what kinds of leaves would they eat? Try maple, sycamore, elm, weeping willow, or beech leaves. Earthworms will also eat bread crumbs, corn meal, and apple parings.

The children could set up an experiment to see what foods worms prefer. Put one each of three kinds of different leaves on the top of the soil. Sprinkle a few drops of water on the leaves, and cover them with a thick layer of soil. Check in two or three days to see which leaf has disappeared.

Look for worm castings both in the habitat and outdoors under logs and boards. Explain to the children that earthworms enrich soil, hence gardeners and farmers like to have many earthworms in their gardens.

Have children check the classroom habitat to look for tunnels that the worms make as they move through the soil. If you put the habitat in a dark room, have the children use a weak light to find a worm eating as it moves along next to the glass.

Children also need the opportunity to study a live earthworm. A worm will die if its body is not kept moist so be sure to keep it damp when handled. Carefully lift a worm from the habitat and place it on a wet paper towel. Have the children examine the head, tail, body. *Gently* feel the worm, and measure it, using a ribbon or string. If the children are older, encourage them to measure the earthworm using metric measurement.

What does the worm feel like? Can the children tell the top side from the underside? How does the top feel in comparison with the underside? Do the sides feel the same the entire length of the body? What parts feel differently? Use a magnifying glass to look at the bristles.

Turn a worm over on the towel. What does the worm do? Try it again. Watch carefully to see how the worm moves along the towel.

Which is the front end of the worm? How do you know? Can you find the mouth? What is it like?

Your children probably will not be able to answer these questions at once. Try a worm observation each day so that each child has a chance to handle and examine a specimen. When your students have finished their earthworm study, be sure to return the live earthworms and earth to the site where they were collected.

A follow-up study might be to observe other worms or worm-like creatures children might encounter. Some possibilities are the worms in apples, corn, or other foods.

Darshan K. Bigelson

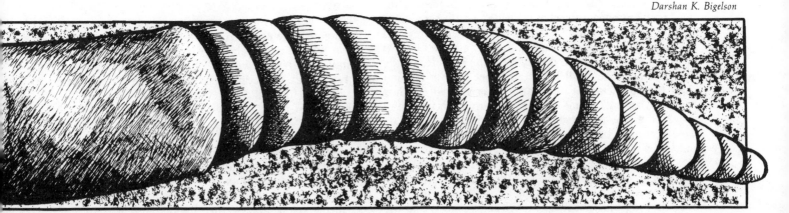

———— Margaret McIntyre ————

Exploring Concepts About Air

YOUNG CHILDREN have limited perceptions about air because it is invisible. A learning center over a period of time could help them develop several basic concepts about air.

Bring to the classroom some small, heavy paper bags, such as those used to carry frozen food purchases home from the store, and some small thin paper bags. Ask a group of children if they think the bag can be full of something they cannot see. Ask them to open up the heavy food bags and look inside. Can they see anything? How can they feel if there is something inside? Can anyone guess what is inside? To find out, suggest they close the bag tightly at the top. Can they feel anything in the bag? Have them hold the closed bag so there is a small opening. If they push the outsides of the bag together, they will be able to feel the air rushing from the bag. Does it make any difference where they push on the bag? What if the push is quick rather than slow? Someone may even want to try it with a regular-sized grocery bag. Have one or two available for children who can handle them.

Some youngsters will want to blow air into the thin paper bag. Who can fill up a bag the fastest? What happens if you let go? How can the air be kept in the bags once they are blown up? One inevitable result is that the

children will want to pop the bag. Why does it make so much noise? What makes the hole in the bag?

These explorations begin to develop concepts about air such as:

You can feel air even though you cannot see it.
You can fill objects such as bags with air.
Air can make a noise.
Air surrounds us.

These concepts are not meant to be memorized or recited by the children, but are given here for information purposes. Much more exploration with these and similar materials will be needed before children truly understand the concepts. Adults can never integrate concepts for children; the children must do it for themselves.

Balloons, Innertubes, and Fans

Another day the center could contain a collection of colored unfilled balloons. Children can blow them up and play with them as they wish. Children enjoy blowing them up and letting them fly free, almost jet propelled. What makes this happen? Who can have a

Reprinted from *Science and Children,*
Nov/Dec 1977, Copyright NSTA.

balloon fly the farthest? This is a good outdoor activity if the wind is calm. Some children will want to tie their balloons shut and perhaps attach strings. Others may want to blow up their balloons until they burst. Why do the balloons burst? Allow only five-year-olds to blow up balloons, under close adult supervision. Younger children may ingest the balloons. Adults can blow up the balloons if there is a mixed-age group.

Can the children tell why the balloons fly up in the air? What would happen if the balloons were filled with water? Would they fly then? Try it.

Bring in an air pump on another day. Let the children play around with it until they understand its operation. Let them feel the air coming out and try their skill at pumping before they attempt to fill such items as a beach ball. Have the children inflate an inner tube. The filling operation gives opportunities for comparing size and talking about change in appearance. Children can also sit on it when it is full. Allow it to deflate with someone still sitting on it and see what happens. The group might want to take a field trip to the nearest garage to see the compressed air hose and watch someone fill a tire. Take an uninflated tube along. Compare filling it there to the chore of filling it with the hand pump back at the center.

These additional experiences reinforce the earlier concepts mentioned and give children insight into additional concepts:

Air can be moved.
Air can make balls, inner tubes, or tires feel hard.
Air pumps can be used to put air into tires.

Set up the learning center with colored paper and crayons, on another day. Have the children make their own fans. What do you do with a fan? Is there any air in the fan itself? Fan yourself slowly, then rapidly. Is there a difference in the air that you feel? Does the size of the fan make a difference in the amount of air that you feel?

What else can you do with a fan besides cool yourself? Can you use it to move pieces of paper across a floor? Even the smallest child can find games to play with a fan. This is a good activity for a rainy or snowy day.

Make Sailboats

If there is a water table or a good-sized sink in the room, use the fans to move sailboats in the water. Children can make their boats from hunks of plastic foam, lightweight cardboard, and a lollipop stick. If the weather outdoors permits, the sailboat experience could be moved outside, using either fans or the wind. In some areas, children might be able to visit a sailing club or harbor to see sailboats or to watch a demonstration. Kindergarten children would appreciate the opportunity to see and feel the sails. The size of a real sailboat and a toy sailboat could be compared.

When outside, let the children talk about what they feel in the way of air movement. Can they see the wind? How do they know there is wind? How many ways are there of "seeing" that it is windy? Do children know the names for wind—breeze, gale, gust? Encourage children to use these words in subsequent outdoor activities and in weather charts.

In the above activities children are beginning to become knowledgeable about another basic concept:

Air movement can move objects; e.g., big sailboats and toy sailboats.

Building on These Concepts

Blowing bubbles is a favorite activity of small children. Provide bubble blowers for the youngest children, straws with split ends for older children, and bowls containing a mixture of water and baby shampoo (in case the bubbles break near the children's eyes). One caution, be sure the children are old enough to know they are to blow *out*, and not suck *in*.

It takes a lot of practice to blow bubbles efficiently. If blown in the sunshine, a rainbow of colors will emerge. What are the bubbles made of? Where does the air for the bubble come from? What makes a bubble pop? What do you feel when a bubble bursts?

These activities are but a few of those possible in introducing young children to explorations with air. What happens to heated air, the presence of air in water, the importance of air in burning, the use of air in sound production, the air in whipped foods—these can be brought in as the year goes along.

Light and Shadow

———————— Margaret McIntyre ————————

YOUNG CHILDREN prefer light to darkness, because they can see what is around them. Darkness may be frightening. Parents or teachers can allay this fear common to two- and three-year olds by teaching them how to use available light sources. Children can be taught to turn on light in a dark room, or carry a flashlight into a dark closet. Permitting the child to control light and darkness by switching on a light or a flashlight at will is both a fear deterrent and a useful beginning in the conceptual understanding that we see when there is light.

Children can use a flashlight to illuminate a peep show or a shadow box they have made, naming what they see. Repeat this activity with different sizes of boxes and with varying intensities of light in the boxes. Can the children note the changes and relationships in both the intensity of light and in the ability to see details when using flashlights of varying strengths?

Another day, in a darkened room, have the children focus a flashlight beam on a chalkboard or a large piece of paper tacked to a bulletin board. Can they tell you the shape of the beam of light? Outline the beam with chalk or crayon. Encourage children to experiment by holding the flashlight closer to the chalkboard or paper, and outline the shape with another color of chalk or crayon. Compare this shape with the first outline drawn. Now try with the flashlight held much farther away, and draw an outline with a third color. Compare this to the other two outlines previously drawn. What are the children's conclusions? This will need to be repeated several times so that many children get a chance to work through the conclusions and see that they are valid.

Can the children block the light path of the flashlight? In how many different ways can this be done? What happens when the light is blocked?

Have available materials such as clear plastic wrap, white and black poster paper, waxed paper, tissue paper, tissue, sheeting, cardboard, and a plastic container full of water. Through which of these materials will the light from a flashlight pass? Encourage the children to guess, giving their reasons. Let them try out their reasons. Let them try out their guesses and observe what happens. The materials can be sorted into two groups, those that light shines through and those it does not. Be sure to allow children ample time to play around with these materials before doing the sorting.

Some older children might want to take a flashlight apart to see what makes the beam of light. Let them locate the bulb and see how small it is. Just watching the bulb light go on and off is fascinating. Can they figure out how the dry cells light the bulb? Can they put the dry cells into the position that will light the bulb? This manipulation will take considerable trial and error, but let the children do it, encouraging them with questions if needed.

Darkness may be frightening. Parents or teachers can allay this fear common to two-and three-year-olds by teaching them how to use available light sources.

Reprinted from *Science and Children,*
January 1978, Copyright NSTA.

Prism Play

On an appropriate day, set out two or three prisms, preferably of different size or shape, in a sunny place. Position the prisms so that the children see the effect of sunlight passing through the prisms and shining on the wall. How many colors can they see? Count them and name the colors. Four- and five-year-olds could be told that this light array is called a spectrum. Have they ever seen a spectrum in the sky or in water spraying from a hose? What is another name for the phenomenon? Encourage the children to talk freely about the exact circumstances surrounding their seeing a rainbow to enable you to understand at what level they are thinking.

Have crayons and white paper available for children who might want to illustrate the spectrums they can make with the prisms. Give all the children a chance to do this themselves. Pull down the shade again. Children need many opportunities to see that direct sunlight is needed to make a spectrum and to observe that spectrum colors are always in the same order.

Some children will believe that any object held in the sun will form a spectrum. Let them try using a clear plastic container and a thick glass jar (the latter with adult supervision). Can the children tell what happens when these catch the sunlight? Have them describe the shapes of the container, the jar, and the prism. Does it make a difference which objects are curved? Only by trying will the children work through this basic understanding.

Shadows Outdoors

Robert Louis Stevenson's "I Have a Little Shadow that Goes In and Out with Me" from *A Child's Garden of Verses* is an appropriate beginning to play with shadows, another aspect of understanding light. By going outdoors to the playground or a sidewalk early in the morning, children can draw their friends' shadows with chalk, measure them, and show the direction in which a shadow points in relation to the standing child. Use large pieces of paper if the children want pictures of their own shadows to keep. Shadows can be drawn on the paper, then cut out. Try drawing shadows at different times of the day. By looking at the drawings on the sidewalk or on paper, children can note the differences in the size of the shadow, as well as direction. Without looking directly at the sun, the children need to be aware of the sun's position at the time they are drawing shadows. Knowing where you have to stand in relation to the sun to get a shadow may take many attempts on the part of children.

Someone is sure to notice that all shadows point in the same direction. By looking at trees, fences, shrubs, and utility poles in the immediate area, children can note the direction these shadows take and compare them with their own. Have the children point in the sun's direction with one extended arm and in the direction of their shadow with the other arm.

Have some children stand in the shadow of the building. Can you make your own shadow there? Go out in the sun again. Can you make a shadow? What happens to a shadow if a cloud passes over the sun? Why?

Shadow Play Indoors

On a cloudy or rainy day, try shadow play using the light from a filmstrip projector. Let the children see what shadows they can make on a screen or a wall using their arms and hands. For the youngest children stuffed animals are excellent for shadow play. Children can discover where they have to place the animals to become shadows on the screen. Encourage movement closer to and farther away from the screen to see the effects. Are children aware that moving the animal makes a like movement on the screen? Have them watch their hand movements in the same manner. How can you tell what makes the shadow? Understanding that a shadow is related to the object that made it is an important concept.

More on Light

If the children are interested, the teacher could provide the materials for further study. What are other sources of light? What can you do with light? Kindergarteners might even be interested in making a simple sun dial showing early morning, noon, and later afternoon. Children could also draw pictures with the shadows of people, buildings, and trees correctly placed according to the sun's position.

Learning to Observe Animals

— Margaret McIntyre —

Teachers frequently invite students to introduce their pets in the classroom. Yet children seldom observe these animals closely; often the creatures seem to melt into the background. To catch children's interest, teachers must ask skillful questions that require more than a mere glance at the animal.

Try the following questions on a small group of children looking at a guinea pig.

- What do we call an animal that looks like this?
- How does it move?
- How does it see?
- How many eyes does it have?
- What color are they?
- Does it have eyelashes?
- How does it hear?
- Where are the ears; what color and shape are they?
- How does it eat?
- What does it eat?
- How does it breathe?
- How can you tell?
- What sound(s) does it make?
- How does it sleep; how can you tell when it is asleep?
- When does it sleep?
- How do we take care of its home?
- How does it exercise?

Children could create a pet book, with each question using a page. Their drawings would add interest and reveal how children see these pets.

Classroom Pets

Hamsters make good pets for the classroom. They need a special cage, an exercise wheel, and a bottle with a tube for drinking. Wood shavings cover the cage floor and need to be changed often. Fresh greens should be added to commercial hamster food. Hamsters easily catch cold, so protect them from drafts and direct sunlight.

Guinea pigs are nice pets too, and have similar needs. Since they are bigger, they need larger cages. For very young children, guinea pigs make better pets than gerbils because they are easier to handle.

Rabbits are gentle pets but require larger cages; newspaper or wood chips should cover the cage floor. Supplement commercial rabbit food with lettuce, carrots, and other raw vegetables. Rabbits can be allowed to hop around the classroom during quiet times, but children must learn not to chase or drag the creatures or pick them up by the ears.

Pet Store

A trip to a local pet store enables small groups of children to observe a wider variety of animals than is found in most classrooms. Animals such as monkeys, parakeets, tropical fish, snakes, and turtles appeal to children. Permitting children to feed certain animals could be a highlight of the trip, if arranged in advance. Again, guide your students' observations with carefully chosen questions. The children will probably have many questions of their own.

If there are no pets in the classroom, a pet store trip can help children select an appropriate pet and obtain proper housing and food for it.

Animal Visitors

Classroom visiting days can be arranged for some of the children's family pets—but do not allow more than one animal visitor at a time. Talk with each child's parents about care of the animal, even if the classroom visit will last only an hour.

Reprinted from *Science and Children*,
May 1981, Copyright NSTA.

"Pets need to be handled with gentleness . . . . Friendly animals that are accustomed to children can help students understand this."

Pets need to be handled with gentleness and consideration. Friendly animals that are accustomed to children can help students who do not have pets at home understand this rule.

Cats and dogs are the usual visitors. Ideally, several breeds of each will visit, to show children the variety within a species. Children can observe dog and cat guests first-hand and (with adult supervision) stroke the coat of each animal. Here are some leading questions to ask students observing dogs or cats in the classroom:

- What kind of a coat does the animal have?
- How does the coat feel as you stroke it?
- What color(s) is the animal?
- How much does it weigh?
- Does it have a tail? Describe it.
- Look at the bottom of the feet. Carefully feel them. What can you say about them?
- What sounds does the pet make?
- Can you name the many ways a cat uses its voice? (purr, meow)
- If the cat is a house pet, where does it sleep at night?
- What is a litter box?
- How do dogs/cats play? (the pet owner can demonstrate these play activities)
- Why do dogs like bones? What do they do with them?
- How can we be sure a bone does not hurt a dog?
- If a dog is a house pet, how does he exercise?
- What breeds of dogs can live outdoors most of the time?
- What does the pet eat?
- How and what does it drink?
- How old do you think the pet is?

Children can and should be involved in planning for the animal's welfare during its visit to the classroom. The child who owns the pet should be especially active in the planning. She gains both self-confidence and self-esteem as classmates question her about the food, water, tags, leashes, or collar required for her pet. Parents and teachers can answer the most difficult questions.

Grooming of animals is another important concept to explore. Brushing can be discussed; the pet owner may let classmates have a turn at this task. The animal's appearance before and after brushing can be seen as well as felt by the children.

Watching a dog chew on a bone raises many questions. Carefully open a dog's mouth so the children can see the arrangement of its teeth. A bone or some biscuits fed to the canine visitor permit children to hear the dog's gnawing, and to see how dogs eat without using arms or hands.

Sometimes pets become ill. This opens up another area for exploration. Where do animals go when they are ill? What are doctors called who care for sick animals?

Some children may have taken pets to a veterinarian. They can tell the rest of the class what happened. Explain that animals sometimes need the same kinds of medical help humans do: rest, medicine, shots, splints, bandages, even tooth care.

Inquire whether a local veterinarian might permit children in small groups to see part of the animal clinic. Learning opportunities abound in well-supervised visits of this sort.

Farm Animals

A visit to a farm or a humane children's farm park acquaints city children with farm animals. Pictures cannot give children the understanding of these animals that the real thing can.

First, the teacher must locate a farm that welcomes children. Classroom preparation for the visit will vary with the type of farm chosen. Provide pictures of the animals you plan to see. Read some farm stories with the class.

On the farm, children need sufficient time to view the animals. They can find answers to questions such as:

- Where does each of the animals live on the farm?
- What do we call the house in which each lives?
- Which animals live outdoors? All of the time? Part of the time?
- What does each animal eat?
- Where does the farmer store feed?
- What crops does the farmer raise to feed the animals?
- What kind of coat does each animal have?
- How does it feel to touch a sheep, pig, cow, duck, or chicken?

Some three-to-five year olds will wonder what male, female, and young animals of each species are called. Help students sort poultry names such as rooster, hen, pullet, cockerel, and chick. Similarly, define bull, heifer, and calf; stallion, mare, and colt; sow, boar, piglet; goose, gander, and gosling; ram, ewe, and lamb. As you walk around the farm, call each animal correctly by name and take time to answer questions. Introduce students to names for animal groups: a brood of chicks, a herd of cattle, a flock of sheep, a gaggle of geese.

In the spring, children will enjoy meeting baby animals on the farm. Observe who feeds the babies, how this is done, and how many young each animal mother has. Point out how babies look compared to their mothers, how babies get around, and the like.

While visiting the farm, do not forget eggs. Can the children tell which kind of fowl laid each egg, based on the eggs' size and weight?

These activities begin a lifetime of learning about animals. Why not start this week?

Bubbles

and Brainwork

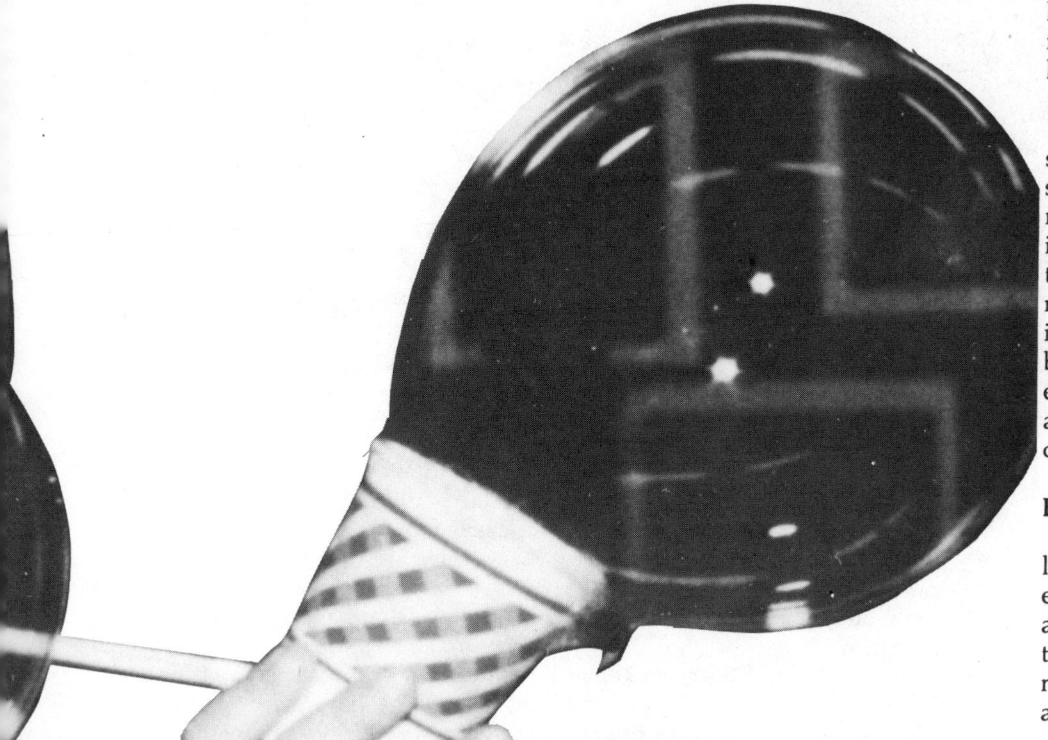

Bubbles are water made into circles.

Bubbles are sudsy.

Bubbles are sloshy.

Bubbles are just bubbles.

Bubbles are fun!

—Comments of six-year-olds

—Margie Mayfield—
Michael Padilla

Simple soap bubbles can be used to have children make educationally valuable discoveries about how materials behave, what their properties are, and how they can be used or changed. Experimenting with soap bubbles can be an extremely pleasurable experience for young children.

Reprinted from *Science and Children*, January 1979, Copyright NSTA.

If a child finds an activity pleasurable, he or she is more likely to continue or return to it. Further experimentation leads to more manipulation and learning of concepts.

Bubble-making does not demand special skills, either. We have never seen a child—or an adult—who was not a successful bubble maker! There is a great variety of experimentation that is possible with bubbles, accommodating a wide range of abilities and individual differences. We have used bubbles and bubble-making experiences with people from three years to adult, including handicapped and special education children.

Bubble Solution

Make a bubble solution of water, liquid dishwashing detergent, and glycerine (it makes the bubbles stronger and longer lasting). The proportion of these ingredients may vary with hardness of water, brand of detergent used, and other variables. Our recipe is:

   2000 ml water
    180 ml liquid soap
     60 ml glycerine

Children should be encouraged to experiment with this mixture. The teacher might mix the soap and water, then have the children add small amounts of glycerine until the mixture reaches the desired consistency. Children can experiment with mixing all three ingredients in various proportions at a later session. If the major goal of a session is bubble-making and not comparison of ingredient variables, then the teacher can premix the solution.

Bubble Makers

Children enjoy making and trying out bubble makers. Some bubble makers are made of plastic straws of different sizes, pipe cleaners, or thin wire

Margie Mayfield is Assistant Professor, University of Victoria, Victoria, British Columbia, Canada. Michael Padilla is Assistant Professor, Science Education, University of Georgia, Athens, Georgia. Photographs by Dr. Padilla.

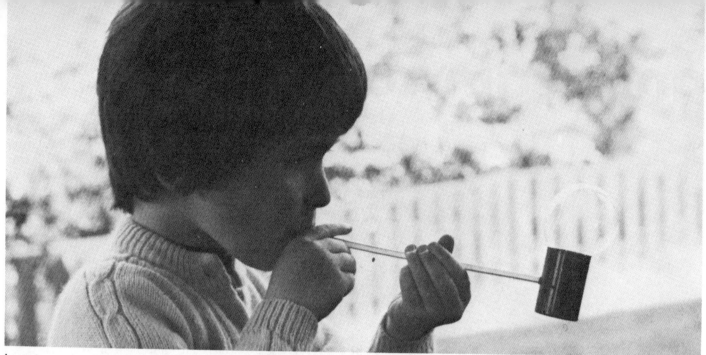

bent into a variety of shapes. Try triangle or pyramid shapes if you think bubbles are always round. Plastic foam cups with a straw pushed through one side or in the bottom make great bubble pipes. Try plastic squeeze bottles with a variety of tops, or plastic tubing with or without a funnel at one end.

Experimenting and Exploring

First exposure to bubbles and bubble-making should be simple exploration of the materials by the children. Then the teacher can guide the experimenting with questions:

Who can make the biggest bubble? How did you do it?

Who can make the most bubbles at one time? How?

What happens when bubbles land? Can you hear them? Do they move?

What happens when a bubble breaks? What does it feel like?

What do you see if you hold a bubble up to the sunlight? Can you see colors? Do they change?

How does a bubble move? What makes a bubble move?

These questions help children to focus their observations on different aspects of the phenomenon. Observations and descriptions are the major observable results of this activity. Can children become better observers by using their senses to investigate bubbles? Can they learn to accurately describe what they observe? Can they describe what they see without using words—perhaps instead pictures, collages, or other art forms?

Testing different brands of soap or the amount of glycerine in the solution are two types of experiments children can perform. By choosing an outcome variable—perhaps bubble size—children can try to answer questions the teacher poses. Several other variables can also be tested, depending on the age level of the children. Try experimenting with food coloring and compare bubble pipes of various sizes. Experiment with the most appropriate size for airborne bubbles.

Experimentation with bubbles and bubble-making is by no means limited to science. Bubbles and bubble-making

can be integrated into other areas of the curriculum. Oral language is encouraged by having children describe what they are doing, what happened, and what bubbles look like. Written language is emphasized by having children make experience charts, written records, or summaries. Creative writing can combine information and imagination. Write (or dictate) a story about the adventures of a bubble. What if you lived in a bubble? How does it feel to be a bubble under water? Bubbles can provide ideas for creative movement activities. Can you move like a bubble floating in the air? Can you move like a bubble in a fish tank? Can you move like a bubble on a windy or a calm day?

Bubbles, in addition to being enjoyed and appreciated, can certainly provide a medium for many positive education experiences.

Resources

Hill, Dorothy M. *Mud, Sand, and Water.* National Association for the Education of Young Children, Washington, D.C. 1977.

McGavack, John, and Donald P. LaSalle. *Guppies, Bubbles, and Vibrating Objects: A Creative Approach to the Teaching of Science to Very Young Children.* The John Day Company, New York City. 1969.

CHAPTER V

Curriculum Needs and Complements

When we speak of complementing the science curriculum for young children, we must accept the premise that "Science Is for All Children." This article looks at children with special-needs who require thoughtful planning to enable them to handle science materials. Teachers can adapt easily to individual needs in a mainstreaming situation with encouragement from administrators and parents and required support services.

The gifted and talented are also children with special-needs, yet we are in the early stages of research relating to these children. "The Gifted Young Child" provides a list of the known characteristics of this type of child. These characteristics are the same as those necessary to understand basic science concepts. This list could motivate teachers and parents to identify, encourage, and nurture these characteristics in gifted children.

If you have youngsters who demonstrate most of these characteristics, how do you encourage individual potential? Check your answers to the questions posed under this heading in the article. The very awareness of your responses will contribute to your own developing skills in understanding children's needs and your ability to provide for them.

"Identifying Children with Potential," a follow-up to the previous article, contains a Checklist for Recognizing a Child's Talent in Science. This checklist is not definitive, however, it does give more specific behaviors for teachers to observe as they watch for science interest and potential. Potential of the child is important. Every child deserves a program matched to his/her needs, talents, and interests at an early age.

Parents are the child's first teachers. The majority of early childhood educators are aware of this key role families play in determining the level of children's interest and achievement in school. "Involving Parents in Science" suggests how teachers can help parents to nurture their own children's natural curiosity about the world. Children like to see how things are put together and what makes them work or function. There are numerous ideas and activities showing children how things are put together and why they work. Teachers will want to try them and consider listening to both parent and child responses.

Priscilla D. Kesting writes of a successful noncompetitive activity in "A Science Fair for Younger Children," which details a hands-on approach. This is a handy reference for teachers who have never attempted a fair. Such an activity is a learning experience for both children and parents as well as good public relations for a school or center.

Science Is for All Children

———————— Margaret McIntyre ————————

IF WE ACCEPT the theory that all children have unique and special needs, positive results can be attained in our relationships with all children. This is no less true in the area of science. What the special child will be able to accomplish individually in the early childhood setting is determined largely by the opportunities provided. Interaction with materials and with adults who are knowledgeable about both science and child development is important.

Adults must let special children work with science experiences even if the child is ultimately unable to manipulate the materials. No progress is made without trying, and this trying can be linked to the working through phase of a science experiment. Adults gain insight into what can be done to provide experiences that will help a child know success.

The teacher must be flexible and creative to come up with something that this particular child can manage as independently as possible. Approaching the situation you may use advice from others familiar with a child's special needs, such as a therapist, resource teacher, special educator, or parent.

Learning for all young children is largely through the senses, but language has a special role. Concepts have to be talked about; children need to express or interpret the sensory intake. For the deaf and hearing-impaired child, the language aspect may be difficult unless one remembers that body language and art forms are means of communication. These children can engage in all tasting, smelling, touching, and seeing experiences. If the adult remembers to face the child while speaking, on his eye level, this can aid the child's language development. Attention to hearing aids is important for those children who have such assistance. Speaking slowly and distinctly is also important, as it is for working with all children who are developing their speech patterns and language. Depending on the age of the child and the degree of hearing loss, the teacher may be able to elicit sufficient language to ascertain the child's comprehension of sorting materials attracted and not attracted to magnets, for example. Usually hearing impaired children benefit from extra adult attention initially.

Visually impaired and blind children present another need, as sight is one of our most powerful sensory experiences. However, other sensory receptors remain active, and if the child is a hearing child, a little extra attention to language description can be most rewarding. Magnet attraction, with blind children would mean more attention to tactile descriptions. Touching the magnet to see if something has been picked up is worthwhile if the child knows each item among the objects to be sorted for attraction and nonattraction. Start with familiar items and be sure nothing is sharp. Possibilities are buttons, plastic and metal zippers, blunt nails, closed safety pins, pencils, paper, and cardboard. How does the child sort the materials as he tries them out? Shallow boxes, one with the usual smooth edging and one with textured edging, facilitate sorting. Once the child can understand the system, he will be able to verify the contents by himself.

Science experiences suitable for sighted children are equally appropriate for children with visual impairments. Water, sand, and mud permit unlimited exploration of texture, weight, simple measurements of both liquids and solids, and flotation. Young children should develop measurement ideas with the metric system s the ultimate—they will not find it difficult as the initial experience. Adult assistance is important at first in helping children with visual impairment to sense the measure-

*Adults must let children work with science materials
even if the child is ultimately unable
to manipulate the materials.*

Reprinted from *Science and Children*, March 1976, Copyright NSTA.

ment relationships. Kindergarten children could use cups and liters with measurements written in sandpaper and coated with shellac. The feel of these written symbols could, over a period of time, tie into the language that other children use.

It's a good idea to help a child to sense a full container. For younger children, filling by dipping into sand or water is more appropriate than pouring from a container. Pouring requires more sophisticated motor co-ordination which, while important, detracts from the objective of sensing that a container is full.

Matching and sorting are other activities. Matching different textures and different sounds are valuable as pre-reading experiences; teaching a child that words he cannot see have referents in reality.

A visually impaired child may help care for animals, especially when he is able to touch them. The rabbits, gerbils, and white mice found in early childhood centers are suitable.

Visually impaired children need the stimulation of sound as well as feeling. Field trips indoors and out will help these children to discuss and distinguish sounds. Insect and bird sounds, weather sounds, sounds of different musical instruments, offer possibilities. Teachers need to be aware of parks that provide nature trails set up for such children, who can later describe what they "see" and feel.

Children with crippling or other health conditions present different challenges to adults working with children. Sand and water are always available and useful. Spills can be cleaned up. Individual plastic pans of water and sand are helpful in the beginning—the pan sets the limits. Feeling, sorting, and matching are possibilities, though progress in reaching and holding may be laborious in some cases. These children need time to work in science experiences as motor coordination may be jerky and some what uncontrolled; holding an object may be difficult. Natural materials such as pine cones, leaves, pebbles, shells, and bark should be used as well as commercial materials. Adapt size and weight to the child's needs.

Children need a great many stimulating experiences if they are to develop to maximum capacity. Concrete materials are important; praise, patience, and precision are

A visually handicapped student in a class with sighted peers manipulates an aquarium into place.

needed. Early childhood teachers should be able to meet the needs of the mentally retarded easily, since the growth and development patterns of very young children are known to them. The teacher should be able to adjust activities given to all children. Concepts build slowly and take time and repetition, using many approaches and a wide variety of materials. The exploratory approach coupled with adult assistance where appropriate seem best.

Depending on their individual needs, all special children can work in gardening activities, cooking, and building with blocks.

Mainstreaming the special children in regular day care centers, nurseries, or kindergartens, is preferred today. Severely handicapped children, however, need interdisciplinary services beyond those found in regular early childhood educational programs. Adaptation to their needs requires more skill, creativity, and knowledge of the child's impairment. It also requires close cooperation with personnel from all the services supporting the child and the family. Nevertheless, the basic philosophy of providing science for preschool children remains the same.

The Gifted Young Child

——— Margaret McIntyre ———

The gifted and talented young child typically possesses many characteristics generally considered important in understanding basic science concepts including:

- good observational skills, with a willingness to observe both the usual and the unusual;
- verbal fluency and a large vocabulary;
- inquisitiveness about the world, wanting to know *why* rather than *what*;
- retentiveness, with little need for repetition;
- commitment to finding out what happens *if* something is done to something else;
- inventiveness and/or creativity in discovering ways to find a solution;
- absorption in self-selected tasks;
- independence, with little or no need for adult monitoring;
- a high energy level with an intense concentration of activity; and
- a wide range of personal interests.

To use these valuable characteristics, it is best if teachers clearly understand and appreciate them. If the classroom is structured so that children can develop these characteristics further, there will be a positive environment.

Teacher-dominated, inflexible classrooms where only convergent ideas are "acceptable" inhibit gifted young children and may turn them off school. If teachers are to be successful, they need to understand, develop, and use teaching processes that build on and take advantage of the special characteristics of these children. Check the processes in the following list—how many are built into your daily encounters with young children?

Encouraging Potential

Do you capitalize on the interests of individual children? Can you help a child find a book about sea shells so that the child can identify and label his or her specimens even if the group lesson plan calls for study of magnets that day?

Do you stimulate investigation into a wide area of science-related topics, rather than force the child to conform to a group plan?

Are you listening to what children are saying as they work on an activity? Do you ask divergent questions to stimulate further study?

Do you lead children to use reference books, films, filmstrips, television, pictures, and trade books to help answer their questions?

Do you allow for self-selection and choice of activities? Do you encourage growth in decision-making?

Do children have freedom to explore materials in their own ways? Do you give children their own chances to learn, rather than always giving them answers?

Is the schedule flexible enough so children can pursue spontaneous interests beyond the normally allotted time?

Are you excited when children make their own discoveries?

Are the children free to make mistakes without recrimination?

Do you encourage hypothesizing?

Can you tolerate a messy room when real learning is taking place? Are you more concerned with order than the child's attempts to master science principles involved in using a siphon at the water table?

Are you stimulating an affective response to learning? Do you let children draw pictures, dictate a story, or dramatize their ideas, thoughts, and activities?

Do you encourage imagination in the fact-finding area of science?

Do you plan for sharing of activities done by children with the rest of the class?

All children can benefit from a "yes" to the items on the checklist, but gifted and talented children especially need an affirmative reply if they are to develop to their maximum potential.

To many curriculum specialists, science is the ideal core subject area around which to develop a total curriculum for children. Science integrates ideally with language, mathematics, movement education, health, nutrition, writing, and aesthetic expression.

Integrated experiences can be planned. Gifted children profit from learning experiences outside the immediate classroom; they welcome change and diversity. They are stimulated by new opportunities to observe, experiment, and discuss with others what they see happening. Chronological age does not determine interest or ability. Teaming gifted and talented children with older children may satisfy the young child's need to know.

Gifted children move at a faster clip than other pupils and lose interest if held back. Try accelerating the pace of classroom activity. Individual learning packets or centers encourage individual pacing. These children are ready to move faster into complex learning levels than other children. Learning is best at the child's level of understanding (so that memorization is not seen as needed for success). Teachers need to be aware of and use the principles of Bloom's Taxonomy, so that children move from the lowest level of knowledge to the highest level of evaluation.

Resources on Bloom's Taxonomy

Bloom, Benjamin, Editor. *Taxonomy of Educational Objectives, Handbook I, Cognitive Domain.* David McKay Co., New York City. 1956.

Carin, Arthur A., and Robert Sund. *Developing Questioning Techniques: A Self Concept and Appraisal.* Charles E. Merrill Publishing Co., Columbus, Ohio. 1971. Chapters 4 and 5.

Sprinthall, Richard, and Norman Sprinthall. *Educational Psychology: A Developmental Approach.* Addison-Wesley Publishing Co., Reading, Massachusetts. 1977. Pp. 365-369.

Phyllis Marcuccio

Reprinted from *Science and Children*, April 1972, Copyright NSTA.

Identifying Children With Potential

—— Margaret McIntyre ——

Is an avid explorer; loves nature.

Tommy lies flat on his stomach intently watching ants building an anthill. Time goes by; Tommy is still watching. Nancy stands by the aquarium in her nursery school, head turning left and right, watching guppies swim. She is fascinated; she hears no one.

Examines pictures in books and magazines to learn about the world.

A Checklist for Recognizing a Child's Talent in Science

Student's name: _____

1. Demonstrates intense absorption in self-selected tasks. _____
2. Is consistently productive; does not await direction from adults. _____
3. Generates questions on his or her own; uses peers and adults as resources. _____
4. Wants to discover what makes things work; takes things apart and reassembles the pieces. _____
5. Manifests curiosity about what he or she sees, feels, and hears. _____
6. Shows interest in a variety of subjects: weather, animals, humans, etc. _____
7. Enjoys collecting items relating to his or her science interests. _____
8. Wants to label items in collections. _____
9. Expresses a particular science interest by devising unique games. _____
10. Invents new ways to work with common materials. _____
11. Possesses a "let's try" approach in play. _____
12. Examines pictures in books and magazines to learn about the world (even when he or she cannot read). _____
13. Is a thorough observer, paying unusual attention to detail. _____
14. Easily and quickly spots details other children miss. _____

Artwork by Katy Kelly.

Wants to discover what makes things work; takes things apart and reassembles the pieces.

Every classroom contains children who find science activities and their natural surroundings absorbing. These youngsters need to be identified and encouraged in scientific pursuits, the earlier the better. A science interests checklist is an effective way to identify children with potential. Consider using the one that follows in your classroom.

Early identification of children who are gifted in science is risky. Until young children have experienced a variety of science activities it is difficult to predict science giftedness and talent with accuracy. A gifted child may merely be precocious—doing what other children do, but at an earlier age.

The purpose of the checklist is to encourage you to observe children's interactions and language development precisely as they relate to science interest and potential. Also important are thinking skills, style of learning, and personal interests. Ideally, more than one adult should observe a child over a period of time, each time recording their observations on a checklist.

Every child deserves a quality education. Highly motivated and gifted young children with science interests deserve this as much as anyone. Early childhood is an appropriate time to assess these talents so that programs can be planned to meet their needs. Too often only children with high IQs or early language and reading abilities receive attention. All too few early childhood teachers consider their students' science interests and potential talents. We must change that.

If the checklist does not contain behaviors you consider important, please incorporate them. Tell me about your results. In particular I would appreciate hearing from day care and nursery school teachers. Let's begin now to identify very young children who have exceptional science potential.

15. Uses words in unique ways to express feelings, observations, and knowledge. _____

16. Uses metaphors or analogies, indicating a linkage of perceptions. _____

17. Talks in a conversational manner; listens and responds appropriately. _____

18. Organizes materials in a way that is meaningful; orders and groups, for example. _____

19. Shows interest in and some understanding of numbers, counting, quantity, and measurement. _____

20. Is an avid explorer; enjoys nature. _____

21. Enjoys exploring materials, both old and new. _____

22. Is easily motivated by field trips, books, and new materials. _____

23. Responds positively to adult suggestions that broaden the task being pursued. _____

24. Accepts a challenge; expresses little fear of the unknown or of the difficulty. _____

25. Is persistent in science tasks. _____

26. Contributes ideas when a problem arises. _____

27. Is imaginative in associating ideas with materials. _____

28. Is independent in thought and work habits. _____

29. Enjoys the spatial challenge of new and difficult puzzles. _____

30. Is self-confident; frequently assumes a leadership role. _____

NOTE: You may wish to designate your own scale for recording behaviors, such as frequently, occasionally, and rarely; or a heirarchy of 1 to 5; or simply yes or no. Variation will depend upon use of the data.

Involving Parents In Science

——— Margaret McIntyre ———

Reprinted from *Science and Children*, January 1980, Copyright NSTA.

The family plays a key role in determining the level of children's school achievement. (2,4)* Early childhood educators are inviting parents to join them in developing an environment that supports children's maximum development. Science-related activities can be an integral part of the child's learning environment, both at home and in the classroom. Wherever the location, children should have a chance to exercise their natural curiosity, to discover, to experiment, and to see how things are put together. Parents are often eager to know how they can help stimulate and nourish this curiosity. Teachers can help them in many ways.

Around Home

A useful way for teachers to make suggestions for at-home science learning is through short newsletters issued regularly. After making applesauce in the school science center, you might feature in the newsletter suggestions for investigations parents and children can do together. Perhaps making comparisons among different kinds of apples such as Rome Beauty, Golden Delicious, MacIntosh, and Red Delicious would inspire the children to talk about color, size, shape, smell, number of seeds in the seed case, and the feel of each apple. How about the thickness of the skin?

Have children wash the apples. Be sure to suggest that parents help their children cut the apples in half for further study. Compare sweet and tart apples. Make texture comparisons. Which apples are crisp and hard? soft? mealy?

You may suggest that parents and children find out what happens to a piece of apple left sitting on a plate. Do the children know what causes the color change? Have parents and children set up an experiment comparing two pieces of apple, one of which was rubbed with a lemon slice. Which changes color first?

You might suggest that parents let children help in other food preparation and cooking. What dissolves during cooking? How do fruits and vegetables differ from one another? How does food change during cooking?

Run the carpet sweeper. What makes it roll? What materials does it sweep up easily? Where does the dirt go? Make ice cream. What happens when a liquid freezes? Wash dishes. What dissolves the grease? How much soap do you need? Are suds different in different soaps and detergents? Sort clothes for the washer and from the dryer. How many ways can the clothes be sorted?

Outside

Homes and apartments often have access to yards, patios, or park areas. The outdoor world provides children with another environment they can explore. Children and parents can plant bulbs and seeds and care for the plants, look for insect life, watch cloud formations, and look for changes in the size of the moon during the course of the month. Why not observe what happens on a windy day, find where puddles form and guess reason(s) why, look for signs of seasonal change, or find animal tracks after rain or snow?

On Trips

Families do a certain amount of "tripping" to keep the household running. These trips are another dimension for parent-child interaction. Help parents make use of the science potential in trips to the airport. What happens during loading and unloading of baggage and mail? when a plane takes off and lands?

In the barber shop, how does the chair go up and down? Can children use the mirror to see all sides of their heads? How do clippers and scissors work? Is the hair on children's heads all the same color? the same texture?

At the zoo, how are animals cared for? What is their diet? How do the different animals move? Compare the differences in their colors, patterns of coloration, ears, tails, and skin.

In a hardware store, how many kinds of tools are there? How are they used? How many can children find? What are the different kinds of wood in the store?

At a dairy, how is milk pasteurized? How is equipment cleaned? How many different sizes of containers are there at the dairy? How is ice cream made? yogurt? cottage cheese?

At a bakery, how many different shapes, colors, and sizes of bread are there? How do whole wheat, oatmeal, cracked wheat, pumpernickel, raisin, white, and French or Italian bread taste, compared with each other?

Science Walks

Not all trips need transportation. The intimacy of parent and child taking a leisurely science walk can be mutually satisfying. Time of day, season, weather, and chance happenings provide daily opportunities, so parents and children never run out of things to discover. Suggest that parents let children decide what they will be looking for during the walk around the neighborhood. Families might walk to see the following:

How many objects with wheels are moving?

How many machines are at work? What noise does each make? What work does each do?

———
* See References.

How many different kinds of birds can they see?

How many different kinds of plants can they find?

Where are the big snowdrifts? Why are they *there?*

Where does ice melt the fastest?

How many evergreen trees are there on the block?

How many houses have snow on the roof?

Using Picture Books

In the newsletter you can point out that the community also has resources for parents. The public library is a valuable resource. Suggest that parents ask the librarian for picture books containing science information and concepts as an integral part of the story. Send home a list of books appropriate to the season, units being used in class, and child interests. Parents can use *Science and Children, The Horn Book,* and *Bulletin for the Center of Children's Books,* among other journals, to find reviews of new books.

Suggestions for Gifts

To help parents sift through the amount of materials available for children you might issue a biannual suggestion list. You could screen material for suitability to age, durability, safety, and opportunity for free exploration and multiple use. Make pertinent annotations. For a beginning suggest that parents offer children:

- several kinds of magnets in varying sizes
- magnifying glass or hand lens
- flashlight
- prisms
- timers
- construction sets that have wheels and axles.

In addition to the suggestions you make to parents to help them offer at-home science experiences to their children, you might ask parents if they want

specific information about any topics. Perhaps your newsletter can become a communication unit between the home and school environment that benefits the children.

References

1. *Bulletin for the Center of Children's Books* is a monthly journal published by the University of Chicago, Chicago, Illinois.

2. Coleman, James, et al. *Equality of Educational Opportunity.* U.S. Government Printing Office, Washington, D.C. 1966.

3. *The Horn Book* features articles on children's books, authors, and illustrators. Park Sq. Bldg., 31 St. and James Ave., Boston, Massachusetts 02116.

4. Jencks, Christopher, et al. *Inequality: A Reassessment of the Effects of Family and Schooling in America.* Basic Books, New York City. 1972.

Roger Wall

A Science Fair

Reprinted from *Science and Children*, April 1981, Copyright NSTA.

————Priscilla D. Kesting————

Hands-on science fairs are nothing new to the American scene; but consider a science fair designed especially to involve young children (pre-school to kindergarten). Our science fair for young children offered individual learning activities in which university students interacted with young children to help them discover the world of science.

Our Early Childhood Education science curriculum class undertook the project somewhat apprehensively. We had never seen such a fair carried out. But as we worked through obstacles and solved problems, our enthusiasm mounted. The final product was deemed highly successful by community and students alike.

Here is one way to create a science fair for young children:

WHERE: A shopping mall, both accessible and inviting to parents and children, is a good choice.

WHEN: We contacted the promotions manager at the mall about two months ahead of time to select a mutually convenient date. Choose a time when parents can be with their children. We selected a Sunday afternoon from 1:30 to 4:00.

WHAT TO OFFER: Each activity selected for the fair met the following criteria: (1) children would be directly involved, (2) the activity would take five minutes or less, and (3) the materials needed were inexpensive and plentiful so that all children could participate. All in all, we offered about 25 different activities. (See list.) We reserved long folding tables on which to display experiments. A supermarket loaned us the square containers used for delivering milk; these we inverted and placed in front of the tables for young children to stand on.

HOW TO ADVERTISE: Submit a description of the fair to local newspapers and radio stations. Duplicate fliers for posting on public bulletin boards. We advertised in grocery stores and all around the mall about a week in advance. In addition, we provided fliers for every kindergarten student in our area. (Packets were made up, taken to the public school administration office, and distributed through the district's regular delivery system to the schools.) We also supplied fliers to some nursery-school and day-care students, including those who attended our school's Child and Family Study Center.

THE DAY OF THE FAIR: Our students arrived about 45 minutes early to set up the fair. Tables were placed in a rectangular shape so that children could move easily from one activity to the next. Large "day-glo" letters spelling "Science Fair!" decorated the mall wall. Colorful posters made by the students hung in front of the tables to advertise the activities. Strolling among the tables, children carried the results of their experiments on styrofoam trays and paper plates.

RESULTS: Young children, parents, grandparents, and students made exciting discoveries about our world.

Science Fair Activities

- Mixing colors
- Fingerprinting
- Planting grass in egg shells
- Sink 'n float
- Will it roll or slide? (fun with rolling and sliding objects)
- Planting marigold seeds
- Feely box (matching shapes)
- Balloons which stick without glue (fun with static electricity)
- Making peanut butter
- Popping popcorn
- Shadow fun
- Sounds of water (water of various levels in soda bottles)
- Chemical garden
- Water changing the way things look
- The clever clip (games with magnets)
- Optical illusions
- Keeping paper dry under water using air pressure (paper in inverted glass lowered into water)
- Telling raw from hardcooked eggs without breaking them
- Smell and guess (identifying substances by smelling)
- Weighing air (experiments with a scale)
- Shake and match (matching and identifying objects by their sounds)
- Sandpaper fun
- Making heat through friction

Priscilla D. Kesting is Associate Professor in Early Childhood Education, University of Wisconsin-Stout, Menomonie. Photo by Kathie Behrs.